A DISAPPEARANCE IN DAMASCUS

DEBORAH CAMPBELL

A
DISAPPEARANCE
IN
DAMASCUS

Friendship and Survival in the Shadow of War

Picador | New York

picadorusa.com • picadorbookroom.tumblr.com
twitter.com/picadorusa • facebook.com/picadorusa

Picador® is a U.S. registered trademark and is used by Macmillan Publishing Group, LLC, under license from Pan Books Limited.

For book club information, please visit facebook.com/picadorbookclub or email marketing@picadorusa.com.

Grateful acknowledgment is made for permission to reprint from the following: Glain, Stephen. "The Arab Street," *Handbook of US-Middle East Relations: Formative Factors and Regional Perspectives*, Looney, Robert E., Editor. Routledge, 2009, 172-173.

Designed by CS Richardson

The Library of Congress Cataloging-in-Publication Data is available upon request.

ISBN 978-1-250-14787-5 (hardcover)
ISBN 978-1-250-14789-9 (ebook)

Our books may be purchased in bulk for promotional, educational, or business use. Please contact your local bookseller or the Macmillan Corporate and Premium Sales Department at 1-800-221-7945, extension 5442, or by email at MacmillanSpecialMarkets@macmillan.com.

First published in Canada by Alfred A. Knopf Canada, a division of Penguin Random House Canada Limited

First U.S. Edition: September 2017

10 9 8 7 6 5 4 3 2 1

FOR RON

An eye for an eye, but always the wrong eye.

WILLIAM SAROYAN

CONTENTS

PROLOGUE

DID I FIND HER or did she find me?

I wrote that question in my reporter's notebook soon after I met Ahlam, the Iraqi woman who was to change my life. It was 2007, and we had only recently begun working together in Damascus. I was the journalist; she was my interpreter and guide—my "fixer"—connecting me to refugees from Iraq. An irrepressible extrovert with a keen sense of the absurd, she was the sort of person who appeared at ease in chaos—always with a dozen projects on the go, always with a cigarette in one hand and a phone in the other. In her early forties, she had a university education and the instincts of a street fighter. As she led me ever deeper inside the hidden world of the war she had fled, and into the increasingly unstable country of Syria where she had sought refuge from Iraq, she showed me what survival looks like with all the scaffolding of normal life ripped away.

When I wrote that question, I had no idea what it would come to mean nearly a year later, when she was taken from me by agents of the secret police. How had I lost her? Was her disappearance somehow my fault? Caught in a web of fear and suspicion, I wanted to run for cover but knew I had to stay to look for her, so I began to question myself as a journalist would, wondering what I really knew—about her, about trust and friendship and betrayal, about the deepening crisis overtaking Syria, about the friends and strangers who surrounded me, about the thin line between courage and recklessness in the face of danger—as I struggled to put together the pieces that would tell me who had taken her and why she had disappeared.

PART **ONE**

Chapter 1

EXODUS

ALONG THE TWO-LANE HIGHWAY from Syria's capital city of Damascus, where it approaches the border with Iraq, anti-aircraft batteries scanned the dome of noonday sky. Here and there an army tank rumbled over hot sand along a barren landscape that looked like the surface of Mars. Next to the highway, a crop of bored young Syrian soldiers slouched on boulders around a commander making diagrams on a chalkboard propped up against another boulder.

Gripped by the anticipation I always feel when I am about to plunge into an unknown situation, I was greeted by a weathered road sign that broke the tension. It read, in English, *Happy Journey*. A lovely sentiment—I had to take a picture. It was the peak of Iraq's civil war, and absolutely no one was travelling *into* Iraq on a happy journey; a million and a half refugees had already fled the other way, to Syria, and they were happy for nothing but to be alive. In the sliver of shade the sign provided from the scorching sun, people stood with their suitcases, gazing back towards the country they had left behind.

Beyond them, past a giant parking lot, more Iraqis were streaming towards me into Syria, disgorged from buses and SUVs. In the early days of the exodus there had been time to make arrangements, to sell houses and cars and belongings. Now the entire middle class was on the run: the doctors and professors and librarians, the filmmakers and painters and novelists, the engineers and accountants and technocrats— the people who thought things, made things, kept things humming. Half the professional class had already left, and two thousand more funnelled through this unimpressive desert crossing every day. Some looked dressed for the office, women in high heels and oversized sunglasses, men in pleated dress pants and button-down shirts, as if they'd walked out of work, grabbed the kids and the cash, and just left.

Watching them, the very people I'd come to the border to talk to, I almost didn't see the border guard as he emerged from a makeshift checkpoint and stepped in front of the car I'd hired. The checkpoint, despite the barred windows, was more shepherd's hut than blazing emblem of officialdom. But officialdom it was. He waved my driver to park in the dirt to the side. As I was getting out—jamming my notebook into the bag that carried my camera and audio recorder, rooting around for my passport, ignoring the furnace blast of heat—a large white press van pulled up beside me. The door slid open and an American TV news crew stepped out.

It was rare to meet other journalists in Syria so I was surprised. I had been doing my best to stay under the radar, to avoid undue attention, and here I was arriving with the cavalry. Waiting in the shade cast by the checkpoint while our documents were taken away to be examined, I asked the cameraman, a frenetic thirtyish guy with a shaved head, where he was based.

"Dixie," he said.

Dixie?

He laughed. "That's our code for the 'Zionist entity,' as they say around here." Jerusalem, like Beirut, was a hub for the international press. "I spend most of my time on the beach in Tel Aviv." For this short-term assignment the news team was staying at the Four Seasons in Damascus. They had taken the same highway from the city to the border crossing this morning that I had.

I glanced in the direction of the immigration building where we would soon be competing to interview the new arrivals. I hate reporting in packs. "Do you ever go into Iraq?" I asked, indicating the refugees.

"Only when I have to," he said. "To justify my paycheque." When reporting from Iraq, the network made sure its staff was heavily guarded. This was good for the staff but bad for journalism. "My bosses want me to leave our base, but I refuse. I'm not gonna get killed so they can get a story."

I couldn't blame him. Next to us was a high concrete wall topped with barbed wire from which wind-blown scraps of plastic fluttered like tiny flags. Beyond the wall was Iraq. Like the refugees, most of the press were getting out of there. Iraq had become the most dangerous country in the world for journalists: they were being hunted, kidnapped, blown up, found in ditches with bullets in the backs of their heads. A few made headlines—Steven Vincent, abducted by men in police uniforms and shot execution-style, his female interpreter shot three times and left for dead; Jill Carroll, kidnapped by masked gunmen, her interpreter murdered—but local staffers, whose deaths barely registered, did most of the reporting now, and even they couldn't be seen with a notebook, much less camera equipment.[1]

The cameraman ventured inside the checkpoint in search of a toilet, so I chatted with his producer. The producer was tall and steel-jawed, just in from Washington, DC, clad in chinos and button-up shirt in the style known as "business casual." Despite the heat he looked depressingly perma-fresh. I had spent several years in the Middle East, reporting from Gaza or Cairo or Tehran, and more remote places where I never saw another journalist. I was suddenly conscious of the jeans I'd been living in since arriving in Syria more than two weeks ago.

I asked him how he'd convinced the Syrians to let them film the crossing. Since invading Iraq in 2003, Americans—journalists at least—came in for special scrutiny in Syria. Getting press credentials for a high-profile news team would require lengthy negotiations and serious clout. I did everything possible to avoid such formalities, but then again, I wasn't hauling around a camera crew.

"We have a big fixer," he said—a fixer being a well-connected local who could leapfrog them over the bureaucratic obstacle course and help them find the information they wanted. "What are you here for?"

I explained that I was writing a story on the Iraqi refugee crisis for *Harper's* magazine. I wanted to see the war from the civilian point of view, to figure out what had turned an invasion predicted as a "cakewalk"[2] into the bloodiest civil war of our times, one that was reverberating through the region. "Iraq is an atomic explosion," a European aid worker in Damascus had told me, echoing the prevailing sentiment. "It's a chain reaction that hasn't ended yet."

While most reporting focuses on those who "make history," what interests me more are the ordinary people who have to live it. I wanted to put a human face to the war. As an immersive journalist, my work, the work I love, involves getting as close as I can for long periods of time to the societies I cover, most recently six months in Iran. But that was not possible for me to do inside Iraq. So I had come to Syria to meet the eyewitnesses. "I want to get a sense of where it's all going," I said to the producer, squinting at him through my sunglasses. I knew what had already happened.

The US invasion of Iraq had toppled Saddam Hussein, the strongman who had run the essentially secular Baath Party state for nearly a quarter of a century using methods of which Machiavelli would have approved. Even members of his own party feared him; many had joined only to save their own skins. On April 9, 2003, the day that US forces captured Baghdad—Saddam having escaped into hiding, to be plucked eight months later, like a derelict, from a "spider hole" in the ground—mobs of poor Iraqis walked out of the slums, saw no one in charge, and started looting whatever they could carry. They ransacked ministries, hospitals, schools, banks, libraries, factories, utilities, weapons depots—even the world-renowned National Museum, home to archaeological treasures that told of the birth of civilization.

"Stuff happens," said US Secretary of State Donald Rumsfeld, mocking the media coverage as a "Henny Penny—the sky is falling" overreaction to what he predicted would be a temporary blip: "Freedom's untidy."[3] But the sky *had* fallen. Within four years a tenth of the population had fled the country. Syria was the only country still letting Iraqis in.

The producer glanced over his shoulder at the bars on the grime-smeared windows of the checkpoint. "We're not actually interested in the refugee story," he confided, lowering his voice. The Syrian authorities, he explained, were eager to show the American public what a fine job they were doing, taking on the civilian burden of an Anglo-American war, so the television network was going along with that. But it wasn't the story the crew had come for. What they were really looking at, he said in a low voice, was how Iraqi terrorists, hiding among the refugees, were using Syria as a base. The refugees themselves probably wouldn't make the news. "We'll shoot B-roll," he said.

The cameraman with the shaved head emerged from the checkpoint. The lavatory, he informed us, was not exactly five-star. We were still clustered in the shade waiting to be allowed to walk over to the immigration building, since the producer had forgotten his passport at the Damascus Four Seasons. Eventually, with the help of a Syrian minder who had been assigned to monitor our activities, we were waved through.

Now we had to pay our respects to the Syrian general in charge. After crossing a dirt field, we were ushered inside the squat immigration building, where he was seated in a dim back office—a fat man behind a fat desk. We sat on chairs around the walls of his office as if waiting for the dentist. The news producer sat next to me, talking about the price of real estate in Washington. Did I know it had gone right through the roof? He counted himself lucky to have bought in when he did.

An assistant entered with a flagon of coffee. On a signal from the general, he poured an espresso-sized cup, passed it to one of us, waited for it to be drained, then refilled the cup and passed it to the next person, going around the room. I was reminded of taking communion in my aunt's church as a child, but the news crew looked awkward, wondering what they might catch and whom they would offend if they turned it down.

The general ran through the numbers of Iraqis coming into Syria. Sixty thousand this month; between a million and a half and two million over the eighteen months since 2006. Damascus—holding out the promise of salvation by the United Nations High Commissioner for Refugees, or UNHCR—was swelling with the largest migration the region had ever seen. There was concern that the Iraqis would bring their war along with them. If that happened, it could tear Syria apart.

It reminded me of the Damascus University professor of economics I'd spoken to the week before. He warned of coming radicalization should the war leave Iraqis destitute and without options. If the international community did nothing to alleviate their suffering, he told me, "we should expect instability and international terrorism that will affect not only the region but the developed countries."[4]

"Questions?" the general asked.

We were as silent as schoolchildren awaiting a dismissal bell.

Released at last into the heat and tumult of the border area, I split off from the TV crew. There was only one minder for all of us, a small nervous man named Basil with a moustache too big for his face. The TV crew was more than enough to keep him busy.

I approached a crowd of several hundred Iraqis lining up outside the immigration building. Fathers held babies, fanning them with pink residency applications. Weary toddlers rested their heads on their parents' shoulders. I walked over to a skinny teenager whose black T-shirt had a single word in English across the front: TERMINATION. He was from the southern city of Basra, where he said Shia militias were murdering barbers and shopkeepers who sold ice, since ice cubes and a clean shave did not exist in the time of the Prophet Mohammed.

"What about cars and automatic weapons?" I asked.

Evidently the militias were okay with that.

He said his dad used to be an official in Saddam Hussein's Baath Party, so the militias wanted his life. "But they don't need a reason. They kill anyone."

Behind him quavered an old woman who had pulled her scarf across her face, not out of modesty, but for fear of being recognized. A month earlier, unknown militiamen had killed two of her sons and three brothers-in-law. Her husband had been driven mad with grief. I wanted to assure her that they could not get to her now. But that was unclear—I was hearing stories of militants who followed their targets across the border and killed them in Syria.

At the far side of the immigration building, a man was pacing agitatedly outside the barred window of a jail cell. Back and forth, back and forth. He looked inside the bars, said a few words, passed through bits of food, and paced. On the other side was his wife, caught trying to cross into Syria on fake documents. Real passports could of course be bought too, but at twice the cost. A man who arranged such things told me that for a thousand US dollars he could get me an authentic Iraqi passport in three days, and no, it was not a problem that I could not pass for an Arab among the blind.

In the lineup snaking out of the immigration building into the dust-choked yard stood three burly middle-aged men, engaged in the endless task of jostling for a patch of shade beneath the lone tree. Engineers from Iraq's state oil company, they told me their lives had been threatened. All of the oil workers, they said, were being kidnapped or killed. It was part of the battle for control of the country's most valuable resource; this, they and many observers believed, was the real reason for the war. "Not Saddam," one of them said. "Twenty-five years ago, Donald Rumsfeld was shaking his hand." That was when the two nations were allies against Iran, and Rumsfeld was Ronald Reagan's friendly emissary to the Iraqi dictator.

Grizzled and weary-looking, the engineer had to check off one of three reasons for entering Syria—business, tourism, or "other." He claimed to be a tourist. "I'm here to take a holiday," he explained, "from the sound of rockets, bombings and explosions."

His colleague interjected. "The Iraqi people are romantics. We like poets, songs, nature, and nowadays we hear nothing but explosions and bombings."

I too had come to Syria on a standard-issue tourist visa. It's what I usually do when reporting from places where journalists are viewed with suspicion. To request an official journalist's visa is to advertise your intentions to those whose job it is to get in your way. In the old days they would have to follow you around, but now they can watch your computer and listen to your phone. They can restrict your movements, decide where you can go, whom you can talk to, how long you can stay, and make trouble for whoever talks to you. Over the past seven years of international reporting I'd learned that the wisest course is to keep your head down and ask permission from no one. That way no one knows what you're up to, and they aren't obliged to think up ways to stop it.

In the letter accompanying my visa application I explained that I was a professor who had studied classical Arabic and wished to see what remarkable sights Syria had to show me. This wasn't a lie. I teach at a university, had studied if never mastered Arabic, and Damascus was a place I'd always wanted to see.

To everyone I met, unless I was interviewing them, I was just a tourist here. To the idle curious; to the sultry neighbour in the apartment below mine, on her second marriage, who told me her life story over tea; to the talented family of artists I befriended after stumbling upon their craggy studio built into the ancient city walls; to the taxi drivers shooting the breeze (or gathering information, maybe)—to all of them I was simply a professor on holiday. I was just interested in art or archaeology or architecture or history or Sufi poetry. Which indeed I was.

A bus with purple velvet curtains had pulled into the dirt parking lot, its passenger windows shot out. Leaving the trio of engineers, I went over to inquire, clambering up for a look inside. The driver told me it had happened in the early hours of the morning in Baghdad; US forces were on patrol and simply strafed the area.

The cameraman I had spoken to earlier ran over to check it out. He poked his head inside the bus but decided it was not worth filming. "This stuff happens all the time."

"That's true." The driver nodded sagely. "It happens all the time."

It didn't use to happen all the time.

Understanding how the invasion of Iraq led to such a chaotic civil war requires some knowledge of the nation's demographics. Iraq is composed of three main groups: Shia Arabs, Sunni Arabs, and Kurds, along with a patchwork of small minorities, some of whom have lived there for thousands of years. The two main branches of Islam, the Shias and the Sunnis, are no farther apart than Protestants and Catholics, which is to say, far enough. The Shia are the majority in Iraq (more than 50 percent, which would win any ballot-box competition), but Sunnis, Saddam Hussein among them, have traditionally held power. (Indeed, the broader Middle East—aside from Iran and Syria—has long been in the hands of Sunnis, who are nine-tenths of the world's Muslims.) Nevertheless, the Iraqi people lived mostly at peace with their neighbours. So much so that by 2003 nearly a third of the population had intermarried, and most major towns and cities were mixed.

Besides envisioning a peaceful outbreak of democracy once Saddam Hussein was toppled, Washington's war planners hadn't thought ahead. Brutal dictator though he was, what they failed to consider when they decided to remove him were the dire consequences commonly observed whenever a strong central power is removed without adequate civic institutions in place. In a diverse society that lacks such unifying structures, there are two tendencies when authority breaks down: a disintegration into communal groups and violence. When governments falter, people turn to anyone who can provide security and basic needs, by whatever means.

With Saddam Hussein felled by George W. Bush's invasion and regime change, Iranian-allied Shia were handed power, along with the Kurds; Sunni Arabs were sidelined, lumped together as if they hadn't also suffered under Hussein. Even worse, and with far-reaching consequences, were two orders issued by the Americans under their chief administrator, L. Paul Bremer III, a former ambassador to the Netherlands who had no prior experience in the Middle East—or any conflict zone for that matter. Taking instructions from a secretive Pentagon agency called the Office of Special Plans,[5] Bremer purged Baath Party members from national institutions including schools, hospitals, ministries and corporations, firing a hundred thousand of the country's white-collar professionals, a Sunni-dominant class.[6] He then dissolved Iraq's army, police and intelligence services, leaving half a million men trained in nothing but war suddenly jobless and afraid for their lives.[7]

The purge amplified as Shia death squads began showing up after dark in Sunni neighbourhoods; torture chambers were run out of the Interior ministry. Before long a thousand bodies a month, most of them ordinary Sunni civilians, were piling up in Baghdad's morgues. Ex–Baath Party officials and ex–army officers were the first targets of the death squads and were first to flee the country, followed by the intellectuals and anyone who had worked for the US coalition forces.

Then, three years after Hussein's removal, came a devastating bombing that launched the civil war in earnest. In

February 2006, the golden dome of an eleven-hundred-year-old Shia shrine was blown up in the ancient mixed city of Samarra. The bombing was blamed on an Iraqi al-Qaeda franchise, a new group of fighters from Iraq and surrounding Sunni states, particularly Saudi Arabia, bent on bringing down the Shia-led government.[8] Later that year, al-Qaeda joined with other Sunni extremists to form the Islamic State of Iraq, the precursor of ISIS.[9]

Before the bombing in Samarra, there had been lists of specific targets, but now any man or woman found to be Sunni or Shia, or a minority—Christian, Mandaean, Yazidi, Palestinian—could be stopped on the way to work, their identities inferred from the names on their ID cards, and tortured to death, or simply gunned down in their homes. At the UNHCR registration centre in Damascus, where crowds of refugees lined up each morning at dawn, clerks took down their reasons for fleeing. "I get sick from the stories," a fresh-faced young Syrian clerk had told me. She meant it literally: she sometimes had to excuse herself to throw up. But with neighbouring countries refusing them refuge (Jordan had already taken half a million or more), Syria was the last exit from the killing fields.

Driving back the way I had come, I watched the setting sun burnish the desert pinkish-gold. Power poles loomed over desert scrub and green patches of irrigated farmland. The highway was calm, my driver silent and brooding; he found the refugees worrisome. "Speaking as a Syrian," he had earlier told me, "we don't want their war to come here."

The refugees would be following in the same direction, many of them bound for a crowded suburb of Damascus where rents were particularly cheap: Sayeda Zainab. Little Baghdad it was being called now. I had been to that neighbourhood a couple of times already. Home to the largest community of Iraqi refugees in the world, it would make an ideal base to research my *Harper's* article on the crisis.

I wanted to immerse myself there, in the lives of the people, but how would I do it? To enter a traumatized community, I needed to find someone the community trusted who could make introductions; I needed a good fixer.

As the lights of Damascus beckoned, it occurred to me that I might already have found that person.

Chapter 2

THE FIXER

THAT EVENING, BACK IN DAMASCUS, I called Ahlam.

I suggested a meeting; she named the time and the place. Nothing more was said over the phone. After that meeting we began working together. She would give me a new way of thinking about war, about what war does, and what it takes to survive. She would become my friend.

I like to work alone, to wander around, look and listen and ask questions, but that is not always possible or wise. Which is when a journalist like me needs a trustworthy guide, someone to act as a go-between, traverse the barriers of language and culture, and gain the trust of people who are unwilling to talk to outsiders. Often the first question put to me by Iraqis in Damascus was—for whom was I spying? They were on the run from strangers who wanted to kill them, so why should they answer questions from a stranger like me?

Given the time it takes to immerse yourself in a culture and do the complex work of observational journalism that requires gathering and cross-checking a complicated array of

sources and material, there are few of us compared to reporters covering daily news. And with the collapse of news budgets and the shutting of foreign bureaus in favour of cheaper
forms of newsgathering (like, say, not bothering at all), even
those are thinner on the ground. To do the work of immersive
journalism means being something of a go-between oneself.
What I strive to do is bridge the gap between the readers of
the magazines I write for, such as *Harper's* or *The Economist*,
and people in troubled places who such readers would never
otherwise meet. We talk about them, make policies to deal
with them, even make war on them, while knowing almost
nothing of who they are or what consequences our actions
might have.

To write a successful story I have to emerge from the field
with an accurate representation of confounding, potentially
dangerous situations. Another way of describing immersive
journalism is "hanging out journalism," which can feel a lot
like "drowning journalism" or "thrashing around journalism," especially at the start when I'm getting my bearings. To
gain the access and understanding on which this work relies
occasionally requires the help of someone informed and connected, whose judgement I trust. In the lingo of journalism,
such a person is called a fixer. If a fixer were European or
North American, he or she would be called a field producer
or a media consultant. A fixer is the local person who makes
journalism possible in places where the outsider cannot go
alone. Arranging interviews, interpreting, providing context
and background, sensing with their fingertips the direction
of the winds, fixers are conduits of information and connections. And when they say, "It's time to leave," it is always time
to leave. Without these local experts, who may be anyone

from a doctor with good contacts to a university student with street smarts, most of the news from the world's dangerous places would not be known, though by the nature of their work, they themselves remain invisible.

Fixers are informally contracted, working for a matter of hours to a matter of months, and tend to fade away once the job is done, but they take risks on behalf of the story that even the journalist might not take. Some fixers, in places where a foreigner would not stand much chance of coming back alive, gather the information themselves while the journalist waits at the hotel to type it up. And when the foreign correspondent goes home, the fixer stays behind. "I avoid fixers," writes the war photographer Teru Kuwayama, "because so many of the ones I've worked with are dead now."[10]

Generally speaking, I avoid them too, preferring to find my own way around. In my *Oxford English Dictionary*, a fixer is "a person who makes arrangements for other people, especially of an illicit or devious kind." That is indeed exactly how the Syrian government saw anyone who worked with Western journalists, and why—on a different level— journalists are wary of fixers. Those fixers who are close to a government (or other power structures, such as rebel groups or political parties) may, depending on their allegiances and the incentives involved, turn out to be more like minders, working as double agents without the journalist being aware of the fact. A Syrian working as an "official" fixer, for example, would have to report to the Ministry of Information in Damascus, a ministry with a mandate the opposite of its name. And since a fixer receiving permission to work from the Ministry could earn in a day or two the same two hundred dollars that a Syrian government employee earned in a month, there was incentive to tell the Ministry whatever the Ministry wanted to know.

I had only been there once since I arrived, to the daunting eighth-floor office of the Ministry of Information, to request permission to visit the border. That day I had carefully dressed in what I thought might pass as professorial garb: grey pencil skirt and black French-cuffed shirt, hair pulled back tautly as if I were about to give a lecture on Baudelaire. When the director, a tall and sorrowful-looking man with a reputation for disliking reporters, asked me directly if I was a journalist, I said no. "I'm a professor and a writer."

If I were to stay below their radar, whoever helped me would have to be below the radar as well. The week I arrived, I had managed to locate two good interpreters: Kuki, a young refugee from Baghdad I'd heard about from a researcher at Refugees International in New York; and Rana, a school-teacher from Damascus who came recommended by an American radio journalist based in Jordan. Rana was thirty-four and unmarried, despite (or because of) being attractive and educated. She had turned down many suitors because she didn't want a controlling husband or a backward one. Though she was studying at night towards a second degree in international law, she still lived with her parents in an apartment where she and four sisters, all university-educated, slept in a single giant bed. "Like kebabs," Rana said.

That first week I camped at the Damascus apartment of a freelance filmmaker from New York who had sublet me a mattress on her balcony. She was a skinny redhead in her early thirties with a finely calibrated register of anxiety—not a bad quality for a journalist to have unless it tips over the edge. Which it did the morning the air conditioner died.

Admittedly, in the midst of a heat wave, this was a crisis. Standing in the bare-bones kitchen, stirring instant coffee into boiling water and still not quite awake, I listened to her screaming over the phone at her landlord. She wanted him to come over and fix the problem immediately so she was layering it on, simultaneously claiming the malfunction had made her ill, praising the great country of Syria, and alluding to having spoken to "officials" and "police" who all agreed that he had overcharged her on the rent. Of course she wasn't ill; Syria wasn't great; and we assiduously avoided officials and police. They considered all foreigners spies, which is how we saw them in return. She had even put a picture of President Bashar al-Assad on the outside of our door, hoping to allay any suspicions about the possible journalistic activities taking place inside. And the rent, though almost as much as she paid for her half of a spacious loft in Brooklyn, was in line with demand: rents in Damascus had suddenly tripled with the arrival of more than a million middle-class Iraqis carrying their life savings in cash.

I'd enjoyed sleeping under the clear moonlit sky on her balcony, lulled by the hum of late-night traffic. But I needed a room, not a balcony, and after much searching I'd found my own place. It was on the fifth floor of a downtown walk-up, since Syrians, the owner wistfully conceded, objected to climbing more than three flights of stairs. Too small for more than one person, it was one of the rare Damascus rentals that didn't have crowds clamouring to pay whatever the landlord wanted. I was glad to be getting out of the overheated apartment and away from a roommate who had recently discovered that the pharmacies here didn't require a doctor's prescription to give her all the Xanax she needed.

I was going to be on the top floor, above everything, looking down on the city, able to see without being seen, invisible, almost omniscient: a writer's fantasy. I was going to understand everything that went on, I imagined, and would avoid being caught up in any of it.

Rana and Kuki weren't fixers: neither had connections or could lead me to sources, though both were game for helping me with whatever I had in mind. Kuki had been an interpreter in Iraq. Not for the army, but for one of the companies that made a fortune supplying overpriced goods to the army. He was young, educated, upper-class, subsisting on money from his parents in Baghdad, a professor and a lawyer whom he'd left behind after a letter arrived on their doorstep threatening to murder the entire family unless their gay son left the country. He came with me on a number of early exploratory interviews and said it made him feel better to see people worse off than he was. Before the war he had been a fashion model in Baghdad—he showed me his portfolio—and he was still vain, refusing to tone down his rock-star attire of tight black T-shirt and white-framed sunglasses even when we were working. Wherever we went, people stared.

One night the two of us went to a bar in the Old City, down tangled alleyways, under a pink neon sign. It was salsa night, hot and smoky, and a steamy, sexy crowd was shouting to be heard. Posters on the wall advertised a visiting European DJ. We drank the pink drinks that came with the cover charge.

I told anyone who asked that I was a professor of fine arts. Or just a "teacher," if that seemed easier. Kuki said—since he would have liked to be one—that he was a VJ for MTV Lebanon. He was shaggily handsome, skinny as a heroin addict, and could put on a convincing Lebanese accent. •

"Do you think anything you write will make a difference?" he asked me at our table looking out over the dance floor, lighting his last cigarette and crumpling the packet.

It was a good question, an existential question, and one I had begun asking myself. I liked to distinguish the work I did from "parachute journalism"—flying in and out and thinking you were an expert when you could have written the same thing without leaving the office—or from the kind of institutional newsgathering that took its cues from press conferences, which meant that whoever gave the press conference wrote the script. But I had been writing long enough to doubt my own contribution. The whole media landscape—so many articles, so much commentary, so much noise—was changing fast, disintegrating. One article, a thousand articles, however in-depth and penetrating, what could they actually do beyond letting me say I had tried?

George Orwell, in his famous essay "Why I Write," said that aside from the need to earn a living, there were four great motives to write. The first is *sheer egoism*: "Desire to seem clever, to be talked about, to be remembered after death, to get your own back on the grown-ups who snubbed you in childhood, etc., etc." The second is *aesthetic enthusiasm*: the perception of beauty in the world; the desire to share a valuable experience; pleasure in "the firmness of good prose or the rhythm of a good story." The third and fourth motives interested me most. *Historical impulse*: "Desire to see things as they are, to find out true facts and store them up for the use of posterity." And finally, *political purpose*: "Using the word 'political' in the widest possible sense. Desire to push the world in a certain direction. . . . No book is genuinely free from political bias."[11] And, thinking about the article I was writing on the refugee crisis, to push the world towards reckoning with the long-term consequences. To show them a human face.

It wasn't too late to find out a few "true facts"—as opposed to the other kind—and store them up for posterity, but it was too late, at least with the story I was writing, to change the present situations of the people whose lives I was documenting. They might, of course, go on to better days, but there was no question that what was done to them was done. The dead were dead; some people really had been driven mad with grief. Observation, recording, documenting, what difference could that make? If the answer was "nothing," was I doing it just for selfish reasons: to make myself feel better, less useless, less angry at various injustices? In which case the whole enterprise was not much more than therapy.

"I don't know," I told Kuki. Salsa music pounded at my ears. A woman with an Afro was showing the dance floor how it ought to be done. "I think," Kuki said, blowing a thoughtful smoke ring, "that people are busy." He knew a fair bit about life in the West and the sort of people who read in-depth analyses in highbrow publications. He had an American boyfriend—they met online—and was trying to get accepted to the United States through the UNHCR. His dream was to live in New York, to become a New Yorker. "You write something, they read it," he said. "Maybe they feel something. But what do they *do* about it?"

Then he turned to his favourite subject. "How's your man?" he asked. "How does he feel about you being away?"

Ahlam and I had been introduced three days before my trip to the border by a Syrian journalist who was on his way to see an Iraqi woman in Damascus's Little Baghdad—Sayeda Zainab—and invited me along. "She might be interesting for you."

Ask Syrians what they thought of Little Baghdad and the word "backward" usually came up, or the joke about the two Iraqis expressing their surprise at seeing something unusual: a Syrian! The last time I had gone there my taxi driver, an avuncular man who believed he was dealing with a confused tourist, tried to talk me out of going. "There's nothing to see there," he insisted into the rear-view mirror. "Just Iraqis."

Home to three hundred thousand refugees, this was where Baghdad had transplanted itself. It was insular, poor and unstable—the Syrian secret police, the mukhabarat, hovered over Little Baghdad the way cops do around high-crime neighbourhoods.

I would love to go with him, I told the journalist that day, but not right then. I was still wearing what I had put on to meet him at his magazine office, a sleeveless shift dress over jeans. This was perfectly fine for the affluent areas of Damascus, which were modern and anything-goes, but not for the sort of outing where I should make an effort to dress modestly and not stand out. Just a glance at my non-Arab face would identify me as a Westerner, so I didn't bother with a headscarf—I'd had my fill of it in Iran; and in secular Syria even the president's wife didn't bother. But when I had time to think ahead I usually wore a wedding ring to visit poor areas, places where marriage was a life event as significant as birth or death. I'd bought the ring for ten dollars at a stand in a shopping mall, preferring to be pitied for having a cheap husband rather than admit that I lived with a man to whom I wasn't married. Unfortunately, the ring sometimes required me to provide vivid descriptions of my wedding: inventing the dresses the bridesmaids wore, the hall or beach where the celebration took place—usually I opted for the beach. Thinking of this made me realize I hadn't called home lately. My boyfriend had emailed to say he had tried my number several times but couldn't get through.

"Don't worry," said the journalist, interrupting my thoughts. "We'll take a taxi to her door." Outside his office he quickly flagged down a cab on the busy street.

Twenty minutes later we arrived at her apartment. Ahlam opened the door—her husband was out, both kids still at school. Clad in jeans herself, she wore a heart-shaped pendant with a photo of a boy around her neck. Her eldest son, she explained, touching the portrait with one hand. He had died last year.

"In the war?" I asked. Later I would understand how hard it was for her to answer that question.

"Here in Damascus. An accident in hospital." He had been eleven years old.

As she beckoned me to take a seat, I apologized for my bare arms. She looked at me blankly. She appeared not to have noticed. She offered me a cigarette as if to say: *don't be so uptight.*

I'd like to say I knew immediately who she was. That she was the most famous fixer in Damascus. But fixers are never famous—not to anyone except those in the know. They work in murky times and murky places. Which is when and where they are needed. And honestly? She didn't look the part. Later, because she lost herself in her work in the same way I did, I would sometimes forget how much she had been through to end up here, but that day she gave me a glimpse of something she normally locked up. When she spoke of her son, she looked like someone with a broken heart.

She told me a bit of her story, in fluent English, explaining what had brought her here from Baghdad, and despite how harrowing it was I couldn't help but admire her attitude. She had a certain flippancy that told me she didn't care about things other people cared about, that she was her own person living by her own rules. She mentioned that she had worked for the international press in Baghdad, and when I said I was interested in meeting more Iraqis in her neighbourhood, she wrote her telephone number in the back of my notebook.

It was easy to miss the gravel turnoff from the paved highway that had taken me from the chic shops and modern restaurants and office towers of downtown Damascus. The taxi driver had to brake and reverse against traffic. Marking the roundabout on the main street of Little Baghdad—recently renamed Iraqi Street after its residents—was a large folk mural of Hafez al-Assad, who had ruled Syria for three decades, painted in the style of a psychedelic rock poster. Every second shop window displayed a photograph of Assad's son Bashar, in moustache and aviator sunglasses and army fatigues, an obvious attempt to make him look less like the nerdy ophthalmologist he had been before taking the presidency in 2000 when his father died. Aside from its festoons of electrical wires and its taxis and sputtering motorcycle carts, the neighbourhood looked medieval.

Drab low-rise tenements emerged like dead teeth from streets of pounded dirt. The air smelled of roasting meat and baking bread. A mule passed by pulling a cart overloaded with watermelons. At the roadside a bearded man with a wrestler's build sold cigarettes, his upper half so hale and robust that it took a moment to register that he had no legs. Farther along were the gold shops where Iraqi widows performed alchemy, turning their jewellery into bread; some did the same with their bodies once the gold was gone.

Looming above it all, aloof from the spectacle, was the magnificent shrine to Lady Zainab, granddaughter of the Prophet Mohammed for whom the neighbourhood had taken its name. With its turquoise minarets and gilded dome, the shrine was the only good reason for visitors to come here. Zainab is a heroine to the Shia for having stood up against oppression after the seventh-century battle that cemented the Sunni–Shia divide. The split began after the death of the Prophet Mohammed in 632 AD, when there was a dispute over who would take his place. The Shia believed it should be the Prophet's direct descendant, and the Sunnis believed any upstanding male was electable. After the murder of the Prophet's closest male relative, Ali, a battle took place on the plains of Karbala in what is now Iraq. Ali's small band of followers, the *shia'tu Ali*, were slaughtered, and his daughter Zainab was taken to Damascus in chains. This was known as a Shia area because of the shrine, but now Iraqis of all sects—Sunni, Shia, Christian—lived here side by side as they used to in Baghdad.

It was Ahlam's suggestion to meet at the main street roundabout. In the warren of nameless alleyways that branched off from it, she figured I wouldn't be able to find her apartment. I waited under the red canvas awning that shaded an electronics shop, willing myself to look inconspicuous. This wasn't easy. Westerners never came to this part of the city except in tour groups to visit the shrine. Fat and pale, they filed out of buses with expensive cameras dangling from their necks, blinking like newborns in the stark sunlight.

As I stood there, glancing at my watch, I felt a rising anxiety. Once, when I'd come here before meeting Ahlam, I had been swarmed by a group of Iraqi men. They were out of work. They were running out of money. They were desperate. They were angry. "I have a question for you," said one of the men, his face inches from mine. "If people come and tell you to get out of your home, if they are killing you based on your identity card, if the international community does nothing—tell me, what will be your destiny?"

I had no answer to give him. The crowd was growing larger, gathering momentum. Crowds like that crave some sort of release, a catalyst, some object on which to vent.

Now, as I stood alone in the shadows beneath the canvas awning, a man walked past. He stopped short to rubberneck, his mouth agape, then took up a post beside me and watched me from the corner of his eye. When I caught him staring, he glanced away nervously. If he was a spy he needed to go back to spy school.

I was relieved to see Ahlam crossing the sunlit main street towards me. She was tall for an Iraqi woman. She wore men's black jeans, men's black shoes, and a man's overcoat that defied the oppressive heat—a style she had adopted when the war began and there were bigger problems to worry about than conforming to fashion. Her broad and high-boned face might have been beautiful if she had paid the least attention to vanity. But her face was unusual here because it seemed cheerful, right at home. As if we weren't walking through a

refugee slum where Syrian agents kept watch for rogue journalists and for any sign of the sectarian tinder that might set
fire to Syria as it had to Iraq.

Phone in one hand, she greeted me with the standard
three kisses—right, left, right—smiling as if our meeting
here was the most natural thing in the world. We might
have been two friends about to go to lunch. No one seemed
to be watching us, but two policemen were standing beside
the Assad rock poster directing traffic, their eyes concealed
behind mirrored sunglasses. Leading the way to her apartment, Ahlam walked quickly but not as if she were in some
kind of hurry. Merely the gait of a busy person. She stopped
to talk to a shoeshine boy whose family she knew. Such boys
were eyes on the street: useful sources of information.

Walking with her into the maze of yellow dirt alleyways,
sweat pooling beneath my clothes, I felt a strange sensation.
I felt relaxed. Almost happy. Like army commanders, sea
captains and wilderness explorers, Ahlam's stubborn fearlessness made those around her feel fearless too.

She had come to Damascus after being kidnapped in
Baghdad two years ago. The conditions of her release were
a $50,000 ransom and a promise to leave Iraq forever. Her
family raised the money—her younger brother Salaam sold
a car; her sisters and sisters-in-law sold their jewellery; her
older brother Samir organized loans to cover the rest. "For
the money," she said, reaching for her cigarettes as we talked
in the sweltering heat of her living room, "they let me live."

She came from a thriving Sunni farming village on the
northwest edge of Baghdad, and spent the early months of
the war working as a fixer for the *Wall Street Journal*. After

that, for the next two years, she had worked at a civil–military affairs office the Americans had built in her district. The General Information Centers (GICs)—the Americans, and anyone else referring to them, pronounced it "gik"—were connected to the Iraqi Assistance Center, which ran humanitarian operations for the US military. Hired as a caseworker on a salary of $450 a month, her job was to translate compensation claims for the families of war victims. A successful claim for someone killed by accident had a maximum payout of $2,500. But the centre, with its all-Iraqi staff, was largely left to its own devices, and since by then she was also a district councillor, she was soon made deputy director, addressing all manner of humanitarian concerns: the wounded, the orphaned, the widowed. A lot of her time was spent locating prisoners who had disappeared into American jails, leaving anxious families who came to her for information on their whereabouts.

Of course it was dangerous to be in any way associated with the Americans, but it was the only way to get anything done. "I had many threats from militias who thought I was a spy."

First came a petrol bomb, tossed through her bedroom window. She returned from work one day to find her bed charred by fire, all her clothing incinerated. She had hidden her savings in her clothing: no one trusted the banks.

Then came flyers, delivered to the homes of her neighbours, accusing her of being a spy for the Americans. "I didn't care. I wasn't a traitor. My aim was to serve my people."

She ignored the signs until the beginning of 2005, when the head of her district council was murdered. A rumour surfaced that another councillor had also been killed.

Concerned that it might be Ahlam, the Americans sent soldiers to knock on doors throughout her village. "Have you seen this woman?" they asked, showing her photograph to the very people who had been told she was a spy. Returning home from work that day, she felt the eyes of every villager upon her. "Now I was trapped."

One cold January evening, a week after the murder of the council leader, she was gathering firewood beside the main road of her village. By day she was a professional woman, working twelve to fourteen hours, consumed by problems that seemed only to multiply, but outside of work she still had the responsibilities of a wife and mother. Since electricity was no longer reliable and cooking fuel now sold on the black market at outrageous prices, she had to cook for her family over a fire.

As darkness approached, and with it a bitter cold, she bundled twigs and branches into her arms. A car pulled slowly up alongside her and stopped. A black Mercedes with tinted windows. She could not see inside. The driver's side window lowered just enough for her to hear a man's voice. "Peace be upon you, sister." A voice she did not recognize.

"And upon you peace," she replied.

He tossed a scrap of paper from the window and the car sped away, its tires tearing up the road.

She walked over and picked up the paper. It was a handwritten letter, hastily scrawled. She read it in the dim light.

Peace be upon you, sister. I am someone who knows what you are doing and respects you very much. For your own safety and the safety of your children, you must leave your home tonight.

She dropped the bundle of sticks. She had received threatening letters before, and ignored them, but this time was different. "I knew I was next." Gathering her husband and three children, throwing their belongings into the car, she moved to a friend's home, and from there they crossed the border and made their way to Syria's capital, Damascus. '

She had thought she would stay in Damascus and keep her family safe, but her two older brothers followed her there to relay a message. Her flight, they told her, was being viewed as proof to everyone back home that she was exactly what she had been accused of being—an American spy. She came from a respected family; her father had been the most important man in their community. Their lives depended on those relationships of trust. If she stayed in Syria it would be like admitting she had done something wrong. For the safety of her extended family at home, she must return to Iraq.

Reluctantly, defiantly, she agreed. She left her husband with the children in Damascus and returned on her own. Before she left she bought new black jeans and a pair of new black boots; she decided she would walk with her head high and prove that she was proud and unafraid. When she arrived back in her village, her father-in-law, in lieu of a greeting, listed off the names of all those who had been killed or kidnapped in her absence.

This time she no longer slept at home but lived in her office at the GIC. She had everything she needed—food, a generator, a mattress, guards to watch over her. The Americans even offered her a car and driver, she said, but this she refused: it would be an obvious target. After her car broke down, she relied on her brothers to drive her around, and when they were busy, on taxis. Taking a taxi was Russian roulette, and one bright summer morning in July 2005, flagging a taxi on the street, her luck ran out.

Four cars surrounded her, each with four armed men inside. Who were they? It would take her some time to figure out the answer to that.

"You're coming with us," said one of the men. The youngest of them, a boy with a machine gun, looked hardly more than fourteen. "He wasn't even old enough to grow a proper moustache," Ahlam recalled. When he lunged at her, she grabbed him by the collar and shoved him hard against one of the cars. The man standing next to him fired a shot between her feet. "I've been tracking you for a year and a half," he snarled.

"Why didn't you just call me?" she told him. "I would have come to see you."

The man didn't like her attitude one bit. "He shot a bullet beside my right ear. He would have liked to put the bullet in my head, but they only had orders to torture me, not to kill me. He told me he'd already tried to kill me several times but he couldn't catch me."

He told her she drove too fast. "I used to drive a hundred and sixty kilometres an hour on the highway."

"You were trying to escape them?" I asked.

"No. I just like to drive fast." She sighed. "I had a Volvo. My dream in life is to have another Volvo."

The next thing she knew, she was bundled into the passenger seat of one of the cars, a blindfold across her eyes.

"I want to smoke," she said, her back stiff as a pole.

"What?" said the boy. He was sitting behind her in the back seat with his machine gun.

"Give her a cigarette," said the driver.

The boy had taken her purse. Now he dug through it until he found a pack of cigarettes. "These are American," he said suspiciously, as if this were proof of her treachery.

"No, they are Korean," Ahlam told him. Pine cigarettes, her favourite brand, are made in South Korea. "You have to learn how to read."

She didn't have time to finish her cigarette. Pulling off the road, the men grabbed her by her feet and shoulders and tossed her into the back of a truck. They changed trucks several more times along the route, tossing her from one to the next. "They were playing soccer with me, like I was the ball." She was handcuffed, the cuffs so tight on her wrists that her hands swelled, and she shouted until they loosened the bands. She was taken somewhere in the desert. The walls of the building were mud and the floors of sand, the wind so hot it burned her skin. She later heard that her boss at the GIC, an American major named Adam Shilling, had sent a hundred soldiers to look for her.

Her captors began to interrogate her. They tied her to a chair and asked about contractors, military bases, interpreters. "I didn't have any answers to their questions."

One of her captors beat her several times a day—"he seemed to be enjoying himself"—but she had the feeling there was some confusion. As if she wasn't the kind of captive they had been told to expect. They had envisioned some high-value American spy, some sort of Mata Hari, and seemed utterly baffled by a mother from a respected family who had become important enough to have information they wanted. They claimed to have reports that she travelled around in a Humvee, that she was having an affair with an American colonel, that she had dyed her black hair blonde.

"Take off my head cover," she told them. She'd always covered her hair, it was how she was raised, and since the war began it was a matter of life or death. "See for yourself."

They seemed frightened by the suggestion. Killing her would be a lesser sin in their eyes than seeing her hair. That's when she knew who they were: al-Qaeda.

For three days she was beaten, pistol-whipped, and not allowed to sleep, but then her captors began arguing among themselves. She could hear them through the walls of her room. The man who beat her argued that she ought to be killed. Another voice, one she had not heard before, agreed. "If I were in your place," he said, "I would just kill her. If she's innocent she'll go to heaven. If not she'll go to hell."

Another voice, younger, objecting. Would God not want them to discover the truth?

The younger one asked her tough questions but he never laid a hand on her. He interrogated her extensively about her central crime, working for the Americans, and she tried to convey nuance. She worked with the Americans, yes, but in fact her work was for the orphans and widows who came to her for help, and for the families of prisoners detained by American forces. She knew nothing of military bases, mercenaries, manoeuvres.

They shouted at her that this was exactly the sort of thing someone in her position *would* say. If she was lying, she would pay with her life. "I said my only request was that they don't throw my body in the river. So my mother wouldn't wonder if I was alive or dead like many of the families of the disappeared."

The young interrogator investigated everything she told him. When she told him she had helped rebuild a school, he sent a scout to check on her story. Then he took her phone and called through the numbers it contained one by one. And in the end, in the strange and circular way life sometimes works, it was the testimony of the orphans and widows she had been trying to save that saved her life.

So the feeling I had about her, that she was fearless, was right. She was fearless though she had plenty of reasons to be afraid. Because after she finished telling me this story she told me something else.

"I've figured out I'm being watched here in Damascus," she said. "Maybe by those same people who kidnapped me in Iraq."

She was wrong about it being the Iraqis, but she was indeed being watched.

Chapter 3

THE APARTMENT

AHLAM'S DAMASCUS APARTMENT REMINDED me of places I had lived in as a student. It was on the second floor of a rundown low-rise at the dead end of an alleyway. Next to the entrance was a modest kitchen with two burners where she could cook, if she were the sort of person who cooked, with a tiny bathroom off it. The four of them—she, her husband, their eight-year-old daughter, Roqayah, and ten-year-old son, Abdullah—shared the bedroom, sleeping on mats next to a locker room–style metal cabinet stuffed with most of their belongings. The large boxy living room had bare white walls and a balcony so small it was pointless. The living room had been furnished with castoffs, including a burgundy velvet sofa with carved mahogany arms that must have been someone's pride before the springs broke through the stuffing. A few stacks of books teetered on a shelf by the only window. Everything else was piled randomly into a doorless closet. On this, my second visit, Ahlam watched me take it all in. "I'm a bad housewife," she said. She sounded unapologetic. She sounded amused.

I am drawn to books. Whenever I go to someone's home and see books, I automatically start to flip through them, ignoring everything else, ignoring even the propriety of looking through someone's belongings, the inner workings of their mind perhaps, their ideals or passions or pretensions. The books they read or wish you to think they read can tell you as much or more than can be gleaned in conversation.

Most of her books were instructional guides—French lessons for Arabic speakers, books on mathematics. A few were more literary, like the copy of *Les Misérables* translated into Arabic, and *Three Cups of Tea*, a book about building schools for girls in Pakistan and Afghanistan (later discovered to be mainly fiction). She said she was collecting them for a lending library.

Fictitious or not, that book's ideas appealed to her. As I leafed through it, she told me that she and a French-American researcher named Marianne, a consultant on contract to UNICEF (and she in turn was on contract to Marianne), had spent the past three months doing fieldwork on Iraqi adolescent girls in Syria. What they learned was alarming: countless stories of sexual trafficking and forced marriage; abduction, slavery, rape. There was also isolation—the girls were often shut up in crowded apartments where they spent all day doing chores instead of going to school as they would have in Iraq. The two of them had come up with the idea of starting a school for these girls. Ahlam was about to start hosting the classes from her apartment.

I picked up an English copy of L.P. Hartley's classic novel *The Go-Between*. Ahlam said it had been given to her by a *New Yorker* journalist she had worked for and counted as a friend. Perhaps the title was a reference to Ahlam's role. And perhaps, I later thought, when I read the book in its entirety and observed how the protagonist failed in his mission and disaster followed, it was a cautionary tale. For now I merely opened the book to that famous first line: "The past is a foreign country: they do things differently there."

I had been weighing whether I could trust Ahlam. As I've said, some fixers can be double agents, not necessarily through any choice of their own but because otherwise they can be prevented from working at all. At which point you might find yourself followed, watched or evicted from the country. Not kidnapped or murdered—that usually only happens when the structures of society break down (which had already happened in Iraq), or when it can be made to look like an accident. When states attack journalists it is typically when they think they can get away with it, which is why they usually focus on their own citizens or on journalists from countries with weaker governments that can't or won't do anything to protect them. The major risk is to your sources—the people who talk to you and help you and face the consequences long after your story has run and you are gone. Especially to your primary source, your fixer.

When I made calls in the evenings to arrange meetings I never said who I was or what I wanted to discuss; the person on the other end always seemed to understand. Everyone knew you had to present your ID in order to get a SIM card for your phone, and a copy of that ID was submitted to the Syrian intelligence. To be caught doing something, even a whiff of something, meant deportation at best. For refugees that could be a death sentence.

Ahlam, however, wasn't reporting to the Ministry of Information. She was working on her own. That afternoon I described the article I was in the midst of writing, a kaleidoscopic portrait of the human consequences of the war. It seemed to me that Little Baghdad was a good place to find the human story. And surrounded by the comfortable familiarity of books, I thought she could help. She had her own story of survival and was working, like I was, unofficially. I believed we could work together.

Ahlam knew the refugees because she was one of them. She was sought out by media and human rights groups who needed accurate, reliable information about the refugees in Syria. I didn't ask her for references—that's not how it works—but if I wanted them I could have talked to the BBC, Reuters, the Wall Street Journal, Al Jazeera, or French or Australian TV— or to Amnesty, Human Rights Watch, Refugees International, the UN, all of whom she helped with their reports.

While we were talking, a friend of hers, an Iraqi professor in his fifties, stopped by to visit. Ahlam invited me to stay for dinner with them that evening. The professor was a famous historian, the author of dozens of books, and had (or *had* had) his own television show in Baghdad on current and historical affairs. He had been friends with Ahlam's family for thirty years. Meeting him confirmed my decision to trust her.

Wearing a brown suit that had rumpled in the heat, his red tie slung over his shoulder like a dog's tongue, he mentioned that a book he had written—about sex in the time of the Prophet—had infuriated the religious establishment. "They call me the Salman Rushdie of Iraq," he said, looking delighted. After the invasion, caught up in the burst of optimism that followed Saddam Hussein's fall, he started one of the first pro-democracy newspapers, *Baghdad Dawn*. Now, after three attempts on his life in Baghdad, he was on the run in Syria.

He said he couldn't understand why the intellectuals—doctors and professors and research scientists—were being systematically murdered, when they were above the Sunni–Shia nonsense. "No one knows who's behind it. The Sunnis blame Iran. The Shia blame Saudi Arabia and the US. They use idiots, teenagers to do the killings. If you ask me, the ideology of the Wahhabis is behind this"—the fundamentalist Saudi form of Islam. But whoever they were, as often happens where dissidents are viewed as a threat, they wanted to destroy the country's brain trust, eliminating those who could prevent the country from slipping into a dark age.

Though the professor was considered an expert on current affairs, he confessed that he no longer understood what was going on. "I say something in the morning and find I'm wrong at night." He preferred to talk about the past. He talked about Alexander of Macedon ("you call him Alexander the Great") who had invaded what is now Iraq in the fourth century BC. Alexander thought he could solve the problems he encountered there by forcing the locals to marry Greeks. "His teacher Aristotle laughed at him. He said, in fifty years you will not succeed in changing these people: you will change the Greeks!"

Ahlam had gone out and brought back takeout. Kebab, roast chicken, roast tomatoes, rice and bread, steaming from Styrofoam. At the smell of food, her children, Abdullah and Roqayah, emerged shyly from the bedroom where they had been watching TV. Sitting cross-legged around a table-cloth that Ahlam had set down on the living room floor, we feasted.

Her husband didn't join us. He had been an engineer before the war and was now unemployed; the family lived on whatever Ahlam earned as a fixer. Like a lot of people, her husband was rediscovering the religion that had been set aside in the days when they lived in big houses, had busy careers and drove nice cars. Now he was where he always was these days: at the mosque. He went five times a day.

"God gets bored with him," Ahlam said, as she emerged from the kitchen with a pot of tea.

The professor laughed. "Ahlam is the model Iraqi woman," he said, turning to me. "I want to write a book about her one day. She's a fighter. Have you seen her get mad?"

I had. Earlier in the day a man had come to her door: it turned out that she was a source of advice and assistance not only for journalists but for other refugees. The man wanted to know which kind of people she helped: was it the Sunni or the Shia? At those words she flew into a rage, shouting at the man to get out and not come back until he stopped talking that way. It was a false divide, manipulated by those for whom it had advantages, was how she explained it to me. She had known Shia who had saved the lives of Sunnis, "and vice versa."

The professor was Shia, Ahlam was Sunni, and both of them hated such distinctions. ⸗

After dinner I took a cab back to my new apartment. I felt the thrum of excitement that came when I knew I'd hit the mark. I had found a hub, a connector, one of those people who knows people, knows what's going on.

The streets of Damascus reflected my mood. I have known more beautiful cities, such as Shiraz or Isfahan. And more chaotic: Cairo, Mexico City, Gaza City, Tehran. More ambitious: Dubai, Doha. More hedonistic: Havana, Beirut, Dubai again. More religiously significant, whether Jerusalem or, with its Zoroastrian fire temple and open-air burial towers, Yazd. But Damascus, vying with Baghdad as the oldest continually inhabited city on Earth, was hard to beat. And I always love places that have remained somehow cut off from the wider world and still have something to show me that isn't available everywhere.

Damascus was even better than expected. I liked to lose myself in the walled Old City with its narrow stone passageways, passing churches fronted by rose bushes and Roman ruins glowing sepia in the setting sun. There was a sense of pride in the city's long history and signs of growing prosperity. Most striking was the way every sort of person melded in the bazaars and the shopping districts, whether secular or any variety of religion or ethnicity. In the cool of the evenings, the city's cosmopolitan residents sat outside on café terraces, men and women mixing freely, the scent of fruit-flavoured tobacco wafting from the water pipes they passed from hand to hand. Through an unpromising entryway—meeting one of my contacts, a logistician from Doctors Without Borders who himself was undercover—I had found myself in a fine old house built for a family of thirty that had been transformed into an elegant restaurant filled with whispering fountains and potted orange trees. Damascenes were warm but shy, intellectual but reticent. When they complained about the influx of Iraqis driving up prices and crime rates, it

was always with sympathy, accompanied by the blunt sentiment: "We don't want their war to come to us."

Nearing my street the taxi was snared in the evening
crowds. American pop music thumped from car windows.
Laughter and wolf whistles. Smoke billowing from a hip sidewalk crêperie. The scent of exhaust and cardamom. From
sundown until two or three in the morning, all summer
long, thousands of young men and women turned downtown Damascus into a nightly Mardi Gras. It was a party that
would end like a fast car hitting an embankment, but it still
felt like it could go on forever.

I paid the driver and got out to walk the last few blocks,
making my way through the crowds, passing espresso bars
where the young intelligentsia hunched over laptops the way
their elders had over backgammon boards. The brand-new
pizza parlour was decked out in red checkered tablecloths
and flickering candlelight. A beautiful girl in jeans and a
bustier perched on the front of a parked car like a hood orna-
ment, surrounded by a bevy of male admirers.

This was the chic modern shopping district of Sha'alan,
where young women in tank tops clustered in front of bright
windows displaying the latest fashions from London and Paris.
The occasional fully covered woman, all in black with her male
guardian, window-shopped too, gazing through the slit in her
veil. The former, in their Western garb, might be Christian or
Alawite; the latter was undoubtedly Sunni. In 2007 it still mattered little in the capital city, where there was only one religion
and it was the same as everywhere else—getting and spending.

I felt safe in Sha'alan. Everyone did. Money has insulat-
ing properties. If the inflation caused by the influx of Iraqis

was forcing poor Syrians to take second jobs and speak with dismay of the skyrocketing price of tomatoes, it was making others rich. One could feel the tremors of discontent in the poor neighbourhoods that surrounded the city, but in affluent Sha'alan all I noticed was a slight uptick in religious sentiment on the part of the Sunnis—striking because religious identities were discouraged by the Alawite state under President Bashar al-Assad. It was considered poor taste even to ask about such things. Yet the man who had rented me the apartment, an educated Syrian gentleman with a son studying medicine in the United States, told me he had recently recommitted to his faith. He apologized for not shaking my female hand.

The war that shook the world four years later, in the spring of 2011, has been often described as sectarian, a revolt by the Sunni majority against the largely secular Alawite dictatorship—the Alawites being an oddball splinter sect of Shia Islam (combining elements of Christian, Gnostic, Neoplatonic and Zoroastrian thought) that is today more cultural than religious. Yet the Sunni business class and most of the minorities would end up siding with the state. That is because its true genesis was a class war: the city versus the countryside.

On the plane over—a packed Syrian Arab Airlines flight from Gatwick—I had sat next to a young Syrian on a break from his studies at the London School of Economics. Slim, clean-cut and urbane, he was emblematic of the new middle and upper classes that were thriving under Bashar al-Assad. Throughout the five-hour flight he regaled me with stories of the ways the economy of Syria was liberalizing, the country finally opening up to the outside world as the nation embraced market reforms. Hence the girls laden with shopping bags, construction cranes hovering over luxury developments, the heady optimism in these streets. Hence the influx of foreign investment, the privatization of state lands and services, the cuts to subsidies that most benefitted the poor.

Meanwhile the countryside, where half the Syrian population scraped out a living, was in the midst of the worst drought ever known. Farmers were abandoning their fields and flocking to the cities, where they found themselves competing for jobs with refugees eager to work for scraps. A decade of migration from the countryside into cities that could not integrate them fast enough brought two disparate worlds—that of "haves" and "have-nots"—into collision.[12] The majority of those have-nots just happened to be Sunni (though the majority of the Syrian army is also Sunni)[13]. While the initial protests inspired by the so-called Arab Spring involved urban progressives, including Alawites[14] and other liberals critical of the ruling clique, the solidarity was short-lived. After government forces fired on protestors, spurring more protestors, and some of the protestors armed themselves to shoot back, Saudi Arabia saw a chance to strike a blow to an ally of its enemy, Iran, transforming what had been a civil uprising into a sectarian proxy war. As foreign jihadists poured in through Turkey, they brought their own interests, neither Syria nor democracy among them. The revolution was over—hijacked by outsiders.[15]

At a corner store I bought necessities: coffee, milk, a bottle of Lebanese wine. Upstairs in my empty apartment, I turned on the air conditioner that served as a kind of white noise, dulling the racket of the street party outside. Pouring wine into a kitchen tumbler, I wandered out onto the terrace. If the apartment was modest, designed as a mother-in-law's suite, the terrace was a wonder. The entire rooftop, twice the size of the apartment itself, was painted flamingo pink, including the fountain that was its centrepiece. It was the kind of terrace where I imagined dinner parties, tuxedoed waiters, champagne in some era long past.

The war was still far off, in another country, and time remained to do things differently here. From the edge of the roof, I could almost see my favourite bakery, closed for the night, where working-class men in thin T-shirts perspired in front of an open furnace from which emerged delicious cheese and zaatar pastries that they never let me pay for. I was a visitor, a guest. "If you have any trouble, just call us," they said, self-appointed guardians of my well-being. I was never able to pass by without being waved over to accept a pastry, hot from the coals, which they made me feel, by their humility and graciousness, was a gift to them as much as to me.

On the rooftop across from mine a troupe of boys, ten or eleven years of age, were singing an American boy-band ballad, choreographing their dance moves in the shadow of a giant satellite dish. The lyrics belted out in accented English floated over to me like a happy serenade. "Girl . . . don't you know?" The night air pleasantly cool, the wine sharp and almost sweet, the moon overhead a spotlight illuminating this performance for its audience of one. .

Chapter 4

THE DEATH DIVISION

WITH AHLAM MY WORK entered a new phase. With her to guide me, as summer counted down, I came to know Little Baghdad's streets, its alleyways, its cramped apartments, dimly lit to conserve electricity. Even when we could easily walk to meetings with refugees we usually took taxis to avoid being seen together. She had noticed a man lurking outside her building, taking photographs of her when she came and went. Two others had followed her when she went to buy groceries. One pretended to take a picture of the other but the flash went off in her face. There were revenge killings between Iraqis, and militias who followed their victims over the border to Syria, so she wondered if it was her kidnappers, putting the fear into her.

Yet wherever we went together we were greeted warmly. Doors opened, pillows were propped behind our backs as we sat down, tea poured. She embraced the women; sometimes they wept while she held them. "You are my eyes," she would say, in the Arabic way. "You are my heart." Afterwards we always ended up back at her apartment to discuss what we had heard and seen that day, and any news she had had from her contacts in Iraq.

"A lot of things have gone crazy down there," she said, tearing open a pack of cigarettes. "Do you know they are putting underwear on the animals now?" She was talking about al-Qaeda, which threatened to kill farmers who didn't comply along with their livestock. "They've started hanging cloth over the animals' backsides. Cows, donkeys, sheep. Only the chickens are exempt because they can't tell male from female."

We laughed at the absurd image, imagining the lengths one must go to in order to put underwear on farm animals. "And you aren't allowed to sell a cucumber beside a tomato in the market anymore, or make a salad with cucumbers and tomatoes, because the cucumber is male and the tomato is female."

Ahlam's apartment was always a hive of activity. Not only her two "monkeys," as she called her children, who turned out not to be shy at all. They were always tussling, playing, or draping themselves around her neck as if she might be taken from them at any moment. And they had to compete for her attention: there were always refugees waiting to talk to her. Sometimes three or four—on more than one occasion I counted a dozen. They would explain their situations and she would promise to see what she could do.

But what could she do for the woman whose husband had been shot in the back by American soldiers while taking his television to a repair shop, who was now responsible for supporting five children while caring for her paralyzed husband? What could she do for the widowed mother of a teenaged boy who had been tortured by militants? His mother was now trying to stop his constant suicide attempts, though she had three other children to care for and he could not be left alone near a knife, a shoelace, an electrical socket. What for the man who brought a sheaf of documents proving that he had worked as an interpreter for the Marines, before his house was blown up? He was trying to get accepted to the United States but was told he needed a reference letter from no lesser rank than an American general. "Why didn't they tell me that earlier, when I was hired?" he asked me. "I can't get one now."

Many of the refugees had received letters ordering them to leave Iraq or die. Often the letters were signed with sinister names that reminded me of heavy metal bands. The Angel of Death. The Death Division. Sometimes they were accompanied by a bullet, drops of blood, a chicken head. As if dictated from a central office, these letters explained that the person belonged to such-and-such a sect, and was therefore an infidel, a terrorist, a "threat to national security."

Sometimes these letters were a tool of the sectarian cleansing that drove out people like the mild-mannered high school history teacher I met through Ahlam. Slim, early thirties, lame in his left leg from birth, he was one of the hundred thousand professionals who lost their jobs in the very first order issued by Paul Bremer in May of 2003. Coalition Provisional Authority's Order Number One—"the De-Baathification of Iraqi society"—was intended to purge the new political system of any influence from the former regime by firing members of Saddam Hussein's Baath Party and banning them forever from working in the public sector. What the order failed to acknowledge was that many people

had only joined the party to keep their jobs or avoid harass-
ment from Hussein's secret police; and anyone who wanted
to pursue graduate studies *had* to join. Bremer's single order
effectively lobotomized the country.

"I learned about it when I went to pick up my salary," said
the history teacher, who was one of forty thousand schoolteachers fired. The next day looters showed up at his house.
"They stole every stick of furniture." Then his life was threatened. He came from a city in southern Iraq. "It's a mixed
city, Sunni and Shia, but the new leaders were sectarian
Shia. I know for a fact that all those killed in my city were
ex–Baath Party members because they had master's degrees
or doctorates, so they had to be. If I show my own face in
town, the authorities have my name and my photograph. I
will be hunted and killed." He spent three years roaming
the countryside with a tribe of nomads who treated him as a
guest until he eventually raised the money to bribe an official for a passport that allowed him to come here. He missed
his wife and three small daughters, but his presence had put
their lives at risk. "They are better off without me."

With the change in regime, Iraq had splintered into mul-
titudes of militias. Some fought the Americans—these were
mainly Sunni—some fought the new government, some
fought one another. (The Mahdi Army, the largest of the
Shia militias, supported by the poorest of the slum-dwellers,
fought the Americans *and* the Sunnis *and* the government,
although they had seats in government.) Some of the fighters were foreign, whether Saudis who joined groups like
al-Qaeda, or Iranians advising the government—it turned out
power had been handed to Shia political activists who had

taken shelter from Saddam Hussein in Iran in the 1980s—but most were Iraqi. And most of them, for all the evil they did, believed they were fighting to defend themselves and protect their communities, which had predictably fractured along tribal and religious lines, since whom do you call in troubled times but family and friends? Plus the militias gave them jobs, cars, phones and protection—and often no choice.

Politics were behind many of the death threats, but as often as not they were simply a cover for organized crime, an excuse to kick people out of their houses and steal their property and businesses. Gangsters were living in the best villas in Baghdad, driving around in company cars. Who was going to stop them? Everyone said the police *were* the militias now.

"We moved from one dictator to a multi-dictatorship system," an Iraqi journalist told me. "People who can harm you, shut you up or put you in jail. A young guy can come and tell you not to walk down this street, and you have to obey. This young man is a dictator. So now we have tens of thousands of dictators."

On the market street two blocks from Ahlam's apartment, which I occasionally walked through on my way home, the scent of fresh baking lured me into the Baghdad Bakery, where glass cases displayed cookies and syrupy sweets. The four Shia brothers who owned it with a Christian friend had recently closed up shop in Iraq and reopened here. They used to live in a wealthy Sunni neighbourhood of Baghdad that they could no longer enter. Their houses and factories had been taken over by gangs. The brothers could not explain what had happened, how the war had turned neighbour against neighbour. "All six of our sisters married Sunnis," said one of them, a grey-haired Scotch-drinker in a madras shirt, "and I don't even know how to pray."

A lot of the people I spoke to seemed disoriented, stunned. "I'm dizzy," a young man told me. "I don't know what I'm doing here." A year shy of finishing a degree in English, he had just lost his father—tortured to death—and his mother spent all day gazing at her husband's photograph, refusing to let go of his clothes. Though his mother was Shia and his father was Sunni, his name was Omar, an identifiably Sunni first name. "And that's big fucking trouble," he told me. "My name is a curse."

Militants had tried to recruit him and so had the Americans, since they needed interpreters. He fled to Syria because he wanted nothing to do with either. "The militias killed my father, and the Americans—they brought this war. Before we never had this Sunni–Shia problem. Now we are like in America, black against white."

Most of the refugees insisted they were "all Iraqis." If I asked which sect they belonged to, they looked as if my words had caused them pain. "We ran from it there," Ahlam explained. "We don't want to talk about it here. Whoever is doing these things is fighting for power and money, not for the future of Iraq."

One afternoon Ahlam and I took a taxi to the end of a dusty alleyway not far from her apartment. It was the home of a former Iraqi intelligence officer who was a Sunni and a captain in the once fearsome Fedayeen Saddam, a paramilitary group made up of Shia as well as Sunnis that had reported directly to Saddam Hussein. The captain told me that the biggest mistake of the war was to "lay the Iraqi army off work." He was referring to Order Number Two of the Coalition Provisional Authority: to fire the Iraqi army and intelligence services without securing the weapons depots. (And to disband the border guard, throwing open the country to smugglers and foreign fighters.[16]) These unemployed soldiers—well-trained, angry and with families to feed—formed the core of the militias that were fighting for control of Iraq.

The man spent his days feeding and bathing his wife, who had been paralyzed when their farmhouse near Baghdad was hit with rocket-propelled grenades by the Badr Brigade, a Shia paramilitary group connected to the new Iraqi government. She was thin, with lustrous black hair that tumbled from her sea-green headscarf. She had been lying on a mat in a corner of their apartment for the past two years, ever since the family had fled to Damascus. "Hysterical paralysis," read the medical report her husband showed me.

Their eldest daughter had been killed in the attack, their eldest son abducted and tortured with electric cables to the head—now he babbled incoherently and was violent unless drugged. Their nine-year-old daughter was left badly burned. They could not afford surgery for her burns, which had puffed up like a topographical map. Nor were they able to send her to school: their presence in Syria was illegal because the family did not have a residency permit. To acquire a permit he would have to cross back into Iraq, and re-enter Syria legally. If he did that he believed he would be killed. "Whoever captures me gets thousands of dollars," he said.

"What about the girl?" I asked Ahlam as we took our leave. Outside, the sunlight was blinding. Her father told us his daughter didn't go outside much because some local children bullied her, taunting her as "the burned girl."

"None of this is her fault," I said. "She's just a child. She should be in school."

"She will marry a man who beats her and have children who can't read," Ahlam said.

The eight-hundred-kilometre drive from Baghdad to Damascus takes twelve hours, much of it through barren desert navigated at high speed to avoid roadside bandits, but it slows to twenty-four tense hours if you are stuck behind army vehicles. Ahlam's youngest brother, Salaam, had spent the past four years as a driver ferrying passengers back and forth in his SUV. "A dangerous job," I said to him. "For sure," he replied. A baby-faced guy of thirty-five with the build of a nightclub bouncer, he showed me his four identity cards—his own, a Shia, a Sunni, and a neutral college ID that bought him time to figure out what to say if the intentions of the men who stopped his vehicle were unclear.

Since the highway from Iraq into Syria passed through Anbar province, a desperately poor Sunni stronghold that had witnessed more violence than anywhere outside Baghdad (it would later fall to Islamic State), Salaam gave his Shia passengers what he called "lessons in how to stay alive," telling them which sheikh to say they knew, which region to say they were from, and which family, in case they were stopped. Once, ambushed by bandits with machine guns protruding from the sunroof of a black BMW, one of his Shia passengers was so frightened he forgot the lesson. He began stammering in front of the gunmen. Salaam slapped him across the face.

"Speak, man!" he ordered. His passenger remembered the lesson and survived.

"Most of my passengers from Baghdad are highly educated people," he told me. "Everyone who returns says they've run out of money, so they have to go back, even if they know they will probably be killed. If they can sell something there, they come back to Syria."

Salaam often stopped by Ahlam's apartment with news from the village where they had grown up. Of their beloved mother who still lived along the Tigris River but would no longer eat fish because she was convinced the fish were feeding on bodies dumped in the waterway. Of the latest viral videos, like the one Salaam showed me on his phone of a young fighter from the Mahdi Army, film-star handsome, arrested by Iraqi security forces while trying to flee in a wedding dress and forced to do a strip tease.

"Do you think they killed him?" I asked, handing him back his phone.

He shrugged. "Him? He's probably back out on the street."

By day I was going out to speak to frightened people, and at night returning to my apartment, my terrace, the moonlight overhead. "Sorry I missed you on chat," I emailed my boyfriend, explaining the long hours. It was impossible to convey what I was seeing in a brief email, so I didn't try. I was meeting people in shock, people needy but asking nothing from me; it would be shameful to ask something of a guest. They were surprised by my interest in their stories because, as they said, quite rightly, "This happened to everyone." The women gave me gifts, shyly, apologizing that it could not be more. On the windowsill in my apartment was a bottle of perfume that made me sad whenever I looked at it because I knew I would never use it. Yet I could not refuse without giving offence, without saying outright that they had nothing and I everything. I felt the awkwardness of taking their gifts, and then taking more: their stories, the accounting of what had been lost.

I had begun to feel like a medieval doctor bleeding his patients while holding out the promise of healing. In my case I knew better: nothing I could write had much chance of solving their problems or changing their destinies. I began to fear that the recitation of memory only reopened wounds.

When I asked Ahlam what she hoped to accomplish in her work as a fixer, she said, "Someone has to open the door and show the world what is happening." I had come to Ahlam because she opened doors, and even as I walked through them I kept looking for something more in what I was seeing and hearing and writing down. I was looking for a gateway into something mysterious that eluded me. A way to understand the foreign country that was the war, and how anyone could survive and yet remain human.

She had. Ahlam had. Of all the people I met, she had somehow managed not to be crushed. Being around her felt, even for me, like a reprieve. I don't know why. Not then and not now. A great disaster had taken place, yet all was not lost. She was proof of that. It was the reason people came to her, although there was not always much that she could do. Just being around her made them feel better, as it did me.

Chapter 5

A FREE BIRD

AHLAM WAS BORN IN 1965, the fifth of seven children: three girls, four boys, all tall and strong like their father, Ahmed. It was a happy childhood, though that might have been a mixed blessing. It gave her dreams that set her up for loss, that placed her on the outside of the culture. That is what her name, Ahlam, means: dreams.

The way she told it, as we talked on those first sweltering afternoons and over the coming year, she had an unusual father. He was her mentor and closest friend. He was the person who protected her from the world and armed her for it, as if he had known all along she would need to be ready.

Ahmed was a self-made man. He was born in a Sunni village northwest of Baghdad, a secluded date grove along the western bank of the Tigris River that runs through the city. He was a second-born son, which meant his older brother was first in line to inherit the land Ahlam's grandfather owned and would eventually become the village sheikh.

Since Ahmed had neither wealth nor prospects, when it came time to marry, none of the girls in the village would have him. So he left the village and married a "foreigner," as they called a girl from another tribe. While he didn't see his bride's face until their wedding day, it turned out to be a happy marriage—a partnership unusual for its time.

The newlyweds set up house in Kadhimiya, a nearby suburb of northwest Baghdad that had grown up around the city's holiest shrine for Shia Muslims: a place of gold shops and libraries and minarets and a bustling economy catering to the pilgrims who came to worship at the magnificent eighth-century burial shrine of the Imam Musa al-Kadhim, descendant of the Prophet. In Kadhimiya, the young family's prosperity grew along with their brood.

In 1958—the year the Iraqi royal family was machine-gunned, ending the monarchy the British had set up after the First World War—Ahmed opened a small service station where he specialized in oil changes. Soon he was doing well enough to invest in a fleet of delivery trucks that brought goods into Baghdad from as far away as Lebanon and Jordan. By the time Ahlam was born he was buying real estate, becoming the landlord of several houses and an apartment building in the rapidly developing suburb. "In ten years he made a fortune," Ahlam recalled.

In 1978, Ahmed's older brother died, leaving the village without a leader. The villagers remembered the younger brother who had left home and made good; they paid him a visit. That year, when Ahlam was twelve and on the verge of finishing primary school, her family moved from the city into the big new six-bedroom house her father had built for them on the riverfront.

The village was a lush green oasis filled with orchards of lemon and orange trees, tall grasses, and sugary date palms that were notched along the trunks so the village girls—who normally left school after a year or two, if they went at all—could scramble up them, right to the top. Some four hundred people lived there in forty or so family clusters, spreading their houses out along the rise above the Tigris. As each new generation married and had families of their own, smaller houses constellated around the parental home. Everyone left their doors open to make it clear that anyone was welcome for tea or a gossip at any time. Their dirt driveways pushed through the greenery towards the paved highway that was a main route into Baghdad. The city was within a half-hour's drive, but seemed a world away.

At the outskirts of the village, near the main road, was a small mosque and a cluster of "everything shops," selling the sorts of sundries they couldn't make or grow themselves. Ahmed's family would farm, of course—that was the point of having land—growing lemons and oranges and apples and dates, raising sheep and cows and ducks and chickens, and Ahmed would manage the village affairs while continuing to tend to his business concerns in the city.

His other children might jump on his back at the end of the day, be carted around on his broad shoulders, but Ahlam was certain she was his favourite. Her brother Samir, two years older, was the closest to her in age, and the two were early rivals. When Ahmed went out on business, it was Ahlam he let tag along. When he presided over village council meetings in the men's reception hall built onto their new house, he ignored the prohibitions against females taking part and allowed his curious daughter to sit by the door and listen. After the men left he let Ahlam ask questions, explaining his rationale for making this or that decision.

As the new sheikh, he was already doing things that struck the villagers as odd. For one thing, he drove around with his pretty wife next to him in the passenger seat rather than seated demurely behind him in the back. For another, he decided to divide the land his older brother had left to him equally among all of his siblings, Ahlam's aunts and uncles, making sure the aunts received an equal share. Traditionally his sisters would not have inherited—what if they married out of the tribe and the land fell out of their hands?—but Ahmed disagreed with this policy. To ensure that there were no accusations of favouritism, he brought in a surveyor to mark off the plots, then allocated them by lottery.

"He was different from the other fathers," Ahlam said. "He raised me like a boy." With the river tantalizingly close to their new house, she longed to learn how to swim, something girls didn't do. When she broached the subject with her father, he called over Samir and one of her male cousins. "Teach her to swim," he said.

"And of course they could not refuse an order, he's the father," Ahlam said. But they didn't have to be happy about it. The two teenaged boys trudged sullenly down to the river-bank with the girl in tow. They drew twelve-year-old Ahlam out to where the current ran swiftest, then released her and swam off.

She fought, thrashing about in the dangerous current. "And in fighting I learned how to swim. But the difficulty isn't to learn to swim in the water," she added, musingly. "The difficulty is to learn to swim in life." Her father taught her that. "He pushed me into the sea of life." Taught her to drive a car, to shoot a pistol, to rely on herself in all things.

He was someone who understood that the hermetic world of the village was about to change. Perhaps because he'd seen the way women in Baghdad were trickling into the workforce: by the 1980s, they were working as doctors, professors, lawyers, running the ministries and public services, because the men were away at war with Iran. He might not have been liberal in a Western sense of the word, but neither was he in favour of a wife walking several strides behind her husband, nor of forced marriages, which he believed ultimately resulted in misery. He alone among the village men allowed his daughters to accept or reject prospective husbands, even if the results weren't always what he would have wanted. One of Ahlam's older sisters married a man who drank and gambled and beat her up. The other moved to her husband's hometown, a severe place where she wasn't allowed to set foot outside the house. Both of them eventually moved back home, divorced their husbands, and later remarried. In any other family this would have been a scandal.

Ahlam liked to quote the "life lessons" her father had taught her:

"Depend on yourself. Wherever you are, begin. Begin and the rest will follow."

"If you're afraid, don't speak. If you speak, don't be afraid."

"There is no difference between Sunni and Shia, and I will never hear you speak of that again."

"That was the only time he ever slapped me." She was six years old and they were still living in the city. At her primary school her teacher had taught the students the difference between the two calls to prayer—the Shia add a line about Ali, whom they see as the Prophet's legitimate successor. Coming home from school that day she saw her father talking to someone. Eager to show off her knowledge, she asked him whether the man was Sunni or Shia. His palm came down hard on her cheek. "May that be a lesson to you. We are all brothers."

"What did you think?" I asked.

"I was shocked. His spoiled daughter slapped? I still feel ashamed to ask that question."

The same went for rich or poor: no differences. "Coffins don't have pockets," he said.

While he raised her like a boy, he also let her hide away in her room all day with a book, avoiding the women's work that didn't interest her. She had been taken to Mutanabbi Street, the literary heart of Baghdad, where amid the tens of thousands of books she found an Arabic translation of *The Old Man and the Sea*. "This is your salary for the week," her father said, handing her enough money to pay for it. With her "salary" she became a regular customer at an enormous bookshop piled high with new and used books from around the world. It was here, on what became weekly visits, that she discovered Shakespeare, Tolstoy, Dostoevsky, Hugo and the author of *Love in the Time of Cholera* whose name she always forgot. She fell in love with the tale of *Don Quixote*, the romantic idealist who sets out to right the world's wrongs. She was an equal opportunity reader, devouring dog-eared copies of Agatha Christie alongside works by the famous tenth-century poet for whom the bookselling street was named.

While the other girls in the village were scrambling up date trees, scything the long grass for hay, dreaming of marriage and children, she was discovering new worlds in books. Aside from her family, books were all she cared about. Later she would reflect on how her upbringing might have made her oblivious to certain matters. She remembered a time in the 1990s when she was completely broke and a pretentious neighbour came to tea at her empty house. "She was wearing gold bracelets, rings, earrings. She kept waving her hands as she talked. I wondered why she was moving her hands around like this, if maybe she had a medical problem, so I asked my sister about it later."

"You're a fool," her sister told her. "She is trying to show you she is rich!"

By the time Ahlam had finished primary school she was fourteen. In those days, that was the age when village girls would begin entertaining offers of marriage. When her parents raised the subject—there was a suitable young man who had asked for her hand—she threw a fit. She screamed. She shouted. She didn't want to get married. Well, her parents asked, what did she want then?

She had a new dream: she wanted to go to high school.

Her mother had married her father at fourteen. She was a country girl who wore gold bands around her slim bronze ankles and believed a pinch of salt would keep away evil. Her father was more worldly, but he himself had gone no further than learning to read and write: that's all the children his age had been taught, and only the boys. Maybe he wanted his daughter to have opportunities he himself would have liked. "And I was the only one of his children interested in school." Maybe he also wanted to protect her from the fate he saw befall so many women—like his uncle's first wife, abandoned with two children after a disastrous forced marriage—made miserable by the vagaries of men and fortune. Because the moment she spoke her dream aloud, he seemed even more excited by the idea than she was.

"I am giving her a weapon," he announced to those who argued that a village girl had no need of schooling in order to tend orange trees and date palms, and that mixing with boys at school could stain her honour. "No one," he told them, "knows what the future holds."

The year was 1979, and no one did. A popular revolution had brought the deeply pious Ayatollah Khomeini to power in Iran, overthrowing the decadent American-backed Shah and his American-trained secret police. A group of Iranian students, worried—given the CIA coup of 1953—that the Americans were about to stage a counter-coup, had taken dozens of American diplomats hostage at the US embassy in Tehran, holding them for 444 days. Meanwhile Saddam Hussein, long known for a scale of violence shocking even for Baghdad, had taken the presidency of Iraq. With the support of the United States, which backed him even when he started using poison gas,[17] he would invade Iran within the year, launching a war that killed a million people, half of them Iraqis.

By then a small war was raging inside Ahlam's house. She had never seen her father like this: smoking cigarette after cigarette, furious at his own relatives, yelling at his sons. Since she was the first of their girls ever to attend high school, the entire village was talking, pressuring him to stop this dangerous and pointless precedent. Usually her father was calm, generous, decisive. Now she could hear him shouting: "She is my daughter and I decide!" And to the astonishment of the men who came to state their objections, even to jeer at him that he seemed to want a daughter who could support him financially, he said, "I trust she will do something great."

That her desire to go to high school coincided with the rise of Saddam Hussein had a lot to do with their objections. Since the assassination of the royal family in 1958, Iraq had been rocked by a series of violent military coups. By the end of the 1960s the Baath Party had consolidated power, having murdered thousands of suspected communist sympathizers based on lists provided by the CIA.[18] Saddam Hussein became vice-president to his cousin, a former general named Ahmed Hassan al-Bakr, but in 1979 al-Bakr stepped aside.

It wasn't so much the change in leadership that upset the villagers—leaders had always come and gone—but his purge of senior members of his own party was alarming. Twenty-two men convicted of plotting against him had been executed. Meetings were held around the country to calm the situation: these men were traitors so no one was to feel sorry for them. Ahlam recalled her schoolteacher, a high-ranking Baath Party member who must have been rattled, telling her class she had seen Saddam Hussein shoot his own brother-in-law in the head.

What really upset the villagers, what affected them directly, was the new leader's education law. It required all children—girls and boys—to attend school to the end of sixth grade. This policy eventually made Iraqi women the most educated in the region, raising literacy rates from one in ten to nine in ten.[19] If the new law was intended to drag Iraq into the modern age, it was also viewed as an attempt to undermine tribal authority. And here was Ahlam, the daughter of the village's most prominent man, intent on going even further than the law required. The struggle to stop her united the village. Her father refused to back down.

"What happened then?" I asked.

"The men shut up. He's the father, the sheikh of the village, so they could do nothing."

To Ahlam he spoke words she would recall for the rest of her life.

"You're a free bird, *lozah*." His pet name for her, almond. "Don't let anyone put you in a cage."

She could continue with school on two conditions. One, that she behave. People would be watching for her to mess up. And two, that she wear the hijab and the abaya, the awkward shroud of black cloth that covered her from head to foot. "The most miserable thing was the abaya." She kept tripping on it and falling down. "Everyone laughed at me. But I had to wear it. If not—stay home."

The school was fifteen kilometres from the village. On the first day her father pressed coins into her hand. He pointed towards the highway where she would find a collective taxi to take her there. Despite her pleas he refused to go with her. "Depend on yourself," he said.

More afraid than she had ever been, grappling with her new and hated abaya, she trudged down the driveway to the main road. Above her, date palms swayed in the sun. She was on her own for the first time in her life. The air was stiff with heat and the sweetness of the fields, with everything familiar and dear. Perhaps this was all a mistake. Perhaps it was hubris. She should have stayed home like her sisters and lived like every other village girl.

It was too late to turn back. She could see the taxi coming from a distance, the future roaring towards her on wheels.

When she got to the school she stepped out of the taxi, caught her legs in the folds of her garment and landed face down in the dirt. Ignoring the laughter of the other passengers, she stood up, brushed herself off and took her first steps into the world.

When Ahlam was a student at Baghdad University in the mid-1980s, her father paid for her to take lessons in street-fighting. She told me this one night as we walked down the dirt alleyway next to Zainab's shrine. It was almost midnight. Almost silent. The golden dome of the shrine, lit from below, glowed like a gas flare.

"I returned to my village from the university after dark," she explained. She wanted to know how to defend herself and had seen a sign at a gym near the university offering self-defence classes for women. There an athletic young woman taught her how to wave her hands as a distraction and knee an attacker in the groin. To throttle a lecherous taxi driver with the handles of a handbag. To aim the pointed heel of a shoe at the jugular. She hadn't had to use her training, she said, except during her kidnapping, when she collared the boy with the machine gun and threw him against the car. It was more of a mindset: knowing you had the tools to fight if you had to.

Her father died of cancer six months before her university graduation. On his deathbed, when Ahlam moved a cot into his room to be near him, Ahmed had been planning her university graduation party. A feast, the new car he would present to her, with all the villagers in attendance. He wanted to show everyone who had opposed her education how proud he was, to show them all. "But he died too soon."

He was the one person who had believed in her without reservation. "With him," she told me, "I felt like I had all the power in the world. He taught me to be gentle, to have a good heart, but in a dangerous situation not to be afraid. He taught me to be wild when necessary." After his death she stopped eating and was soon so thin that people began warning her mother that she would join her father in the grave. But she marshalled her strength and completed her studies; it was what he would have wanted. She brought her diploma to his graveside. "Here it is," she told him, holding it out to the air.

She had been the first girl from the village to finish high school and the first, man or woman, to earn a university degree. Four other girls from the village later followed her to the university. "What's so great about Ahlam?" parents began asking themselves. "Our daughter is just as good as she is." What had been taboo was now a status symbol. When American soldiers later came to the village, they were struck by how educated all the girls were.

But instead of the brilliant career her father had predicted, Ahlam went straight from university to the family farm. The war with Iran had shattered the economies of both countries. Sanctions were about to start, barbed wire around the country's trade that would have devastating consequences for the newly educated middle class. Her mother, ill since the death of her father, was unable to manage alone. Ahlam, as the only unmarried daughter—even her youngest sister, Roqayah, or Tutu, as she was called, had married by then—was the one to whom the duty fell.

The scent of green fields at dawn would always remind her of her father. It was him she would think of as she rose from her bed at first light, as she took on the labour of tending their orchards and fields. She had known nothing until then about back-breaking farm work.

Slowly, watching the other girls, who laughed at her clumsiness but were eager to teach her, she learned to scythe the hay and load it onto the back of the donkey. Awkwardly, but growing in physical strength, she shimmied up the date palms to pick the golden fruit. Neighbours came to watch. "Look at the scholar!" they gloated. "A lot of good your education has done you. What a waste of time."

Her tongue was as sharp as the scythe that cut her untrained fingers. "Education is a weapon!" she shot back, echoing her father's words. "I'll use it when I need it."

"And that," she told me, smiling broadly, "is what I did."

She dreamed of becoming a flight attendant and seeing the world. But she couldn't afford the bribes for such a career, and wouldn't have been hired anyway: a country girl with no connections who wasn't about to sleep her way into a job. She thought of working at an embassy abroad, though the same contraventions applied. But when the world came to Iraq she could meet it. In the years between university and marriage, eager to give her mind something to do, she took English classes at the British Council in Baghdad.

That stopped when Saddam Hussein invaded Kuwait in the summer of 1990. Everything stopped and went into reverse. The people were told it was a revolution in Kuwait, not an invasion. When a friend burst into her house to tell her about the revolution she went to turn on the radio. There was no news, no signal, no BBC Arabic, nothing but static. Then, suddenly, the markets were filled with looted Kuwaiti air-conditioning units and Kuwaiti furniture. A cousin returned from the war with hair that had turned completely white. People ran out to buy all the food they could find because they feared another war was coming.

I had been in the region during that war—I was a foreign student taking Middle Eastern Studies at Tel Aviv University when Saddam Hussein invaded Kuwait, thinking he had a green light from the United States. He did not. Throughout the Gulf War that followed, when his Scud missiles sputtered towards Tel Aviv, I carted around the gas mask all students had been issued, sealing up the cracks of my dorm room with packing tape whenever the air-raid sirens sounded, waiting for the chemical weapons we feared would be deployed by Saddam Hussein. The campus was all but empty—everyone bunkering at home with family or having caught the first flight out—except for me and one other student who lived upstairs. Staring out of our gas masks, we watched the bombing of Baghdad on CNN as a series of flashes against green-glow night-vision cameras, the sound of our own breath roaring in our ears. When the war ended, and the news moved on to other stories, we returned to our studies and forgot Iraq.

But for Iraqis the international trade embargo imposed by the United Nations Security Council from 1990 until 2003 was an extension of the battlefield, with ordinary people on the frontline. Hunger and disease swept the country. Corruption and smuggling became normal, even essential, laying the foundations of the mafias that would flourish after 2003 when the dictator and all restraints were gone.[20] Where a schoolteacher's salary had been US$1500 a month, it was suddenly worth $2—enough to buy a plate of eggs—so a stupid rich boy could now pass his classes without bothering to show up. Any crime could be cleared with a small payment to police, so only the poor and the political were jailed. As the state's authority withered, people depended on family to survive. Ahlam learned to roll cigarettes in newsprint. The mushrooms sprouting in her yard tasted like miracle food.

The sanctions were supposed to force Saddam Hussein to disclose the non-existent weapons of mass destruction and make reparation for the war against Kuwait, with the tacit goal of persuading Iraqis to rise up against him. But in fact they only crippled his opponents. "*His* people had everything they needed," Ahlam said. Whatever they didn't have, they took.

The riverfront of her father's property had already been confiscated in 1983. Men with hard faces appeared one day and fenced off the land below their house. There was no question of negotiating. The men were armed. The land was for Saddam Hussein's half-brother, a man named Sabawi, who wanted a country estate—during the Gulf War Sabawi became head of the secret police.

Southeast of the village, Saddam Hussein had taken more prime riverfront. His son Uday, known to the villagers for sending his men around the city to kidnap beautiful girls for him to rape, held parties there whenever his soccer team won a match. These parties, which the villagers could hear at night, were unabated by sanctions. "Here we were barely surviving," Ahlam said, "and every time his team had a victory he had singers and dancing and feasts that could have fed our entire village for a week."

Ahlam married in 1994 at the age of twenty-nine—very late for a traditional woman from a rural family. The only reason she married at all was because, at the already ancient age of twenty-eight, she had refused a doctor's hand and announced to her mother that she wanted to do a master's degree. "I saw the look in my mother's eyes. She was so worried about me. She imagined I was going to be alone, my chance finished." A curse, as her mother saw it, for a woman to be without a man.

So when an engineer some years older proposed, she gave him a choice. He knew she was educated, active in the community, had many male friends. She was not, like other women, bound to hearth and home. If he accepted that, and did not insist that she conform, she would marry him. If not, they should go their separate ways. He accepted, and only a small number of times—three that she could think of—did he bother with the thankless task of trying to control her.

A year later came their first son, Anas. Another son and a daughter followed, each two years apart. They were hungry but they still had enough land to grow their own food. In the poorer south of the country—undeveloped, and punished for backing a failed Shia uprising against Saddam Hussein by having their historic marshlands drained—people were moving to Baghdad in search of work.

The year after she married she went with her husband to visit a friend of his who lived in Saddam City, a Shia slum in Baghdad, since renamed Sadr City. What she saw there shocked her. People lived in shelters built from stacks of empty oil drums. Their floor was a sheet on the ground. "They lived in the open. A gust of wind could blow down their homes. How could they send their children to school?" Education was free but they had to buy uniforms—impossible. And the kids had to earn. Girls and boys were set to manual labour from the age of five or six; their mothers and fathers joined the Fedayeen Saddam militia in exchange for a salary. "Nobody cared about their poverty. Later they were among the main looters."

Her older brother Samir had finished high school behind Ahlam, since during the war with Iran their father had ordered him to fail his exams so he wouldn't graduate only to die on the battlefield. Samir went on to do a PhD in economics, though the most lucrative part of his education was learning English. He began working as a driver and fixer for foreign journalists, employing the charm and resiliency that was a family trait. It was Samir who first introduced Ahlam to the correspondents who came to report on the sanctions. The first one she worked with was Stephen Glain, an American reporter for the *Wall Street Journal.*

Glain met Samir for the first time in 1999. He had been directed to the Al Rashid Hotel, a base for international reporters made famous during the First Gulf War as the headquarters for CNN. He was instantly mobbed by the fixers, drivers, translators and prostitutes desperate for foreign currency.

A scrum of men surrounded me as I disembarked from the GMC I'd hired for the fourteen-hour drive to Baghdad from Amman. I waved them off and they reluctantly parted to reveal Samir . . . in faded khaki pants and a polo shirt. He was standing ram-rod straight as he strolled over and casually extended his hand.

"Welcome to Iraq," he said. "May I be of assistance during your stay?"

There wasn't a trace of servility in his voice. I liked him immediately.

"You're hired," I said.[21]

Glain's impression was deepened when he asked Samir his opinion of a staged patriotic event they had attended. "That?" Samir told Glain. "Fuck." At a time when almost no one dared criticize the regime, Samir had named his two dogs Uday and Qusay, after the dictator's sons. He invited Glain to dinner at his home, but suggested they go fishing beforehand.

> I asked him what kind of reel he used.
> "Reel?"
> I nodded. "What kind of rod and reel do you use when you fish?"
> [. . .] Samir then explained that he and his brothers catch fish by extending a metal wire into the Tigris River and electrocuting it with a car battery.
> "That's not very sporting," I said.
> Samir looked at me as if he was appraising the village idiot.
> "We don't want sport," he said. "We want fish."

The fishing trip was unsuccessful but Glain had a wonderful dinner at the family house along the river. Ahlam was there, trying to bake bread in a clay oven, giggling every time she burned herself. She told him that after finishing university she never thought she'd have to bake bread like her mother and grandmother.

Samir had already begun to subcontract work to Ahlam, at first just the translation of documents. Sometimes she even washed the journalists' laundry. As more reporters came, too many for Samir to handle alone, he put his economics training to work. Perfecting the bait-and-switch, he would take one of them around for a while, then pass him off to Ahlam so he could work with another. It was through Samir that Ahlam met people like Khaled Oweis, the Reuters journalist who became the news service's bureau chief in Damascus and later recommended Ahlam to correspondents there.

At first, Ahlam told me, she was shy about working with strangers. "Get over it," Samir said. She had no choice: she had a family to support, a husband with a talent for money-losing ventures. And besides, she was good at this, good at connecting this person to that person in pursuit of a story, good at dealing with all kinds of situations, crazy or sane. A natural fixer.

Chapter 6

FRIENDSHIP

HOW DO FRIENDSHIPS EVOLVE? In part through shared experience, intense experiences of the sort Ahlam and I encountered in Damascus. Shared risk forges strong bonds.

We began talking in shorthand, inside jokes, the private language that develops from esoteric knowledge, as we walked down dusty alleyways, stared at by curious children, buzzed by rickety motorcycle carts and the occasional Pepsi truck, the scent of roast peanuts and diesel in the air. Once, when I asked Ahlam whether she felt safe here in Little Baghdad, she said curtly, "Nobody's safe here," but when we were working together it seemed as if nothing could harm us. It was as if we were encased in a cocoon of mutual trust. There was no other way to work here. And there was no one else who knew exactly what it was like to do this work, no one who understood completely what it was we did.

Ahlam and I were very different. We had sprung from different soil, from civilizations that were said to "clash," but we were both outsiders to our own cultures. A writer usually is, and the unusual life she had led set her apart.

Maybe we were similar, too, in ways I couldn't have foreseen. She was older than me, but both of us had grown up in communities that told us who we were going to be and had managed to rebel. Both of us came from large families—I'm the eldest of eight—from small towns (mine on the outskirts of Vancouver, hers of Baghdad) where what we *should* do or *should* want were burdens we had worked hard to shrug off. We had both made it out through education. She had the help of her father against the barrier of culture; I had the help of my schooling against the barrier of my father.

When Ahlam told me of learning to swim, fighting the current, thrashing not to drown, I remembered an event that took place when I was about the same age, twelve or eleven. We were at a lake in the Pacific Northwest on a family vacation. My father had been shoving my younger brothers into the water from a boat, perhaps our new boat—he, too, was a self-made man who had become well-to-do—and whenever they scrambled out, he threw them in again, laughing as they sputtered and choked. I was sitting behind him, watching him torment my brothers. It was nothing new, it was how he always behaved, always the bully. But that day was different. That day some demon made me want to let him see what it was like. He was leaning over the edge of the boat precariously. I stood up, placed my hand on his back, and pushed. I still recall the feel of his back, the give as he fell into the lake, my astonishment at my part in it, that it had actually worked. Soaking wet and furious, he hauled himself out and turned on me, pushing me into the water and holding me under. I fought to breathe, sinking under, over and over again, his hand on my head holding me down.

A year later I was sent to private school, an attempt to reform me that turned out to be a saving grace. Since I was a good student, which might well have been lost on the mediocre school my brothers attended, there was an assumption on the part of my teachers and peers that I would go on to bigger things. Ahlam and I both left behind the world we knew for educations that forever put a distance between where we had come from and where we were going. We learned early to rely on ourselves.

And though we were both well-read, we were also drawn to empirical experience, to the turmoil of the tangible world. For me, in order to bear witness to it; for her, I think, to solve it.

Neither of us liked being told what to do either, a mentality that is characteristic of freelancers who prefer to go their own way, follow their own stories, which is to say their own minds. We shared a disregard for convention and other people's ideas of what it meant to "behave ourselves," which is usually code for "shut up." You could see it in her smoking, something women in her society didn't do (or if they did, it was in secret), and in the way she talked to men as equals, ordering them around when necessary, cajoling them otherwise. Shouting at the younger men if they were unruly, mocking them with an ironic word, keeping them in line. I enjoyed watching her conduct herself with such finesse and good humour, managing the refugees who treated her apartment as a gathering place, wanting her to resolve their life problems as if this were the same village council she had watched her father run and she were now the patriarch.

And we both liked to immerse ourselves in the lives of other people, gripped by the human drama, though she had lived that drama in ways I couldn't even begin to share.

It is possible, even probable, that our similarities blinded me to the vast chasm of our differences. For I had come here by choice. I chose where I went and when I left. "Because of your passport," an Iraqi man had said to me, pointing out the irreconcilable difference between him and me, "you can go anywhere."

I had the status of a lucky birth in a lucky country at a lucky time for women, when I could carve out the life I wanted. I had a home to return to whether I appreciated it or not. If I didn't like something, or the going got rough, or when I'd wrapped up my research, I could just leave. Though I often felt broke, a plane ticket on a credit card was not beyond my means, nor would my passport be turned away at customs. I had a foot in her world but one step could remove me from it; it couldn't envelop me; I couldn't fall far. Barring something extraordinary happening, there was too much holding me aloft.

The truth was that Ahlam was one of the people I was writing *about*, one of history's casualties, a refugee from a war planned and executed by *my* culture; a person who, because of *us*, no longer belonged anywhere.

In the evenings I always landed back at my apartment. It was another life. At night I transcribed interviews, made notes and phone calls, read a biography of the English explorer Gertrude Bell, who famously drafted the previously non-existent borders of Iraq for the British after the First World War, defining the country where Ahlam was born.

One night Ahlam asked me if she could come over. The water had been off in her apartment for several days. She was longing to take a shower.

When she arrived I gave her a towel, soap, shampoo, and put on a kettle for tea. While she was in the shower I turned on the small television my landlord had left for me, watching Al Jazeera with the sound off. A flash of White House spokesman, his mouth opening and closing.

When she emerged, we sat on the pullout sofa, drinking tea while she let her hair dry. It fell halfway down her back. She held up a thick sheaf of it in one hand and looked at it critically.

"I wish I had hair like that," I said. Mine is fine and fair.

"You know," she said, "when I was a teenager I wanted to cut it off. It was down to my waist. So hot in the summer. But my family loved it so much."

Was I married? Ahlam asked. I told her the truth—no, not officially. Children? No. What does your boyfriend think of you going away all the time? I confessed that it was a strain. But I loved my work. It wasn't about choosing one thing over the other; I had to work like I had to breathe.

She agreed with me: the work gave life meaning, it was the essential. "I would have been just as happy if I had not got married," she said, lighting a cigarette. She turned the subject back to me. "Your boyfriend misses you."

I reached for her cigarettes and shook one out. "Maybe that's the problem," I said.

She looked at me sympathetically and waited for me to go on. I was hesitant to burden her with my concerns. The gradual demise of a long relationship that showed obvious signs of deterioration whenever I was in the field for too long, and nagged at me even as I ignored it, was petty by comparison to what she dealt with every day.

"We have a nice apartment in Vancouver," I said. "Small but nice. Near the beach. He's a good person." I described how he had ingeniously created an office for me from a series of bookshelves organized at right angles so as to carve out an extra room. "I sometimes think, if there's an earthquake, I'll be killed by falling books."

I described how we had met a dozen years ago, when we were still sorting out who we were. We took turns putting each other through university, all the way through graduate school. Until now, one of us had always been studying, the other working. We were different people now than when we had met, arguably better people, but not the same.

"What's he like?" she asked.

"Intelligent. Good-looking. Driven. Works in technology. Sometimes in Silicon Valley. Where they work with computers, that sort of thing." I couldn't be sure she had heard of Silicon Valley. "He can explain string theory, the Grand Unified Theory. Physics." I paused, wondering if I was losing her. "The thing is, he's always been supportive of my work. Whenever I'm getting ready to head somewhere, like here for instance"—I indicated my apartment with the cigarette—"I have a few bad nights where I think I must be crazy, because normal people don't do this kind of work. And he's always told me just to go. But I go away too much." Going back was getting harder.

"The worst was Iran. A year and a half ago I was reporting a big story. I went everywhere—Khuzestan, Kurdistan, Bushehr. I wanted to know everything so I could write about the people there. But I was away for six months straight, living a completely different life. When I went home it was so"—I struggled for the right word—"disorienting." Returning had left me with what anthropologists call the shock of re-entry. "For a while I could only sleep if I lay down on the floor." I had felt a craving for something solid beneath me.

I had never told anyone about that, even my boyfriend who thought I was sleeping on the living room sofa, which was challenging enough. That time away had been especially troubling for us. Towards the end I had been threatened with arrest and called him in a panic, then been cut off when my phone card ran out. I hadn't been able to call back for three days. In that time he had not slept, imagining all the scenarios—jail, torture, death—yet helpless to do a single thing about it. While I was active, absorbed in keeping myself out of prison, he endured the terrifying anguish of the person left behind.

I stopped talking and got up to pour us more tea. She was holding the pendant she always wore, that held the small photo of her son Anas who had died the year before. She placed it back around her neck, then tucked it into her shirt.

"Why do you do that?" I asked, handing her the tea glass. "Put it inside your shirt?" When I first met her she used to wear the pendant with her son's picture on the outside of her clothing.

"Abdullah"—her middle child—"has been becoming upset remembering his older brother. So now I put his picture away, by my heart."

Her eldest son had been a fine, tall, obedient and clever boy, as she described him: "My right hand." Anas was eleven years old—"eleven and a half"—when he returned from school in Damascus last May complaining of pain in his side. This from a boy who never complained, who had left behind his home and friends without a word. Other kids threw fits, begged to be allowed to bring computers or toys or refused to understand why they had to leave their homes at all, but not him. So at first she wondered if he might have been beaten up at school, a foreigner in a wildly overcrowded Syrian classroom, taunted by other boys who resented the newcomers. A bit of schoolyard bullying, the sort of thing a boy that age knew to keep to himself; his parents had enough problems. The doctor at the hospital in Damascus said he had a kidney stone and gave him an injection. Within moments Anas was dead.

A supervisor at the hospital came to investigate, calling in the doctor. The pair began discussing the case in English in front of her, thinking she wouldn't understand. The supervisor said the medicine was not meant for a child of that age. "I felt what it was to stand in front of the person who had killed my son, and because I was a refugee, be afraid to open my mouth." She paused. "After that you can only take care of the people around you, nothing else."

Would it have been better if her son had been killed by the war? At least that would have made a kind of sense, even if a terrible sense, because everyone knows that children die in wars. You can talk about it, rage about it; people understand it. At Ahlam's apartment I had spoken to a woman whose only child, a boy Anas's age, was killed on the fifth day of the war when air strikes dropped a missile on their house. But Anas's was a death without reason, a death that cancelled out meaning.

Something else had changed when Ahlam stood next to her son's still-warm body in the hospital. She looked across the bed at the face of her husband, who stood there helpless, immobile, unable to do what he ought to have done in that moment and take her in his arms. In such cases parents either grow closer or break apart. The distance across the bed, the slight boy lying there between them, no longer breathing—in that moment she slipped off her wedding band and dropped it into her pocket. The end of something, the silent breaking of a bond.

"That's when I said, it's finished." Later she gave her wedding ring to a young man in Little Baghdad who was planning to propose to a girl he loved.

Ahlam's extended family had insisted that Anas be buried in his homeland. She had promised her kidnappers she would not go back, but it was tradition, and the family would not relent. Her brother Salaam, the driver, organized a convoy of vehicles: Ahlam and her husband and the two younger children in one SUV, her son's body in another, a third filled with men Salaam had organized to guard them should they come under attack. They left Damascus at three in the morning and arrived in their village on the outskirts of Baghdad thirteen hours later.

She never learned the exact site of the grave. Though she begged her family to take her there, they refused. She was treated, she said, as a foolish woman who would collapse, when she only wanted to see her son for the last time. "He stayed eleven and a half," she said. "He will always be eleven and a half."

For the funeral ceremony her house was guarded by armed men from her village. In the room with the other women she turned herself to stone. Some of the villagers, some of the women who sat offering words of sympathy, were among those who had lauded her kidnappers, who called her a traitor behind her back. She stared straight ahead, refusing to shed a tear. "They would have said my son's death was God's punishment for my work with the Americans." She refused to give them the satisfaction of witnessing her pain.

When the family returned to Damascus she went right back to work. "I didn't even have time to feel sorrow for my son. I had two children to care for. I had the landlord knocking at my door for the rent. So I contacted the journalists I had known in the past to look for work. I didn't surrender." As she spoke she touched the cord around her neck.

Perhaps all empathy comes from a wound. That hard lump of grief, which she took out from time to time, usually alone, fired her public activity, her obsessive drive to solve problems that had no lasting solutions. And there was no one among the refugees who had not lost someone dear. Her son's photograph, dangling from a blood-red cord, bound her story to their own, and without a word said everything.

In the weeks after her son died, Ahlam couldn't stand being in her apartment so she would leave her other two children in the care of her husband and visit Zainab's shrine to be alone with her sorrow. One day, a girl of sixteen saw her there, weeping. "What's wrong, Auntie?" the girl asked. Ahlam told the girl about her son's death and the girl started crying.

"At first I thought she was crying for me," Ahlam told me, "but she said, 'You are so concerned about your children, while my parents force me to do this work.'" The girl was the youngest of three daughters in a family of ten. Her father rented a three-bedroom apartment to which he brought the men, mainly pilgrims holidaying at the shrine. If she or either of her sisters refused, they were beaten. The girl had turned twelve the year the war began. That year her father made her lose her virginity to her cousin. "A foreigner," he told her, "should not be the first."

At night the dry brown hills above Damascus were lit up by nightclubs filled with tens of thousands of Iraqi girls and widows. Customers at the clubs exchanged thousand-pound Syrian notes, worth about twenty dollars, for monopoly money they could safely shower on the dance floor without fear of an errant high heel disgracing the face of the president's father. Inside, beautiful entertainers in glittering dresses sang songs of Sunni–Shia brotherhood. After some hours of drinking, the Iraqi clients started fights outside: "You are Shia, you people killed my brother!"

Rana, my schoolteacher-interpreter, always impeccably turned out, went to a good salon even if she covered their handiwork with a scarf. She told me she had seen a dozen Iraqi girls there the last time she had her hair cut. Hovering over a girl who looked about fifteen was an older woman who might or might not have been the girl's mother. She was advising the hairdresser—do it this way, move the tendril so it falls across her cheek.

In Little Baghdad there weren't any nightclubs. Most transactions took place behind the shrine, where Afghan opium was sold by pilgrims from Iran and refugee women came to negotiate the so-called temporary marriages that expired after an hour.

Ahlam had met two sisters—"Good girls, they had never spoken to a man in their lives"—whose parents were old and sick and had run out of money for food and rent in Syria. Each night the girls waited for their parents to fall sleep, then slipped out to the shrine, returning at dawn. Their parents believed the money was being sent by a generous cousin who had long ago moved to Europe. "They will never know how those girls sacrificed to keep them alive," Ahlam said.

On another occasion a boy had come to see Ahlam and told her he was planning to murder his uncle. His uncle had sold the boy's two cousins, his daughters, who were thirteen and fourteen years old, to rich men in Saudi Arabia who came in search of virgin brides—"pleasure wives," they were called. The boy was enraged. His cousins were his friends and he missed them. He would stab his uncle, perhaps strangle him—he hadn't made up his mind. Ahlam was trying to talk him out of it. "What will it accomplish? You will go to jail and it will not bring your cousins back."

While reporting for UNICEF on Iraqi adolescent girls, Ahlam and the French-American researcher, Marianne, whom I'd not yet met, learned the many ways the girls were being bought and sold. There were those, often orphans, who were trafficked by gangs; those prostituted by their own families; and a third category who on their own supported their families or themselves in order to survive.

Fearing such a fate, other families locked up their daughters to protect them. Their mothers had been engineers, accountants, librarians, teachers, but now it was as if time had rolled back a hundred years. In previous decades, when girls typically went to university and had careers, the marriage age had risen, but now it was dropping fast. Better they be married, before they became damaged goods. Better they be married and eating someone else's food.

Iraqi students could enroll in Syrian schools as Ahlam's had, but most had not been able to bring their school records with them or had missed too many years or simply had to work. A blue-eyed boy from Baghdad who sold fruit at a side-walk stand on the market street told me he wanted to study biological sciences. "To study," he said solemnly, "is the most precious thing." After we had spoken he chased me through the market, startling me because I heard his pounding foot-steps before I turned my head. Could I help him? He had to support his parents, they were old, and he had missed the last four years of school. He wanted to finish high school and go to university. Perhaps I could take him to my country, or help him get to a university in Dubai? Listening to his earnest pleas I felt the helplessness of his situation and the uselessness of my own: I'm just a writer, I said.

Just a writer. A useless profession. Sometimes it seemed to me that all writing could do was comfort those who already understood what was wrong with the world by letting them know they weren't alone. To simply watch the loss of an entire generation—a generation that would otherwise have gone on to study something useful like dentistry, or even become writers and journalists themselves—was a position I was coming to despise. Nothing would change the fact that my interpreter Kuki expressed to me in one of our late-night discussions. "A little kid in Baghdad now, all he talks about is war. He knows the names of all the weapons, the names of everyone killed. So what will that kid be like at eighteen? They said this war was going to end terrorism but it will only bring more war, more terrorism."

Ahlam saw what was happening to the next generation, but she was doing something about it. She explained that that was how the idea for a school had begun: she and Marianne had come to the same conclusion—that the international aid organizations had their hands tied, whether by lack of funds

or the rules they had to follow in order to be here at all—
so they had come up with their own plan to create a space
where the girls could meet one another and their parents
would know they were safe. Marianne, who had a master's
degree in International Affairs from Columbia University
and had worked on development projects in several countries, donated the start-up money; Ahlam had offered up
her apartment and spoken to qualified refugee teachers who
were willing to volunteer their time. She was planning an
opening ceremony and invited me to attend.

But there were concerns. Group meetings, even of schoolgirls, were against the law. "The mukhabarat are asking
enough questions about all the people coming here," she
said, gesturing at her apartment.

"How do you know?" I asked.

She reached for her cigarettes and searched around in
her bag for her lighter. "They told me to come see them."
Clicking. Clicking. Tossing the lighter down. "Not told—
ordered. To headquarters." I saw a lighter on her windowsill
and passed it to her. She lit a cigarette.

"They want to know what I'm doing," she said, exhaling.
"It's strange for them, to see a woman who is active." She
shot me an amused glance that spoke of our shared awareness of what it meant to be thought strange as a woman.

There were certain things she kept from me. It's normal
among colleagues. It is possible she didn't want to worry me
with things I could do nothing about. Or, more likely, make
me doubt the wisdom of working with her altogether. She
may have noticed the way that certain journalists she used
to work with were starting to keep a distance—an American
reporter who stopped calling; a war photographer who used

to visit but no longer did—yet she never spoke about it. I only heard about that later, from the journalists themselves. In the meantime—and this was how the subject came up—she was contemplating ways to get the necessary permission to run the school.

The intelligence captain in charge of Little Baghdad was a pale man with a thin Syrian moustache who called himself Abu Yusuf. "A captain who wants to be a major," as Ahlam described him. She had answered his summons, going to his office, taking the chair opposite his desk.

Who was she, Abu Yusuf demanded to know, about whom he had heard so much? "You are running around from six in the morning until midnight. We sent three men to follow you and they can't keep up."

So the men who were following her were Syrian intelligence agents? She kept her expression neutral, as if this was not a surprise. "They must be out of shape," she replied.

He was not amused. He had been watching her with mounting perplexity. With his next question he tried to fit her back into a category he understood. "Are you with the Sunni or the Shia?"

She wasn't with either side, she told him. She was with whoever needed her help.

But that made no sense to him. There must be something else at play. Abu Yusuf was a man who understood self-interest, games, hatreds, deceit. These were his stock-in-trade. He was, she thought, a careerist. A small man in the big system who wanted to make a name for himself. Later, when it became clear that he was not merely a temporary annoyance, I pondered this characteristic. How many catastrophes, how many wars, have been enabled by exactly these sorts of careerists: diligent, ambitious, calculating, loyal to the basest forms of power, who use whatever levers they can grasp to prove themselves.

That day he took a copy of her passport and made her write out a detailed autobiography: family history, reasons for coming to Syria. "He was mainly interested in my work for the Americans in Iraq."

Now she would need his agreement if she was going to run the classes. Otherwise trouble. There would be even more people coming and going. "Suspicious activities," she said.

She told me she had found an ally, however, and this eased my mind. A Syrian woman named Mona who was, like her, a fixer for journalists. Some time after Ahlam's visit with Syrian intelligence, a young Iraqi filmmaker Ahlam knew had introduced the two of them, and they had hit it off. Mona too had covered the refugee crisis and she told Ahlam she wanted to "give back." I was relieved to hear about this development; I hadn't met Mona but somehow I could immediately picture her: middle-aged, plain, perhaps with grown children and a hard-working altruistic air. Her involvement took a weight off my mind. I couldn't do much to help, and I wouldn't be here forever. Ahlam needed an insider. A Syrian professional who knew the lay of the land was a gift.

With Abu Yusuf watching her, Ahlam wanted proof that what she was doing was nothing he should worry about. To that end she asked me to go with her to the UNICEF office to request a formal letter acknowledging the field research she had done with Marianne. Marianne was out of town, but the stamp of officialdom would legitimize Ahlam, make it obvious that she was an expert on the issue of refugee girls, the classes a natural extension of the work she had done.

"If you come with me," she said, "it will be harder for them to say no."

I was pleased to be asked. Here was someone who was actually doing something, not just writing about it. Ahlam's usefulness was a counterpoint to my uselessness, set it in stark relief, and she was offering me a way to be of use. I could be part of what she did, do something practical and tangible rather than merely observe, and use my status as a Westerner to good effect.

We met at the UNICEF headquarters in Damascus one sun-blasted afternoon. I arrived by taxi; Ahlam was already there, watching for me on the street outside. We waited together to be ushered into the director's office. He was Egyptian, with a long sallow face. I could tell right away that he was sorry to see us. Rather than speaking to her in Arabic, as I expected, he directed himself to me in French, as if she wasn't there.

This time I was the translator, explaining what she needed. Just a letter stating that she had worked on the report. He sighed, leaning back in his chair, and spoke in ponderous French of the "process" of the "formalization," and the need for a study in order to formalize the process, and then committee meetings, and budgets and more studies. . . . It was clear he was only giving her an audience because I was there: a Western journalist who, having brought out my notebook as a prop, was ostentatiously taking notes.

Afterwards Ahlam and I sat in the park opposite the office. It was hot and dusty but pleasant, sunlight filtering through leafy jacaranda trees. Ahlam bought two coffees from a small stand and we sat on a bench smoking. I was angry but she was not. She said, "I knew it probably wouldn't work."

Ahlam didn't blame the sallow-faced director. She reminded me that she was not employed by UNICEF—foreign NGOs like UNICEF could not hire Iraqis, who themselves were foreigners in Syria, "guests" without legal permission to work. Marianne was on contract and Marianne had hired her. But she had no contractual structure, no rights. And in such a situation there is nobody to come to your aid. It wasn't the director's fault. He must have felt he was being made the fool, asked for something he could not grant even if he wished.

As we finished our coffees, her phone buzzed with a text message. She pulled it out and looked. A friend in Baghdad, a British journalist. *You are a tank*, she'd written. *You are a Humvee*. Ahlam read it and laughed. She looked as if she had already forgotten the meeting.

We got up to leave. It had been a waste of time but not a waste. Perhaps because we had switched roles. Perhaps because I was now invested in the success of her efforts. This time I was the translator and fixer, even if the mission had been a bust.

We went out to the street so I could find a taxi. We would go our separate ways. I had a dinner meeting with a Swedish diplomat who knew a lot about human smuggling. Then I would leave to spend a few days in the ancient city of Aleppo, the largest in Syria, a trip I had been planning for some time. Ahlam was heading back to her apartment. She would not, she told me as we parted, waste any more time. She would go straight to Abu Yusuf and tell him about the school before suspicions arose.

She looked happy. "If he says yes, okay. If he says no, I continue!"

Chapter 7

ANOTHER COUNTRY

AT THE BARON HOTEL in Aleppo, a five-hour journey from Damascus by crowded bus, I sat on a cracked leather armchair next to the dusty bar, drinking a lukewarm vodka tonic. The cars honking on the streets, overlaying the call to prayer, sounded like a mutinous brass band, but the Baron was quiet, almost dead. With its atmosphere of faded grandeur and indifferent service, it was a forgotten way station on the road to conquest. A group of loud Germans sat on the stone terrace outside, drinking beer. A British tourist wandered in expectantly, as if into a museum, and left looking underwhelmed. Not much had changed here since the hotel opened a century ago, hosting Germans and British as they vied for control of the Middle East.

The Baron, Syria's oldest hotel, had witnessed many of the crucial events since then. In its heyday it had hosted the founder of modern Turkey, Mustafa Kemal Ataturk; the Shah of Persia; Mr. and Mrs. Theodore Roosevelt. Agatha

Christie, more famous than all of them, was said to have written parts of *Murder on the Orient Express* while staying here with her archaeologist husband.

I had come to Aleppo to escape my work in Damascus for a few days, but found myself thinking of the war anyway—where it had started, how it could possibly end. Framed in a dusty corner of the hotel was T.E. Lawrence's unpaid bar bill from 1914. Lawrence had stayed here on breaks from an excavation for the British Museum. It's hard to separate the young man he was—handsome, intellectually curious, probably gay—from the legend of Lawrence of Arabia that made him the most celebrated hero of the First World War. But it was as a young archaeologist learning Arabic in Syria that he first came to sympathize with the Arab struggle against foreign domination; at that time, the fading Ottoman Empire.

I had spent the day at the Aleppo souk, wandering through vaulted archways lit by elaborate hanging lanterns, the air heady with the scent of spices piled in bright little pyramids. Sheep, freshly killed and sharp with the smell of blood, hung from chains in open cases; others were tethered in the stony crooks of dark alleyways, unaware they were next in line. Veiled women gathered around a fabric stall, expertly thumbing bolt after identical black bolt, measuring out to the inch exactly what they needed to cover themselves head to foot.

Lawrence had visited this bazaar to seek out artifacts. Though short of money, he loved beautiful old things, and couldn't resist haggling with men like the antiquities vendor who coaxed me into his cave-like shop. I sat on carpets, drinking strong coffee as the man tried to sell me Assyrian figurines that he said dated back three thousand years. It was possible they had been looted from collections in Iraq and just as likely that they were made last week in a workshop owned by his brother-in-law. But there was no mistaking the authenticity of the old Iraqi currency he showed me with the face of Saddam Hussein, and those bearing the regal visage of Lawrence's close friend Faisal, briefly King of Syria and then—when that didn't take—of the newly minted country of Iraq.

You can see almost everything that has happened in the Middle East today in light of Lawrence and the First World War. The Ottoman Turks, by the time he came here, had ruled Arab lands for four hundred years. Their secret was simple: they mainly let their subjects run their own lives. In 1916, one of those subjects, Sharif Hussein of Mecca, launched a rebellion against them. He owed the Turks his job as director of the Islamic holy sites in what is now Saudi Arabia, but disagreed with the progressive Young Turks whose ideas, such as the emancipation of women, were not ones an old-fashioned tribal leader like Hussein could abide.[22] The British, at war with Germany, needed help defeating the German-allied Turks, so they agreed to give Hussein gold and guns and, if all went well, an independent Arab kingdom of his own.

T.E. Lawrence, assigned as a liaison to the Arab revolt, later said he suspected all along it was a ruse. In his memoir, *Seven Pillars of Wisdom*, he wrote, "I risked the fraud, on my conviction that Arab help was necessary to our cheap and speedy victory in the East, and that better we win and break our word than lose."[23] Yet he was drawn in, trading his military uniform for the robes of an Arab prince, and befriending Sharif Hussein's son—the dashing Faisal—whom he helped to blow up Turkish railway lines.

When the war was won and the time came to make good on promises, it emerged that France and Britain had secretly agreed to divide the same territory between themselves: Syria (including Lebanon) falling to the French; Mesopotamia (what is now Iraq) to the British; with Palestine under international administration—though it would later be claimed by the British, to repent at leisure.

In *Paris 1919*, Margaret MacMillan's masterly account of the post-war division of spoils, British Prime Minister David Lloyd George is overheard musing aloud about the creation of the modern Middle East. "Mesopotamia . . . yes . . . oil . . . irrigation . . . we must have Mesopotamia; Palestine . . . yes . . . the Holy Land . . . Zionism . . . we must have Palestine; Syria . . . h'm . . . what is there in Syria? Let the French have that."[24]

Just as cavalierly, I exchanged a few Syrian pounds for some Saddam Husseins and left behind the Faisals, though both were worthless now.

During the Arab revolt Lawrence met a young American journalist who brought back pictures of the blue-eyed blond in Arab dress, and made him the subject of a sensational multimedia show that seized the public imagination—the dashing young Englishman leading the proud natives to liberty. But by 1920 Lawrence saw the British occupation of Iraq turn ugly. The Sunni and Shia, supposedly so at odds, united in an armed uprising against the lack of representative government. In response, Britain razed entire villages with the new technology of aerial bombing; they debated using poison gas. Lawrence thought the British even worse than the Turks. "How long," he wrote in the *London Times*, "will we permit millions of pounds, thousands of imperial troops, and tens of thousands of Arabs to be sacrificed on behalf of a form of colonial administration which can benefit nobody but its administrators?"[25]

He had gone with Faisal to the Paris peace conference in 1919 to press for Arab independence, but neither the British nor the French wished to hear another word about it. Nor did they wish to hear the American president encouraging self-determination for national groups. (God was content with Ten Commandments, the French president quipped, but Woodrow Wilson had a list of fourteen.) The French insisted on having Syria as their share of the spoils, and the main lesson Britain seemed to have drawn from the war was that no future war could be won without oil.

Faisal claimed Syria anyway. In March of 1920, from the balcony of his room upstairs at the Baron Hotel, he proclaimed himself King of Syria. A few months later French forces drove him out.

The following year Lawrence and his friend Gertrude Bell—having met on that early dig outside Aleppo—persuaded Colonial Secretary Winston Churchill to place Faisal on the throne of a new country to be named Iraq.

Above my leather armchair in the bar of the Baron was a pastoral painting of an idyllic Arab village. I was reminded of the nine-year-old girl I had met through Ahlam whose farmhouse outside Baghdad had been fire-bombed. Her father had called her over to show me her burns. Clearly anxious to get back to the kitchen where she was tending to her paralyzed mother's chores, she relaxed only when her father pulled out a photo album. Leafing through it, she gazed dreamily at pictures of her family on their farm.

Happy times, smiling faces, herding the cows, harvesting their crops.

Her father thought the biggest mistake of the war was the American decision to lay the Iraqi army off work. Others had their own theories: allowing the looting; not sending enough troops; not enough planning or enough fluent Arabic speakers. As if, had any of these factors been different, things might have turned out well. Perhaps the biggest mistake of the war was none of these. Perhaps the biggest mistake was the same as in the First World War. The war itself.

The French went their own way in Syria. It turned out no better. Having carved Lebanon from Syria as a separate state for their Christian allies (without considering how the Muslims there might feel about that), they ceded oil-rich Mosul to Britain, gave 40 percent of Syria's coastline to Turkey, and shaved off Palestine and Transjordan from Greater Syria.[26] In what remained of the weakened country, they recruited Syria's minorities into their occupation forces in order to divide and rule. Chief among these were the poor rural Alawites, long the victims of discrimination, for whom joining the military was the only way to move up in the world. After the French left in 1946, there were democratic elections. But the results did not please the United States, which had replaced Britain as the leading imperial power following the Second World War. In 1949, no longer championing self-determination, the US engineered its first Middle Eastern coup after the democratically elected president waffled on approving an American pipeline for Saudi oil. They put the head of the Syrian army in charge.[27] He was murdered in less than six months, and successive military coups continued until a group of mainly Alawite army officers seized power in 1963. Among them was an ambitious air force pilot named Hafez al-Assad, who became president in 1971.

It was here in Aleppo, a decade after that, that the Sunni Muslim Brotherhood rose up against his rule. With Syria poised on the brink of civil war, Assad brought his army out against the Brotherhood, massacring as many as twenty thousand, including civilians, in the city of Hama in 1982. For nearly three decades the rebels were driven underground.

The Aleppo I saw as I walked through the city is finished now—bombed and shelled and shot to pieces. Syrian forces barrel-bombed civilian neighbourhoods; rebel forces burned down the ancient souk. The Middle East fashioned a century ago has become what the Ottoman Empire was before it: fragile, quaking, rife with rebellions. Like the First World War, the Iraq War upset the balance of power in the region, a horrifying illustration of the impotence of power to contain what it sets in motion.

The Baron Hotel, as always an eyewitness to history, found itself on the frontier between opposition and government areas in the embattled city. By 2014, its roof pierced by shrapnel, the rooms stood empty except for a few displaced families. A hundred years after Lawrence visited, the Baron quietly closed its doors.[28]

Chapter 8

AHLAM'S WAR

FOR AHLAM, THE WAR began on April 8, 2003, the day she watched the first Abrams tank rumble past her house along the main road into Baghdad. Until then all traffic had been in the opposite direction, cars and buses carrying people out of the city to the north of Iraq to wait out the invasion. When the bombs began to fall, the villagers panicked. Men rushed to organize cars, filling them with women and children. She refused to join them, or to let her husband take the children from her side. The two of them had argued before he left. He pleaded with her to change her mind. "No one has the right to kick us out of our house," she told him. "It's our country. If I die, I will die in my home." A handful of men—her cousins—stayed behind to safeguard their property, but for the next several weeks she was the only woman left in the village.

Now, as the huge tank rolled past, beige as a sand dune, she felt a profound sense of loss. From a loudspeaker, a pre-recorded voice blared orders in Arabic: *Stay away from the main roads! No one is going to harm you! Avoid gathering in large groups! Don't shoot at us and we won't shoot at you! Any suspicious activity will be viewed as threat!* More convincing than any news headline, it was proof that Baghdad had fallen. "We had lost our country."

US ground forces were pouring into the Iraqi capital. Until that day the war hadn't seemed real. In the first three days of the invasion a dust storm had swept in from the desert. She taped plastic over the doors and windows against the dust. All she could hear through the thick copper haze were sporadic explosions several times a day. She hoarded food as she had learned from other wars. In her garden she dug a bomb shelter, scattering dirt over the tin roof. From overhead came the roar of F-18s and B-52s. She taught her children to plug their ears and shout "Ahhhhhh" to save their eardrums.

Anas was nine, Abdullah seven, and Roqayah, her "angel," just five. The countryside north of Baghdad was being heavily bombed because the Iraqi military hid armaments there, but her children thought the war was a game. They waved at the fighter planes, shouting greetings. "Look, Mum!" they said, pointing in the air, jumping up and down. They slept soundly through even the loudest explosions.

Once, six planes loomed over the dusty date palms, flying in formation. From the B-52 came a powerful screech as it released a payload of cluster bombs over their fields. "It was enough for us adults to hear the bombs drop on our fields," Ahlam said. "The sound, like opening the gates of a thousand-year-old castle, scared even the biggest man. But my children didn't give me a chance to be scared."

As the tank rolled on towards Baghdad, a half-hour away, Ahlam turned her attention back to her household. She had been standing in her garden after lunch that day when she saw young Iraqi soldiers hiding in the brush. "Please, Auntie," one of them called to her. "Can you help us?" As they emerged from the tall grasses around the orchards, she saw there were about fifty of them. They were eighteen, nineteen years old—just children, she thought. They were tearing off their army uniforms and needed civilian clothing, since the Americans would otherwise kill them on sight. They had been drafted only recently, with little or no training, and their commanders had slipped away to avoid the US military, knowing their old weaponry wouldn't stand a chance. Her heart went out to them.

Bringing them inside, Ahlam handed out what clothing her husband had left behind when he had fled north. She arranged to billet them among her cousins' houses along the river. Her own house had many bedrooms, so ten of them stayed with her. "If the Americans come to my door," she promised them, "I will say you are my relatives." One of them sat on the floor next to her television set in the living room, crying and asking for his mother.

A lone civilian was among them, a quiet young man named Adem. He had been on a bus full of civilians fleeing Baghdad along the main road when it was struck by an American helicopter. Wandering from the wreckage, he saw that he was the only survivor. A bullet had torn through his hand so Ahlam brought him inside, cleaned the wound, and managed to stop the bleeding using the first-aid kit she kept for cuts and scrapes. "You need a doctor," she told him. "They'll have to operate." But roads and hospitals were closed.

For two days and nights, Adem and the teenagers remained in the village. She cooked meals for them but they were too frightened to eat; they only wanted cigarettes, nervously smoking every last one she had. They wanted to go home but they could hear the helicopters whirring overhead. One of the boys collapsed in terror, sobbing helplessly.

On the third day, one of Ahlam's cousins swam the hundred-metre breadth of the muddy Tigris to borrow a rowboat from friends of theirs who lived on the other side. It was a calm night, no helicopters. After dark she left her children in the care of another cousin and led the boys down through the orchards to the riverbank. Under a sliver of moon, she helped ease them, five at a time, onto the boat.

It took three hours to row them all across. For two of the trips Ahlam took a turn at the oars. The current was rough and she worried that the boat would sink. For days afterward her arms ached, but it was worth it. From the far side, as the boat bobbed up against the riverbank, she watched the last of them run headlong across a field and disappear into the night.

All along the main road near her house were the bodies of those who had been killed while fleeing the city. A few had been soldiers but most were civilians; they appeared to have been shot from American helicopters with the kind of bullets that explode inside the bodies. The first looters had begun to appear, pulling the dead from their cars and driving off; they were armed so no one could stop them. Now the dead, lying in the hot sun, were attracting the dogs that roamed in packs along the riverbank. Ahlam and four of her male cousins held a meeting to discuss what to do. "It was a hard decision but the right one. It was that or let the dogs eat them."

The five of them worked as a team. Two of the men dug the graves, two carried the bodies, and Ahlam took charge of registration. She made a logbook, filling it with identifying characteristics: names (if the dead had identity cards), estimated height, weight, age, a description of their clothing or the vehicles where they had been found. Because of the cluster bombs that now lay concealed among the trees and tall grasses, they couldn't bury them in the fields, and instead dug holes along the roadside. On the makeshift graves they placed markers wrapped in plastic and held down by rocks. The logbook they stored in the village mosque. They knew they could be killed at any time but they reasoned that no one would attack the mosque so at least the records would survive.

A few weeks later the roads reopened and families began searching for the missing. For most of them, the main road was the last option, after they had exhausted all other routes going north. Ahlam led them—confused, relieved, anguished, full of despair—to the graves. They had searched with the hope that they would discover their family members alive, and even when faced with the description in the logbook they found room for doubt. Perhaps this was the grave of a different father and a different set of children, aged nine and eleven, discovered in a different red car near the bridge?

The family of Adem, the civilian wounded in the bus attack, came to speak to her. They wanted to know if he had told her anything about his brother-in-law, who had been seated next to him on the bus—Adem had told them he couldn't remember anything. But Ahlam wondered if he might be trying to protect them from the truth.

An old man came to find his son, a soldier of eighteen. He stood on the grave where they had buried the boy.

"Tell me, are you my son?" he shouted. "Speak! Even if you are not my son, I will care for you, I will bury you! Just tell me!"

While they were burying the dead, an American tank stopped. The soldiers asked what they were up to and since they had no translator Ahlam interpreted. Despite their weapons she wasn't afraid of them. "It's my land, not theirs." They seemed surprised to hear her speak to them in English.

Ten days later another tank was stationed on the main road. This time, surrounded by a group of men from the village, it was Ahlam who approached the soldiers. She explained on behalf of the villagers that they were out of electricity, drinking water and medical supplies. Their orchards were dying because the irrigation system relied on electricity, and their land was covered in unexploded cluster bombs so they could not set foot there. "People are becoming angry," she told them, "watching their fields die."

She also asked them to collect the weapons left behind by the Iraqi Army when they fled. "There were weapons everywhere—in the schools, the streets, the military camps, even the hospitals. The shrine in Kadhimiya had three rooms full of weapons—rocket-propelled grenades, explosive devices, anti-tank mines—and there were long-range missiles just sitting there in our fields, ready to be used. We asked every American troop unit to remove the weapons before the looters did, but they didn't listen."

Nevertheless the soldiers told her they would speak to their commander.

The next day a tank pulled up in front of her house. A soldier stepped out and called out to one of her nephews who was standing in the yard. He pointed at her house. "English," he said.

The boy ran inside to get her. "Auntie," he told her, "this man from the Americans wants to talk to you!"

She went outside.

"Is there anything you need?" the man asked. And before she could say a word: "How come, in the middle of this village, we find a woman speaking English?"

She laughed at him.

"What did you tell him?" I asked her.

"I said, 'What do you see in front of you?' He told me that back home they learned that Iraqis were all wild, like animals."

If Iraqis all seemed the same to Americans, to Iraqis the Americans all looked "like creatures from outer space," since only their mouths and noses protruded from their protective gear. She could not distinguish their ranks at a glance, but she had the impression this man was in a position of power. That day he gave her a radio that worked with solar, battery or hand-crank—a gift that pleased her because she could once again follow the news.

The next morning she looked outside to see two tanks pulling up beside her house. One was filled with medical supplies and foodstuffs—cakes, sweets, orange juice, coffee, jam. The second had come to protect the first. They were part of an armoured tank battalion with the 3rd Infantry Division, which had led the invasion of Baghdad. They had been reassigned to stabilize a large area northwest of Baghdad, from the urban Shia area of Kadhimiya where Ahlam had spent her early childhood to the rambling Sunni countryside known as Al Taji. The northernmost part of their sector, where Ahlam lived, was one of the most heavily bombed, so medics from the battalion came to treat some of those injured by coalition attacks. Among them was a little girl badly burned after air strikes hit her house, a father and son who both lost their legs to cluster bombs dropped on their farm, and an old man shot through his Achilles tendon.[29]

After that day the soldiers were fixtures at Ahlam's home. Even in their desert camouflage she could see how young they were, barely older than the soldiers she had rowed across the river to escape them. Over the coming weeks they brought toys and treats for the awestruck children, and English books for Ahlam to read. Black, white and Hispanic, they were curious, eager to learn, to have new experiences. They asked her questions about Iraqi culture. "Why is it that y'all fire guns in the air?" one of them wanted to know. She told him it was a traditional way to summon people to a meeting or a celebration such as a wedding, since not everyone in the world had mobile phones.

Their company commander, a genial ginger-haired captain named Jason Pape, in charge of about a hundred men, hit it off with Ahlam and with her husband who had by then returned home. "Ahlam and her family were the favourites of all the men," he would later tell me. "We went there as often as we could." The meals at her house were simple fare, nothing like the "over-the-top, ridiculous feasts" served to them elsewhere. That was part of the draw: "They weren't trying to impress us or ask for anything." Perhaps because of the relaxed atmosphere, a pleasant change from urban areas where they had to be on guard, Pape's men began removing their cumbersome gear and took to swimming with the local children. Some of them held competitions in the river. One of them swam all the way across the Tigris and back. A twenty-year-old Mexican named Mendoza watched one of Ahlam's sisters cooking and took to preparing Iraqi dishes himself in Ahlam's kitchen. He told her he had joined the military to get his American citizenship and maybe a scholarship for his education.

Since she didn't have any ammunition for the gun that, like most Iraqi families, she kept to protect their home, another of the soldiers gave her ten bullets. "Don't tell anybody or they'll put me in jail," he told her. "If anybody asks, I'll tell them I shoot bullets, not give them away!"

A month later, in May, David Luhnow, a reporter for the *Wall Street Journal*, was put on to Ahlam's brother Samir through a correspondent who had used him as a fixer in the past. Samir did the usual—taking him around for a few days, then "outsourcing" him, as Luhnow put it, to his younger sister. Luhnow was furious at first, thinking he'd been shafted, but as he got to know Ahlam and her husband he quickly changed his mind. It turned out to be a lucky break. "I was happy," he recalled.

Luhnow had arrived in Baghdad on the day that American president George W. Bush stood on an aircraft carrier off the coast of California under a banner stating "Mission Accomplished," and boasted—rather prematurely as it turned out—that major combat operations in Iraq had ended. It was the reporter's first visit to the Middle East and he was supposed to be chronicling American reconstruction efforts. What he saw in Baghdad convinced him that not much of the kind was happening. If anything, Baghdad was being *de*-constructed. He needed to figure out what the hell was going on.

Ahlam, with her husband at the wheel, drove with him through the post-invasion landscape. There was only one cassette in the car, Frank Sinatra, whose greatest hits played in a loop as smoke poured from burned-out buildings and looters roamed the lawless streets. This view of Baghdad was a reminder that the problems in the village were paltry compared to what was happening inside the city. On the sidewalk by a hospital, an X-ray machine had been claimed by somebody's grandmother. Street markets had turned into arms fairs—machine guns, RPGs, missiles, anti-tank mines pillaged from abandoned stockpiles. "American GIs were just standing around," Luhnow would recall. "When I asked them, they'd say they had no orders to intervene. They only had orders to guard the Oil ministry."

At a power plant where a pre-sanctions General Electric turbine, held together with spit and ingenuity, was the only thing keeping the lights on, they met a delegation of portly middle-aged executives from American power companies. The executives mooted bringing in three new turbines, but this would require congressional approval. Months it would take, perhaps years. "We don't need this fancy stuff," one of the Iraqi employees protested. "We need hammers, wrenches, pliers. They've all been stolen. Is there a way you could tell them to bring those first?"

One day, on a street corner, they came across a magnificent white stallion. The stables of Uday Hussein had been looted, and this stunning creature had been hitched to an impoverished street vendor's rickety cart. Spooked by gunfire, the horse bolted, launching itself into a barrier of razor wire the Americans had set up. The soldiers scrambled for a forklift while a crowd of Iraqis watched the horse bleed to death on the sidewalk.

Luhnow interviewed the American officials who were in the midst of disbanding the public service and firing the Iraqi Army, anointing this person enemy and that one friend. His reporting took him in and out of the Green Zone, the recently fortified administrative centre of Baghdad. The Coalition Provisional Authority had taken over Saddam Hussein's Republican Palace with its swimming pools, ornate ceilings and elaborate cupolas—gaudy excess of the sort Luhnow associated with nouveau riche bad taste. Security was tight but he had press credentials. In this way Ahlam, the village girl who had once been terrified of ever having a flat tire outside one of these palaces and disappearing from the face of the Earth, was free to "run around" (as Luhnow put it) the former dictator's residence. One ostentatious room had been turned into a barbershop where soldiers were taking turns getting shorn, but Ahlam couldn't shake the feeling that at any moment the ex-dictator would pop out from behind a polished marble wall.

As she gazed around her, a haggard-looking woman swanned through the palace dressed in the finest clothing: a gorgeous robe embroidered in gold thread, gold bracelets from wrist to elbow, on each hand at least three rings. "That's the maid of Samira al-Shahbandar," an Iraqi woman working for the Americans told Ahlam—Saddam Hussein's second wife. "She's taken over her villa as well."

In this upended world a boy rode a donkey past Ahlam's house with a brand-new laptop strapped to the donkey's

hindquarters. At the library in Kadhimiya where Ahlam had
passed so many precious hours during her student years, an
old woman carted out a wheelbarrow full of books, saying
she would use the pages as wrapping to sell seeds.

Ahlam had seen enough. When a pair of teenaged boys
pulled a horse and cart up to an Iraqi tank abandoned near
the main road to scavenge for parts, she called together a
group of the village children. "Each of you pick up a rock,"
she instructed them. She and the children threw stones at
the looters until they drove them off. The mothers of the
children were furious with her. It was reckless. They could
all have been killed.

All the traffic police had disappeared—the US Army had
suspended the Iraqi traffic code because it had made excep-
tions for Baath Party members[30]—and the streets had become
anarchic and dangerous, filled with new cars, new drivers,
and military vehicles that treated the roads as an obstacle
course. Once, Ahlam got out of the car herself to direct traffic, frustrated that no one was left to do this most basic of
jobs. And then one day, someone was. He appeared suddenly
in the middle of the street, waving his hands and signalling
to the cars, focused on the job, alone against a world gone
mad. No one had ordered him back to work. He must have
woken up that morning and decided to put on his old grey-
and-white uniform and return of his own accord. Watching
him go about this impossible task, risking his life to bring
order to chaos, Ahlam felt tears in her eyes.

"It was the first time since the war began that I wept,"
she told me. "That man represented a country that recognized its duties, its responsibilities, order. Before the war you

understood the rules: avoid the government and you will be safe. After the war there were no rules, only chaos. He symbolized a governing system. Without that we were lost."

That month—it was June now—two other events stood out. The first was a protest outside the gates of the Green Zone. Several thousand Iraqi army officers had gathered to ask for the same fifty dollars the lower ranks received after Paul Bremer fired them. "It was a small amount of money but it was symbolic," Ahlam said, "and they were starving." Their military service had been mandatory, and the international sanctions that preceded the invasion had erased other forms of employment. "Now they were out in the street without hope, hunted from one place to another—on one side by Iraqis who wanted revenge, and on the other by Americans who wanted to arrest and interrogate them."

Luhnow was in a hurry that day—he had an interview scheduled inside the Green Zone. Ahlam urged him to take a moment, to speak to the protestors, to listen to what they had to say. Surrounded by a throng of shouting men, he spoke to an ex–army captain. "You don't understand what a massive mistake this is," the man told him, his voice almost pleading. "You are putting the army on the street. They will form the backbone of the resistance." Luhnow, preoccupied and hardly able to pay attention, would later hear those words echo in his mind with the force of prophecy.

He went into the Green Zone. Ahlam waited for him outside on the outskirts of the crowd. While she was waiting, she saw American soldiers open fire on the protestors. In the uproar that followed, protestors began overturning cars and setting them on fire. Ahlam ran back to her car. She pulled the "Press" sign from the window, stuffed it under the seat, then leapt in to move the car farther off. While she was parking, a woman stepped out of her home. "What are you doing here?" she asked, suspicion in her voice.

Ahlam thought fast. "I went to ask the Americans about my brother. He's missing."

"Oh, you poor girl," the woman said sympathetically. "This sort of thing is happening to everyone."

Ahlam hurried back on foot to look for Luhnow. With his mop of light brown hair, his American style and bearing, the reporter was as much a symbol of foreignness as the press sign. She always kept a steel pipe under the seat of her car in case they were stopped, because in the back of her mind was a vision of her charge being pulled from the car and dragged away. The enraged protestors might kill him as soon as he emerged from the Green Zone, but she figured if they saw him with her, they might leave him alone. She searched for his face at the gates until she saw him. He was looking quite relaxed—he had no idea what had happened while he was inside. Together they pushed through the raging crowd and made it back to the car.

The second event, a short time later, was an explosion that blackened the sky across the river from her village. An army transport vehicle had driven over a roadside bomb. No one was hurt but it was a sign things had changed. When Captain Pape's unit was reassigned, the soldiers who took their place preferred to stay inside their tanks. "They were frightened," Ahlam said, "and they were right to be." But she saw where this left ordinary people: caught between the US military and the Iraqi resistance.

She had not asked the Americans to come to Iraq, but she knew that nothing could be accomplished without them. In sweeping away the state, they had become the state. And though their ranks included some fine and decent people, and others whom she saw as simply desperate, she had enough experience of war to know that soldiers followed orders. She also knew that the Iraqi people had expected the Americans to swiftly organize elections, then leave. But a new realization was dawning: the war had just begun.

"I remember one of the nicest afternoons in Iraq was at her house." David Luhnow was talking to me over Skype from his office in Mexico City, where he was now the Latin American bureau chief for the *Wall Street Journal*. I had contacted him to get his understanding of their work together, for the writing of this book. He seemed pleased by the prospect of talking about Ahlam. He was full of praise for her work, for how meticulous she was—her powers of observation and recall—and especially for what she had taught him about her country. Though he wondered if her open mind, her "can-do" attitude, the way she scorned the "Sunni–Shia–Kurd thing," had made him more optimistic about the future than he ought to have been.

It was a lovely afternoon in May when Luhnow went to Ahlam's house. He sat in her garden drinking tea with the Americans who had "set up camp" in her home. They had yet to be reassigned, and their tanks were parked in her yard. "They were sort of based there. She had welcomed them and helped them reach out to the neighbourhood on projects and security. It was very encouraging to see that dynamic."

Some of the guys had gone swimming in the Tigris. He remembered Ahlam shouting to warn them about the current. The atmosphere was warm and relaxed, but a part of him wondered what other Iraqis would think.

"She welcomed the Americans in terms of helping her own people," he told me, "because they were the de facto authority. She was very much a community leader and tried to organize people immediately after the war and in the first months of the occupation. She was very smart about what needed doing. I think some of that ended up getting her into trouble."

He had already begun to have his own doubts about the war. "If you're going to decapitate a government and try to run it from afar I'd think having the institutions intact to run it would be very important. There was none of that happening." He remembered the protest outside the Green Zone, shortly after that visit to Ahlam's home, and how stupid he felt not to have paid more attention. "Those days were the critical turning point." It would not be long before the first Iraqi civilian walked up to an American soldier and shot him in the face.

On that golden afternoon, such problems seemed far off. As they drank tea and talked and the soldiers dried off in the sun, Ahlam discussed ideas and plans that still seemed possible and Luhnow talked to Captain Pape's superior, a lieutenant who had joined them that day. They both agreed that there were good signs and bad—it was alarming that nobody in the occupation forces seemed to have a plan for post-war Iraq—but even so there were reasons for hope.

A year or so later the lieutenant wrote him an email. He wanted to know if there had been any word from Ahlam. "I remember he told me there were flyers and graffiti in her neighbourhood saying derogatory things about her. There was ill will because she was the main go-between for the Americans and the people." By that time she was deputy director of the GIC set up by Civil–Military Affairs, and it was clear that the problems she had seen with Luhnow were just the beginning; that Iraq was the white stallion they had watched bleed to death on the street.

"I went through my own journey in Iraq," he added. "I had some hesitation about the war but I basically supported it. I guess I was one of those naive Americans who tend to believe what they're told, and I guess I had that beaten out of me, largely because of Iraq."

Ahlam, he said, personified the sort of people they had let down. "Someone very much willing to build bridges and create a future." He was quiet for a moment. "We left those people swinging in the wind."

The situation in Baghdad continued to deteriorate after David Luhnow left. The reporter who replaced him didn't want Ahlam as his fixer—he preferred a man who could function as a bodyguard. Looking for work, Ahlam applied to be a translator at the GIC, newly opened in nearby Kadhimiya. Her job, she was told by one of the Americans who led her training seminar, was to be the "missing link" between Iraqi civilians and the US occupation authorities. Meanwhile bodies had begun appearing on streets or dumped in rivers, often so badly mutilated they could not be identified. She carried a pistol in her handbag for a while, but then gave it up, since people were usually either shot from a distance or blown up. From her new office she observed that the Americans were arresting people "right and left" and jailing them based on suspicions and anonymous reports. "That was enough," she told me, "to keep you in Abu Ghraib or Bucca for a year."

It was at Camp Bucca, through which a hundred thousand prisoners passed, that the future leaders of Islamic State met.[31]

Thrown together in numbers too large to supervise, their incarceration provided an ideal opportunity to forge bonds and spend time conspiring under the oblivious gaze of the Americans who had inadvertently brought them together. Indeed, without the American prisons in Iraq, Islamic State would not exist. Housed alongside the radicals were many more who were innocent of any crime. A neighbour with a grudge had only to make an anonymous report to have his enemy arrested. "And if you were wealthy," said Ahlam, "forget it! You would be arrested for supporting terrorism. By the time you were released, everything you owned would be gone." Even when the Americans had good reason to arrest someone, if they arrived when a neighbour had come to pay a visit, the neighbour would be arrested as well, as a matter of course. Detained without trial, without lawyers, without permission to phone their families, the prisoners appeared to have vanished. In her new office, their families besieged her, demanding to know their relatives' whereabouts.

She had recently agreed to serve on the governing council for northwest Baghdad. Captain Pape, who was responsible for rebuilding the local political system from the ground up, had taken note of her leadership qualities: she was educated, fluent in English, a take-charge person—and despite coming from a rural Sunni community known for its conservatism, "she came across as very liberated," he later recalled. Her position on the council allowed her to expand the contacts she needed in her work at the GIC. One day, at a council meeting, she met the general in charge of the military base at the Baghdad airport, where many prisoners were being held. She introduced herself as a councillor and humanitarian worker and requested a moment of his time. Families were coming to her to look for their relatives, she explained, and she had no information to give them.

"Please put yourself in these families' places," she told him. "They have no idea if the missing person has been kidnapped or killed or imprisoned. Telling them where their family members are held will improve the American reputation in the eyes of Iraqis. I don't need their charges, I just need their names."

"I'll do my best," she recalled him saying. "I am not the only one responsible for this, but I'll do my best." He ordered her supervisor, Major Adam Shilling, to give her the names. And each day a list of the latest detainees arrived by email so she could inform their families.

A kilometre from the GIC was Camp Justice, which housed a prison that had been used to torture political prisoners under Saddam Hussein, and would revert to that purpose after the Americans handed it over to the new Iraqi government. She tried to convince the commander there to give her the names of the prisoners and he promised to deal with it, but nothing happened. She knew the Iraqi translator responsible for registering incoming prisoners at Camp Justice, where they were detained until transferred, so she invited him to a meeting in her office. She told him she had a problem he could help her solve. She told him of the old men who came looking for their sons, how she watched them lose weight week by week until they shrank inside their clothing, slowly dying before her eyes; of the women who wept in her arms, not knowing whether their sons or husbands or brothers were alive or dead; of the professional women, distinguished professors, arrested on anonymous reports. She explained that she had asked the Americans for help and been turned away, that they were ignoring the growing anger their actions created.

She knew what she was asking him for was dangerous. "Because he would be in big trouble, actually. He would not only lose his job but be detained himself and face a trial." She would understand if he was too afraid, and would not ask him again, but if he agreed it was not only she who would be grateful, but all the families who had someone inside.

He promised to think about it. "If I call you tomorrow, come to see me at the gate. I'll ask you a question. Then you shake my hand."

The next day he called her. She met him outside the main gate of Camp Justice. "Do you have the medicine for the prisoner?" he asked her loudly in English. It was a perfect cover. She replied, in English, that she had the medicine and would bring it for him. Then they shook hands. In her palm she felt a twist of paper. She surreptitiously tucked it into the pocket of her jeans.

After that they met each day at noon outside the gate. They exchanged pleasantries, always in English so the soldiers on guard would not be alarmed, and shook hands before going their separate ways. If those in charge of the prison wondered why people no longer clamoured outside the gate, demanding information about their relatives, they said nothing to her. These meetings continued until she was kidnapped. After her ransom had been paid, she could no longer stay in Iraq. She would have to build a new life in Syria.

Chapter 9

A SMALL TRIUMPH

THE OPENING CEREMONY FOR the school in Ahlam's apartment turned out to be much more fun than I'd expected. I had envisioned a sad little affair—demure war-shocked girls like those who watched silently while I talked to their mothers or fathers. And I had to admit that part of me had doubted whether the launch would come off at all. People often talked about doing things here, and even planned them, but follow-through was another matter. There were a million obstacles to getting anything done in the refugee community.

It was a stifling blue-sky Sunday afternoon in late August, and the apartment was an un-air-conditioned hotbox even without the twenty or so teenaged girls who crowded in excitedly, along with at least that many adults. The white walls ricocheted with conversation and competing perfumes. The girls had all dressed for an occasion: colourful frocks, chunky necklaces, bright scarves, lipstick. They must have borrowed the finery from sisters or mothers, taken makeup tips, absconded with eyeliner pencils.

The preliminaries were short. After everyone had finally settled into the white plastic chairs lined up in neat rows, and the stragglers standing at the back quieted down, Ahlam stood up at the front to address us. Her face was beaming, her dark eyes glossy. To rapt attention she outlined the schedule—a roster of times and teachers, classes in English and French to be held on weekends so those who were enrolled in Syrian schools could also attend. This was followed by a solemn moment when one of the parents in attendance, a dignified-looking doctor in a grey suit, stood to give a small benediction. "Some people want to turn back the centuries," he said. "That is why they murder our teachers and professors. We want to cooperate with each other to protect our children, girls *and* boys, from the looming darkness of the future." Then an interlude of silence, after which the room broke into what felt like a garden party.

Girls talking; girls laughing; girls snapping up books from the lending library and tucking them into their handbags. One girl stood out from the rest, as much for her aura of reserve as for her loveliness. I realized I had met her briefly, through Ahlam. I recalled what her parents had told me at their apartment, speaking softly only when their daughter was out of earshot. She had married an engineer a year ago, when she was just sixteen. A month after their wedding, her husband had kissed her goodbye in the morning and left for work. He was shot that day along with four of his colleagues by an unknown gunman in his office at the Baghdad electricity department. After that she had moved with her parents to Damascus.

Today she was standing and talking to another girl her age. When the other girl said something, a subdued smile brightened her serious face. It may have been the first day in a year that she had worn a pretty dress, or talked to anyone of anything other than tragedy.

I had taken a seat in the back row, where it was a surprise to discover that I was only one of many Westerners Ahlam had invited to the event. In total there were about a dozen of us: journalists, photographers, anthropologists, aid workers. Ahlam, I realized, had a gift for making friends. We were all in our thirties, dressed in jeans and button-down shirts like members of a visiting tribe. And we were all here to witness something rare: a small triumph.

She had been to the intelligence headquarters to talk to Captain Abu Yusuf. He had, quite remarkably and fully out of character, granted her permission to hold the classes. "I have a feeling he will want something later," she told me, before turning back to her girls. But I paid no attention. Because it was remarkable to see this one thing, this thing that had been talked about like a daydream, actually happening.

Marianne was there, back from her travels, with her Italian-Dutch fiancé, Alessandro. Ahlam told me how they had bought the chairs, along with whiteboards and markers and books for the library, and I was pleased to meet them. They were a striking young couple, at once aristocratic and down to earth. Marianne was willowy, even statuesque, yet the kind of beautiful woman who would rather no one noticed. She radiated a gentle shyness that contrasted with Alessandro's gregarious nature. While Marianne had immersed herself in fieldwork with Ahlam, he had spent the summer working on an educational project for Palestinians in Damascus and studying Arabic. Between the two of them they had six or seven languages.

Marianne tucked a strand of fair hair behind her ear and talked, so soft-spoken I had to strain to hear her, about the rationale for setting up the school. It was about education of course, but it was also about creating a community for vulnerable girls who had so few opportunities to leave the house. It was a chance to make friends with others who had been through similar experiences, and perhaps find something to hold onto, the possibility of a different life. "The school is a small measure in the face of great need," she said, as the party swirled around us, "but it addresses their isolation and loneliness while allowing them to learn."

"Two targets with one rocket," was how Ahlam had put it.

Ahlam's children, Abdullah and Roqayah, were there, their high spirits muted in the presence of sophisticated teenagers. And for the first time I met her husband. Tall and thin, with a shock of white hair, he had a gentle face marked by worry.

No one else that day seemed worried. For the Westerners as for the girls, the opening ceremony was a social occasion. It was refreshing to be around people who didn't need any explanation for what you were doing here, in the middle of Little Baghdad on a ferociously hot day. Refreshing to not have to answer questions about what you were doing with your life that you could hardly answer yourself. And to be here to celebrate something all of us wanted: a better future for the people we had come to care about.

As the noise level rose to a conversational roar, I chatted to a tall blond Frenchman who had recently left his job with the Red Cross in Iraq. He was spending a month in Damascus to work on his spoken Arabic. "Where to next?" I asked. He shrugged. "Not Iraq," he said over the din. Next to us a woman with an intense expression was taking pictures with an impressively lensed camera. This was the American war photographer Ahlam had told me about, a close friend who was living in Syria. Ahlam had told me she hadn't been by in a while because she wasn't feeling well. She looked well. Lowering her camera as I introduced myself as another of Ahlam's friends, she told me the real reason she wasn't coming around anymore: "Ahlam's name is a red flag." She had been warned by a Syrian official to stop associating with her if she wanted to renew her visa. She had come today, just this once, because she didn't want to let Ahlam down by missing the opening.

It must have been the festive mood, or the fact that Alessandro and the Frenchman were conspiring to find us some beer and a place to drink it—this neighbourhood was *dry*—but I didn't give much thought to the photographer's concerns. As we prepared to leave, Ahlam's husband called her over: he asked us to please be careful when we left the apartment building, to take different routes so as not to be seen. Ahlam rolled her eyes, giving the impression she was only humouring him, but we listened, nodding agreement. The problem was there was only one route out of the dead-end of the alley where she lived.

The sun was already falling behind the rows of low-rise buildings as a group of us made our way downstairs. I realized that this would be my last visit for at least a few months. I was heading home soon—I had other assignments to juggle and would return in the winter to follow up—and this was the best possible note to leave on. Whatever the future held, whether the concerns of the war photographer or the fears of Ahlam's husband were justified—and paranoia was normal here, how could it not be?—something good was happening. I was glad to have seen it for myself. The school had grown up by dint of hard and thoughtful work from the grassroots. If Marianne and Alessandro had helped to set things in motion, it remained an organic achievement, created by a woman who was not sitting around awaiting rescue, because rescue, as all of us knew, would never come.

The night before I was due to leave Damascus I threw a dinner party. I wanted to invite everyone who had made my work here possible, all of whom I considered friends. I wanted everyone to meet and to like one another for the reasons I liked them. And I wanted to use the flamingo-pink terrace for what it seemed made for. I bought wine, for those who drank, from the nearby liquor store, pickled mushrooms from the downstairs grocer who used to live in Paris, and, using the limited utensils in the tiny kitchen, made a fettuccini Alfredo that I could serve from a single pot.

Kuki, my interpreter, showed up first, wearing his uniform of skin-tight black T-shirt and artfully distressed jeans, carrying a bootleg CD of James Blunt as a going-away present. He was followed by Rana, the schoolteacher-interpreter who usually accompanied me anywhere that required dealing with Syrian officials, where Kuki certainly wouldn't do. She was elegantly dressed as always in a lime green skirt that matched her headscarf that matched her handbag.

Rana was a natural diplomat, but I worried that Kuki, who hadn't met Ahlam yet, wouldn't get along with her. Generally speaking he liked nothing to do with other Iraqis, hating to be mistaken for a refugee except when he was recognized ("Aren't you that model from Baghdad?"). It was dangerous to be photographed, I would tell him, lifting my hand to shield him from yet another fan's camera phone. But vanity, I realized, can also be a survival strategy. It allowed him to exist as an individual, to remember himself as he had been, be greeted with admiration rather than resentment or pity.

I had given Ahlam taxi fare so she could join us, but she took a collective taxi anyway to save money. Soon Kuki, Rana, Ahlam and I, plus a handful of Westerners I knew, were all sitting in the cool of the evening on the large terrace beneath the stars, exactly as I had imagined. I set my laptop on the edge of the roof, the music tinny on the speakers. I handed around plates and refilled glasses for all but Rana and Ahlam, who didn't drink. The streets below pulsed with the carnival of Damascus nightlife.

"You'll be back?" everyone asked.

I smiled at them all. "In three months." I knew I wasn't finished here—I like to follow stories over time. "I'll fly to Jordan and come in by land, probably, rather than flying direct. I had to talk my way onto a Syrian Arab Airlines flight to get here that'd been booked for months—I don't want to go through that again."

It was strange to see Ahlam outside of her native environment, in this upscale neighbourhood where the party never ceased. For a moment I could see her as others might: her clothing shabby, the same well-worn jeans and men's shoes she had worn since the day her son died; her exuberant laughter ringing out. But I could see she didn't care, didn't even notice. Ahlam fitted into this neighbourhood as she did anywhere, because it didn't cross her mind to think that she didn't.

I have found this in journalism too: that if you believe you have the right to be somewhere, or talk to anyone no matter how powerful or barricaded, nobody blinks. It's a certain aura or manner that erases questions. As I watched, Ahlam made herself at home, but without changing herself, without adapting, as if she was accepting everyone else rather than the reverse. Rich or poor, urban or rural, Western or Eastern or Martian, we were all the same to her. I have never met anyone so oblivious to the social divides of our modern world. It could have been seen as a kind of blindness, but I realized it was a kind of sight.

She borrowed Kuki's lighter and lit a cigarette. The two of them were soon talking as if they had known one another a long time. She was in the mood for a celebration. The music was turned up and the conversation flowed.

Chapter 10

ASSASSINS

AT JFK AIRPORT, THE MERCENARIES bound for Iraq via the New York flight to Jordan were easy to spot. Clad in Oakley wraparound sunglasses and Quiksilver T-shirts, the uniform of the off-duty hired gun, five of them did tequila shots at the bar next to the Royal Jordanian boarding gate, where I was nursing a glass of water and a hangover.

"I'm always shit-faced when I fly transcontinental," the one who looked like a *Top Gun* pilot boasted to his friends. "We rule two-thirds of Iraq and all of Afghanistan!" shouted his nerdier colleague, proposing a toast. They talked of being "assassins."

I was booked on the same flight, having spent the previous days in New York meeting with editors and friends. Over lunch with Luke, my editor at *Harper's*, we discussed the structure of my piece on the refugee crisis and the reporting I still needed to finish it. He drew a complex diagram in marker on a placemat and I nodded as if it made perfect sense. I told him I was going to start in Jordan, then check in on Damascus for a week or so. I was planning to focus a segment of the piece around the refugees who congregated at Ahlam's apartment; their situation could only have worsened in the last three months as they burned through their savings. After that I would go to Beirut where I had learned that tens of thousands of Iraqis were paying smugglers to take them over the border from Syria to Lebanon.

The night before had been a noisy reunion of the Westerners I had met in Damascus through Ahlam. I embraced Marianne and Alessandro, who had finished their work in Syria and were settling into life together in Chelsea. Their wedding was planned for the summer in Italy, a logistical challenge joining families across countries and continents, but they seemed very happy. At their apartment, with its high ceilings and ornate plasterwork, Alessandro uncorked a bottle of red while talking animatedly about an Iraqi film festival he was organizing in Milan. The focus was the plight of media workers in Baghdad, but he hoped that some of the filmmakers who were planning to attend would be granted asylum. That way, he explained, regardless of who came to the screenings, something good would come of it.

Marianne had moved on to other development work after finishing up with UNICEF—adolescent girls remained her focus, they were so vulnerable, she said, and tended to slip through the cracks—but she worried about Ahlam. "If anything happens to her," she told me later in the evening, as one of the guests clambered out onto the fire escape for a smoke and another struggled with a corkscrew, "at least Mona can keep the school going." Mona, she reminded me, was the Syrian woman who had offered to help Ahlam run her classes. She hadn't been at the opening ceremony so I hadn't met her, but what struck me was the first part of Marianne's statement—the acknowledgement that something *could* happen to Ahlam.

Not possible, I thought. Of course I remembered the meetings with Captain Abu Yusuf, and how surprised Ahlam was to learn that the Syrians were sending intelligence agents to follow her around. Yet the school had opened without a hitch, so perhaps the worst was past. "Nobody's safe here," Ahlam had told me during our work together, but compared to other refugees she seemed invincible—a force of nature. Besides, she had so many friends. Before I left that night, Marianne slipped me an envelope to give her. "For the school," she said. "Or whatever she needs."

At the airport bar, the men had sent the only woman at their table, a hard-looking blonde in a short denim skirt, to the barman for another round. When she returned I noticed her tattoo: a snake winding up her calf.

Jordan was a transit hub for contractors heading into Iraq— men you always saw in airports like Frankfurt or Dubai. A lot of them worked for KBR, a spinoff of Halliburton, whose former CEO Dick Cheney helped mastermind the invasion of Iraq after becoming vice-president to George W. Bush. If there was an undisputed winner of the war in Iraq, it was KBR, which took in multi-billions in no-bid contracts. Others worked for Blackwater, the most notorious of the dozens of private military and security firms who made up a shadow army that for the first time ever outnumbered traditional troops. These included firms you'd never heard of until you listened to their employees talk about "killing bad guys" as if they really believed that. Some earned in a day what a grunt, which many of them had been, earned in a month. They counted when it came to their paycheques, but not when they died. Conveniently, their numbers were left out of the body count back home.

This group was from SOC, which I learned when they toasted their employer. Special Operations Consulting, when I looked it up, was a Nevada-based company started by six Navy SEALs that specialized in "international force protection." It had recently been expelled from Namibia for illegally attempting to recruit low-wage guards for US military bases; other SOC recruits alleged abuse on the bases, with female contractors passed around for sex.[32]

On the ten-hour flight over I was seated next to a woman with a wailing baby. My head throbbed, so I asked to be moved to an empty seat in the back. On one side of me sat an Arab girl reading a book called *God's Answers to Life's Most Important Problems*. On the other side was a bearded contractor, approximately six foot six, wearing a T-shirt with a skeleton brandishing an M16 and the words *US Army: We're the Ultimate in Body Piercing*. Hemmed in by religion and militarism, I tried to get some sleep.

Chapter 11

DAMASCUS IN WINTER

THROUGH THE WINDOW OF the taxi, the city rose abruptly from the desert, veiled in cold white mist. At the outskirts, the driver, who had brought me all the way from Jordan, nosed into Sayeda Zainab, sloshing through potholes filled by recent rains. He had trouble finding the Kuwaiti Hotel, which had been recommended to me with the words "cheap" and "clean," and was forced to circle the block several times, stopping to ask for directions. Finally I spotted a narrow glass door, wedged in next to a kitchen shop. I pulled my bags out of the back and hauled them up the stairs to the manager's office on the second floor.

I looked around the room he offered me with satisfaction. It was a lodging for pilgrims: two single beds, furnished kitchenette, bathroom, prayer rug. A little settee for guests. A sharp chemical scent assured me it had recently been sprayed for cockroaches. Just a block from the shrine in Little Baghdad—luxury.

I called Ahlam from the phone in the manager's office. In a matter of minutes she flew in the door. Breathless, as if she had been running. "You came back," she said, dissolving into tears. I felt embarrassed but pleased, standing to embrace her as the manager, who had made tea, watched us with amusement. No one had ever cried with happiness at seeing me. I come from an inexpressive culture, where tears are private matters reserved for sadness or self-pity.

It was late, well past dinnertime. I needed bread, coffee for the morning, a new SIM card for my phone. Ahlam and I headed outside to the market in a tumble of words, arm in arm like mismatched school chums—she, the shorter one, all in black; I, at nearly six feet, the ponytailed giantess in jeans.

She had been ill, she said. After her kidnapping back in Iraq, she'd suffered a heart attack, and since then experienced intermittent heart pain. I said I had been . . . busy, away, on assignment in a rainforest on the other side of the planet. I never knew how to explain my life to someone for whom it must sound so carefree. And anyway, I was happy— glad to be here, now, to be absorbed and fascinated. That in itself defied explanation. She was happy too to tell me she was now a neighbourhood representative for the UN High Commissioner for Refugees. The refugee agency had recently brought over an Egyptian rock star as a goodwill ambassador and she had been showing him around. The work was voluntary, but it gave her a monthly stipend for expenses, and just as importantly provided connections, access to information and a sort of legitimacy. The staff there had to return her calls. She laughed. "Maybe now the Syrian intelligence will leave me alone." Abu Yusuf was still calling her in for meetings, still flummoxed, but it appeared to me that she was in a more stable position.

At the market, electric light from stalls and shops splashed over darkened streets and illuminated faces at close range, like a farm fair at night. It was so densely packed that we had to unlink arms and wedge ourselves into gaps. As the crowd surged around us, we were stopped by a woman, a widow who wanted advice on obtaining food rations. Then another woman approached her through the crowd. Also a widow.

"So you're, what, the mayor of this place now?" I asked after they left. Ahlam grimaced, then laughed. "You're the mayor of Little Baghdad," I said, laughing even harder, throwing an arm around her back. "Congratulations. No one else would want the job."

A few weeks earlier I had been sailing through the Great Bear Rainforest off the west coast of Canada to write a travel piece for *Canadian Geographic*. The rainforest, stretching across an archipelago of thousands of islands and webbed fjords, is one of the last inhabitable places on the planet that, on satellite images, still turns black at night. For nine days there was no phone reception, no email, no headline news. I was about as far off the grid as you can get.

It wasn't my usual sort of assignment, but it was a once-in-a-lifetime chance to see a place with few human footprints, so when an editor dangled it, I bit. From the boat I watched grizzly bears with great bands of muscle across their hulking backs rear up along the shoreline. I perched astride the bowsprit while two Dall's porpoises raced alongside the ship, their silvery skin almost near enough to touch. I looked for and found the famously elusive white Kermode spirit bear, the rarest bear on earth.

In the rainforest, history is written on the rings of thousand-year-old red cedars. Human endeavour is the golf balls shot off cruise ship decks that wash up on rocky outcrops. And plastic, so much plastic, is our culture's legacy. Sleeping in the wheelhouse of the hundred-year-old schooner through a violent storm, I dreamed about the death journey of the salmon. The salmon, as it battles upriver to spawn, grows fangs and a snout, turning from Jekyll into Hyde. After spawning and giving up its life, it floats downstream, providing food for bears, eagles, trees, for every living thing.

If the rainforest seemed like a vision of the deep past, Sayeda Zainab—Little Baghdad—seemed like the future. Masses of humanity, on the run from our own species and our uniquely destructive abilities. Here, I was about as far as it was possible to be from that place of natural cycles. Here, when someone died, it was almost always for nothing.

As we made our way through the market, passing carts selling soccer jerseys and cheap colognes with names like One-Dollar Man, Ahlam caught me up on recent events, which had become more dire. The conflict in Iraq was reaching deeper into Damascus. Three refugee ex-generals had been found in an apartment nearby, hog-tied and strangled. Another ex-general, in a neighbouring apartment, fled upon hearing the news; no one knew where he ended up. A widowed mother of three who was working as a prostitute to feed her children was murdered by a family member who had come from Iraq to protect the family "honour." And an Iraqi television director who made programs critical of the political situation in Iraq had been stabbed thirty-seven times outside his Damascus office. His name had been on a list of "cultural targets" published by an Iraqi militia.

On the edge of the market was a stand piled high with fresh-baked bread. I stopped to buy some. The vendor looked at me as if couldn't quite believe what he was seeing, the only Westerner around. "Who is she?" he asked in a shocked whisper.

"A professor," Ahlam told him. She needed no prompting from me. Not to answer would be to leave a vacuum into which rumour would flood, and rumour was the main source of news.

On the second morning, awakened early by the call to prayer, I dressed and walked the winding alleys over to Ahlam's apartment. She'd be awake—sleep did not come easily to her and she was always awake. Nearing the gold dome of the shrine I passed the only other person who was on the street at this hour, a young cigarette vendor who was slapping his arms to keep warm. He beamed a broad smile, shouting his greeting through a fog of breath. "Welcome, *doktorah!*"

I had been here less than thirty-six hours. News travelled fast.

December mornings were cold and damp, fingers of mist transforming the alleyways into a medieval film noir. The mist draped itself around the neighbourhood the way it had over the rainforest, guarded there by eagles atop tall cedars, here by minarets.

Since the summer, I had become familiar with the Escher-like maze of streets and alleyways, though I took back routes, never lingered. I was no longer on top looking down, but had burrowed my way to the centre of Little Baghdad. I tried to make myself invisible, and at times felt I must be succeeding. When a knot of Iranian pilgrims emerged from the shrine chanting, arms swinging, they flowed around me like a river around a stone.

I rarely bothered going downtown except to visit Kuki or Rana, and they were not eager to come to me. When I went to dinner with Rana and her family—a boisterous clan who were always trying to force-feed me—I told them where I was living. One of Rana's sisters, a pharmacist who wore too much makeup, shouted something I couldn't follow. She pantomimed striking her forehead, then collapsed into laughter.

"What did she say?" I asked Rana.

"It's an expression." Rana smiled. "'May God fix your head.'"

"But I like it there," I protested. "You'd be surprised."

I was teaching Ahlam yoga. Since her kidnapping, when she was thrown from truck to truck, Ahlam had found moving her shoulder to be painful, so while her husband and children were still asleep in their bedroom, we stretched our arms up, up, up. Now bending, now touching toes, then up again. "Bend your knees," I said, watching her and illustrating. "Just slightly, when you turn." Then lifting the arms up and over, up and over, breathing from the stomach. She joked that we could offer classes: one for the victims of Saddam Hussein, one for the victims of the Americans, one for the victims of the militias. We would have lineups around the block.

I had planned to stay for a week, catch up on the latest developments, then leave to continue my research in Beirut. But a week became two, became three, and still I stayed.

Each morning I descended the stairs from my hotel room with a wave to the slim moustachioed hotel manager, who looked like a waiter in a French restaurant. I bought a pack of cigarettes for Ahlam from a sidewalk vendor, and bread and cheese to share, and spent my days at Ahlam's apartment. I didn't need to hustle anymore. I had the base I had been looking for. I treated the burgundy sofa as a theatre box seat, taking notes as people talked. Since she was more or less the mayor of this community of exiles, her apartment the town hall, I could simply sit there while their stories came to me.

Ahlam was still running the classes from her apartment, although the school was on winter break. There were seventy students now coming on weekends, divided into classes that ran from nine in the morning to nine at night: a morning class for girls in English, a noon class in English conversation, an afternoon class for boys in math and English, then French lessons for girls in the evenings. She had introduced the class for boys after a group of them had made the case that they, too, deserved to learn. Ahlam was the headmistress, but the classes were taught by volunteers—some of them Westerners, others Iraqi schoolteachers. Roqayah, her precocious daughter, now nine, was learning English in her mother's classes, and was always quizzing me on my Arabic, correcting my deplorable accent. She had chosen a line from one of the textbooks, making me say it back to her in Arabic. "The monkey," she said in careful English. "Lives. In the jung-le. Now you."

Meanwhile the apartment had become a temporary warehouse for donations from a mosque in New York. All day long mothers came by to rifle through the wall of black garbage bags filled with used winter clothing, fitting warm coats onto the stiff arms of children. They heaved up packages of donated foodstuffs. "Write your names here," Ahlam said, handing them a list, making them sign and pose for a photograph. "So the donors know I did not steal," she explained.

"Now," she told the recipients, "you won't tell anyone where these things came from?" She made them promise. If word got out she'd be mobbed. "I will have to put a notice of my death on my door," she told me. "Some will cry for me; some will cry for their packages."

Pacing around her apartment in a green army surplus jacket, a phone to each ear, cigarette between her lips, Ahlam looked like a guerilla fighter commanding operations. While she shouted orders and handed out packages, her apartment was the centre of lively activity, laughter, commiseration.

"The problem with these kerosene heaters," she said, looking at a stack of them that had been given by a famous Syrian actress to honour the death of her grandmother, "is how to afford kerosene." Even so the heaters were gone from her apartment within hours.

People came to get news, advice, their packages. And mainly, I think, to feel as I did—less alone. When I had told my boyfriend I was going to be away for December—and Christmas—he had assured me that he would be fine. But almost as soon as I had left his tone changed. He recounted in an email a dinner alone at a restaurant when he was pierced by the sight of a couple holding hands. He wrote: *Maybe I just have to find a way to accept this. We will talk when you get back and try to sort this out.*

I did what I usually did: gave myself over to the work. Things were much worse since I had been here in the summer. Walking down the alley towards Ahlam's, I was trailed by a morose teenaged shepherd who was earnestly trying to sell me one of his flock—just a small one, he suggested. During the holidays of Eid al-Adha, Muslims are meant to butcher a sheep the way Abraham did after proving to God that he was willing to kill his own son. (This story always struck me as reflecting badly on both Abraham and God.) But Iraqis were too broke this year to eat lamb. "We are becoming veg-et-ar-ian," Ahlam said, laughing, her tongue stumbling over the unfamiliar word.

One day her neighbour's son disappeared, a young Iraqi on the run from the Syrian police. Some said he had been selling forged Syrian residency permits, others that he was running a network of girls. All we knew for sure was that a sympathetic police officer had warned his two brothers to stay out of sight lest they be rounded up in his stead.

The two young men, breathless and pale, came over to hide out. Years later I would learn that one of these brothers, a devoted nationalist and family man, would return to Iraq, where he would be killed by Islamic State militants while attempting to get his wife and son out of the ISIS-controlled city of Mosul. The other brother would make it to the United States, where he would become a successful drug dealer.

For now their futures were undecided. As they joined us, a woman in a full face veil walked in the door, sank into a plastic chair, tore off her veil and waved her fingers in the air for a cigarette. One of the brothers scrambled to give her one, standing up to light it for her. Inhaling deeply, she fluffed out her dyed blonde hair with her fingers. Even in Little Baghdad, where almost every woman but me covered her hair—no one seemed to care—I hadn't before seen anyone fully veiled. And underneath she looked like a femme fatale. It turned out that she was a widow who had recently solved the problem of single motherhood by becoming a "second wife." The veil came about because her new husband, a well-to-do businessman who worked between Baghdad and Damascus, wished to hide his second wife from the first. In this way his neighbours had no idea she was not the same wife he kept in Baghdad.

Suddenly, everyone knew someone who had made it out. Some walked through the mountains into Turkey, bound for Greece, their gateway to Europe, paying smugglers $9,000—half up front and half on arrival. For $15,000 the teenaged son of a businessman made it to Sweden, said to be the Promised Land. Others were conned by swindlers and lost their life savings, or ended up stranded in Nigeria or Cambodia or India without documents. Yet others died en route, trapped in meat lockers or the backs of transport trucks. "Ninety-nine percent of us want to be smuggled out to a country where we can live in peace," an Iraqi Mandaean told me. "The problem is money and safety." They lived in terror that something would happen to force them back to Iraq—which it did when the Syrian war began in earnest, sending others scattering to surrounding countries or joining the exodus of Syrians to Europe.

While Europe tried to staunch the flow—the Swedish police were active in Damascus, trying to stop the smuggling—ever more innovative escape routes were being set up by the mafias who ran the lucrative human trafficking trade out of Syria; it was they who pioneered the underground networks that would later be used by Syrians themselves. One of the widows who frequented Ahlam's apartment left for Cyprus by smuggler's boat, carrying her newborn daughter in her arms. She made it over safely.

Good, I thought when I heard that. Good for them.

I felt myself, slowly, become part of the background. Part of the scene, where I like to be. Not that I completely disappeared—that wasn't possible. Around the subject of human smuggling in particular, the number one topic of conversation, I was assumed to be an expert. I had come from the West, after all—I ought to know something about how to get there.

"I have an idea," said an old man, standing before me to outline an improbable plan by which he would pose as a tennis coach and convince customs officials to let him into Canada.

"Have you ever played tennis?" I asked. I imitated a tennis serve with a swerve of the wrist.

Well no, he had not. But could it be done?

Another plan, one that was clearly making the rounds, was to "rent" an authentic passport from a US citizen and give it back when he got to America. He'd be rich then, obviously, so paying for the smuggling service would not be a problem. Everyone thought, despite the lessons I tried to impart on economic and social policy, that all Americans lived in mansions, drove fancy cars and lived like movie stars. When I suggested otherwise, they smiled indulgently. They knew what they'd seen on TV.

One night we went to a restaurant in the Old City to meet a group of Ahlam's friends. The Old City was festive: young couples holding hands, families out for a stroll dressed in their best, shops decorated brightly for Christmas. A guy walked by wearing a jaunty Santa hat. I thought of the recent emails from my boyfriend, and tried to remember whether this would be the second or third Christmas in a row that I would spend away from home. I had sent him an email, telling him about the widows who were becoming second wives. He replied that he had had a dream that he had two wives—one who went away, like me, and another who stayed home.

The restaurant was smoky, with white tablecloths and waiters in pressed white shirts, like an Italian supper club. We were ushered to a large table in a semi-private room in the back. Ahlam brought her children, who for once behaved themselves, excited at the novelty of menus and ordering. I had given Ahlam the envelope of cash from Marianne and Alessandro in New York, and her children were both proudly wearing the new track suits she had bought them for the holiday of Eid.

Several Iraqis were already seated at the table. One of them, shaved head, leather jacket, young and flashy, stood up with a drink in his hand. He greeted Ahlam with a brilliant smile. "Do you have any money I can borrow?" he asked her. Tarek worked, when he worked, making documentaries and freelancing for foreign media.

"You can afford to drink in a restaurant and you ask me that?" She laughed. "Go away," she said, and sat down.

I took the seat beside her and introduced myself as a journalist writing about Iraqis in Syria. An older guest, speaking no English, with a pockmarked face, was eager to talk to me.

"He wants you to interview him for your story," Ahlam said, setting her phone on the table next to her cigarettes. "He is an artist from Baghdad."

"Why does he want me to interview him?" I asked. I had done many interviews already, in the hundreds, and I distrusted those who sought me out—it usually meant they wanted something more from me than to tell their story.

"He thinks it will help him sell his paintings. And help him get to the United States."

"Thank him. Tell him, later. Another day."

I glanced over the menu. Good—there was mezze, the tapas of hummus and baba ghanoush and fattoush and moutabel. These starters were as inexpensive as they were delicious and filling, unfortunately for restaurateurs who had me as a guest and expected them just to whet the appetite, not sate it. Good, also wine—alcohol was perfectly legal in Syria but in conservative Sayeda Zainab the only liquor store was so well-hidden that I never found it. We had just ordered when another guest joined us. Ahlam stood up and kissed her warmly.

"Deborah, this is Mona," she said, as I stood to greet the newcomer. "Mona is helping me with the school."

So this was Mona? She wasn't what I had expected—the stalwart, middle-aged woman I had imagined when Ahlam first mentioned her to me. Mona had a luxurious mane of dark hair that fell in tendrils down her shoulders, a face like a spoiled doll, and a belted raincoat that emphasized her figure. She was in her mid-twenties and looked like the kind of woman who makes a sweeping entrance in a detective novel with a tale that seems plausible until the trouble starts.

She spoke English, but her manner with me was aloof, as if she were Ahlam's friend and had to figure out whether she could trust me. Curiously, I felt the same way. She had brought a friend with her, also Syrian, her dark hair pulled up into a lazy bun. Both of them were fixers, Ahlam told me.

The fixer mafia. It was a small world. Fixers often knew one another, just as journalists inevitably do when our turfs overlap. The day before, a fellow fixer had stopped by

Ahlam's apartment when I was there, one I had immediately liked. Hamid was a gruff man of sixty with a square impassive face and thick old-fashioned glasses. I had heard of him before meeting him—he had worked for a journalist I knew in situations of extreme danger in Iraq. He was known as tough and reliable, solid as a block of granite. He was accompanied by a photojournalist, a Czech-American named Gabriela whose project was to photograph the refugees. As Gabriela and I talked—it was rare to meet other journalists around here, and I gave her my email so we could stay in touch—Hamid and Ahlam exchanged contacts and information with the fluency of colleagues. He had a voice like raking gravel. Hamid was the only Iraqi I met who came to see her on an equal footing, not asking for anything.

Mona and her colleague sat across from us at the table, lighting cigarettes. They talked in low voices while Ahlam attended to her excited children's meals—their mother wasn't much of a cook.

We had begun to use the term "if anything happens." *If anything happens* was shorthand that neither of us decoded, any more than we had to discuss why Ahlam introduced me to everyone as a professor. Any more than she needed to explain why she had two phones. The first, which rang incessantly, a hundred times a day, was kept for regular calls from people in the neighbourhood or her family in Iraq. The other she had bought for her work as a fixer and the UN refugee agency.

It may be she was already looking around for a replacement for herself, but I don't think her intentions were that fully formed. She was just ensuring that there were backup plans for backup plans, the way people with experience of things breaking down know to keep spare generators and extra batteries on hand. Mona, she told me, had become her primary backup plan, *if anything happened.*

For a while, she had also been talking to the mild-mannered high-school history teacher I had met in the summer, the one who had lost his job and home and nearly his life after being fired for having been a member of the Iraqi Baath Party. He was gentle, intelligent, cared about children, was a qualified teacher—an excellent choice as a backup to run the classes, if anything happened. But Mona was Syrian, and thus, in these precarious times, a better long-term backup for Ahlam.

The next time I saw Mona was at Ahlam's apartment. It was late afternoon and the small heater barely dented the cold. I wore fingerless gloves, warming my hands over the red-hot wires. It was almost as cold indoors as out, and almost as dark, the sky pressing greyly against the only window. The small apartment was full of refugees, as usual. Ahlam told me with concern how crowded it was becoming—hosting the classes in her apartment, with her and her family living there, the place not their own. Every weekend, dozens of teenagers were coming in and out, along with the volunteer teachers. She had noticed that there was another apartment for rent on the ground floor of her building that might be suitable, but it was beyond her means.

Mona was wearing high-heeled boots, looking like a film star slumming with the extras. She seemed as surprised to see me there as I was to see her. "I'm here all the time," I said, which was more or less the case, but my words must have come across as a challenge, because she bristled. It occurred to me that she and I were the only two people who were here by choice rather than necessity; we were neither lost nor destitute. My reaction to her made me examine myself: Was I defensive of my right to be here? Suggesting to her that Ahlam was as much my friend as hers? Could it be as simple as that?

Mona settled tentatively on a chair near the heater and lit a cigarette, talking to me woodenly about the school. I said I thought it was a hopeful project. It was, she agreed.

It struck me as odd to find her so eager to help with nothing obvious to gain from it, but I reprimanded myself for my ill will.

However, my confusion deepened on the visit Ahlam and I paid her a few days later, at a downtown apartment rented by a couple of her friends—tough-looking Serbs in leather jackets who said they worked in the oil business. Mona was helping the men prepare for a party, showing them where to pile the boxes of booze. She stood on a chair to pin up decorations, her skirt riding up her thighs.

"Do you want a drink?" she asked me, when she climbed down. There was no wine or beer, only spirits. She poured two glasses, handing one to me. Ahlam, phone at her ear, declined with a wave of her cigarette and walked into the kitchen where I could hear her talking.

Mona and I talked about why observant Muslims don't drink. "They smoke to make up for it," I said, smiling.

"Or take drugs." She proceeded to explain the logistics of smuggling drugs from Lebanon into Syria, wonderfully detailed information that I supposed she had gleaned from her work with journalists.

Later that week Ahlam and I were invited to a party at the home of Tarek, the young Iraqi I had met at the restaurant who made documentary films. Tarek and Ahlam were friends, even though she thought he spent all his money on drink so wouldn't lend him any, even if she had it to lend.

Tarek rented a cellar apartment that was built into the stone walls of the Old City. Before he got into film and journalism, he was in a rock band in Baghdad called Black Rose. "We were horrible," he told me, "a shame to music history."

Bottles littered his flat. He had nearly destroyed a book he was writing about the war by spilling a drink on his laptop. He talked a lot about returning to Baghdad, regarding it with the romantic idealism of someone longing for a destructive relationship that might have been okay once, even good. Did I know the taste of the fish that came from the Euphrates, how good it was? Had I any idea? He was determined to go back despite having been kidnapped twice—the second time by Shia like himself who meant nothing personal by it, were just making a living. They loosened his wrists so he could drink with them, then cried about the girls they had loved.

Seventeen of his friends had been killed, artists and journalists, part of the eradication of the intellectuals, but he said it would be better to die in the Baghdad he loved than to endure the soul death of exile. He liked to see Ahlam because she reminded him of home. "You *are* Baghdad," he told her.

I had had a work obligation before the party. Tarek's friend, the artist with the pockmarked face who had asked me to interview him, had been phoning Ahlam repeatedly, needling her to get me to talk to him. I ignored him for a while but it was easier to agree than put him off indefinitely. "May as well get it over with tonight," I had told Ahlam, "since I'm sure we'll be seeing him at the party." So we met him at a café near the Old City gate of Bab Touma. The interview revealed nothing but his narcissism. "He is telling us," Ahlam said, stubbing out a cigarette, "that the woman who is working on his resettlement file at the UNHCR thinks he is a very great artist. She bought one of his paintings. He says she wants to have an affair with him." He watched her proudly, nodding solemnly as she interpreted his words.

The three of us went to the party together, descending the stone stairs to Tarek's cellar. Ducking through the low doorway, I saw Mona. She was drunk and passed out on a bed. Was this the backup plan? If so, it wasn't very solid. That Ahlam seemed to trust her was the main reason I didn't dwell upon my misgivings. I would have plenty of time to do so later on.

The next day I left for Lebanon to complete my research. A few tens of thousands of Iraqi refugees had paid smugglers to take them west across the Syrian border, whether to find jobs in Beirut or another route to Europe. They were living in hiding in Beirut but I wanted to talk to them.

In the next ten days I made a lot of contacts—including "the Emperor," a swarthy Greek-Lebanese ex–guerilla fighter who ran MusicHall, a famous cabaret that was a watering hole and listening post for European ambassadors, politicians of all stripes, shady tycoons and even shadier James Bond characters. Most of what happened in the hive of conspiracy that was Beirut was never known, except here, where red velvet curtains parted on a young Arab man in a white suit who sang a perfect, plaintive Edith Piaf.

I was running out of time, exacerbated by a hassle of my own creation. In Beirut I misplaced my passport—a serious mistake that required making an intelligence report at Beirut's gigantic General Security complex. Escorted to a windowless holding pen in the basement prison, told to sit tight next to downcast men in handcuffs, I found myself with the very refugees I had come here to find. Iraqis in Lebanon, I learned while I waited for the intelligence officer to complete my report (in longhand, there were no computers), were being arrested and forced to choose between indefinite imprisonment and deportation to Iraq. They chose prison.

I was lucky: the taxi driver who found my passport had brought it to the Canadian embassy, which I discovered when I arrived there with the Lebanese intelligence report in hand. My freedom of movement was returned to me, and the next morning I made the four-hour drive back to Damascus. My flight home would be leaving from Jordan late that night, which meant another four-hour taxi ride from Damascus to Amman to bookend the day. But I wanted to spend the few hours I had left with Ahlam. Between the summer and the winter I'd spent three months talking to refugees. I had everything I needed to write. I was saying goodbye.

"Here," I said while the two of us had tea at her apartment. I handed her an envelope—money from a fundraising event in Vancouver where I had given a talk and mentioned the work she was doing. A donor wanted it to go to supporting the school, and had arranged for me to pick it up in Lebanon, since Syrian banks were under sanctions. "You should hide it somewhere," I said, standing up to look beneath the battered burgundy sofa for a hiding place. "Otherwise someone will take it from you." All sorts of people came through her apartment. Most were desperate, a few no doubt prostitutes or thieves, doing whatever to get by. She didn't judge. But I worried.

"Maybe you can rent a proper space for your classrooms," I said.

"Yes," she said. She clapped her hands together. "Yes!" Now she could move the whole thing downstairs.

I waited until she had proven to me that she'd found a place to hide it, on the underside of a padded armchair where she could affix the envelope beneath the wires and no one would think to look.

Ahlam seemed happy, and that made me happy. The money would help cover things here for the next few months. But I understood, with some shame, that it served me too: it lessened my guilt about walking away.

By late afternoon, as darkness fell, her apartment was even busier, more frenetic than I remembered. It was like a railway station crammed with travellers who keep arriving but never leave. There were at least twenty people hanging around, talking and smoking in the dusky light, faces lit like Rembrandt paintings, and quite a few I hadn't seen before, when I thought I knew all the habitués. I didn't see Ahlam's husband, but then again he was often gone, and half invisible when he did turn up, lost in depression.

Abdullah and Roqayah were there, watching all the people demanding their mother's attention. "The monkey lives in the jungle," I said to Roqayah in Arabic, as greeting or secret handshake. She was an exceptionally pretty child, with green eyes that startled, and had already begun wearing a headscarf because men bothered her in the streets. It made her seem older than her happy-go-lucky brother, more watchful.

The apartment had the air of a party that had sped up when it was supposed to be winding down. One of the young men I recognized was there, along with two or three other guys his age. Ahlam sent them out to find a driver willing to take me to Amman.

But something seemed different, though I couldn't say exactly what. Maybe just the fact that I had been away and then returned, the slight alteration of perception. It always happened when I returned home as well, and saw everything differently—amazed at the easy certainties, the unquestioned faith in the way things were, the values that struck me as absurd. In a few days the feeling usually passed and I would revert to normal, behaving just the same way.

As night fell, blanketing the neighbourhood in darkness, Ahlam accompanied me downstairs to the taxi that would take me to Jordan and a flight home. For a brief moment we were alone. She buried her face in my shoulder and for the first time I noticed how exhausted she seemed, as if some force had been leached from her character.

"Is something wrong?" I asked. I almost didn't hear her muffled words as she helped me put my bags into the back of the car, then almost wished I hadn't.

"I need you so much," she said, "in these dark times."

I felt embarrassed and inadequate. We had become friends but I was leaving. The fieldwork for my article was complete; my own work was done. We would keep in touch, exchange occasional emails, but the chances were good, I knew from experience, that I would never see her again.

"You have to go," she said, as the driver stood next to the open door, waiting. She looked stoic, resigned. I got into the car.

Driving through the blackness of that winter night I could see my own face reflected in the window of the car and the moon bobbing up over the desert like an unanswered question.

PART **TWO**

Chapter 12

THESE DARK TIMES

IF AHLAM HAD NOT stopped answering my phone calls and emails that might have been the end of it. You do a story, get to know people, even to care about them, then you leave. It's always this way. You think it won't be but it is.

I finished my story for *Harper's* on the refugee crisis. As usual, the writing process was painful and took longer than expected. Ahlam made an appearance, though I changed her name. It is something I usually do when writing about vulnerable people who might not foresee the consequences of talking to international media, a media that can easily reach those who wish to do them harm. In the words of her father, which I quoted in the piece: "No one knows what the future holds."

The article was well received. It went on to win an award. I gave a couple of television interviews in New York and was invited to moderate a panel at the National Press Club in Washington, DC. I was busy, new opportunities were presenting themselves. I should have been satisfied. It should have been enough.

Usually when a piece is published the fever breaks and I find myself wanting to move on to another subject, the past neatly wrapped up in words. This time that did not happen. My customary life held no interest. "Even when you *are* home," my boyfriend pointed out, in one of our increasingly frequent arguments, "you aren't really here." As he spoke he proved his point, because my thoughts were elsewhere: with Ahlam, who kept her silence. I had a feeling that something was not right.

In these dark times. She had seemed distracted, distraught. I had been too absorbed by my impending departure to work out what it meant.

Weeks passed without a word. The muted buzz of overseas calls ricocheting through satellites and back to Earth, unanswered. Emails floating in the ether. Did anyone open them?

After the *Harper's* piece ran, an editor at *The New Republic* had asked me to pitch them ideas. I suggested something on the psychological effects of the war on civilians. PTSD was widespread: that story had been told about army vets, but what about those who didn't have armoured vehicles or battle training? What about those at whom their guns were aimed? The editor was tentatively interested and asked for a formal proposal.

In my makeshift office, behind the wall of books, I contemplated aloud what to do. I could go back to Damascus, make sure Ahlam was okay, and get going on a new story, somehow make it all work financially.

"You should go," my boyfriend said from the other side of the wall. It was what he always said, but this time his tone had an edge. "If you don't, you'll be miserable," he added. "That means I'll be miserable too."

Would I have listened if he had argued otherwise?

In April I finished teaching a class. I bought a plane ticket and was gone.

I arrived in Damascus to the warm embrace of spring. The scent of jasmine hung thickly in the better neighbourhoods, the jacaranda trees about to bloom. I could feel the energy returning to my blood, a quickening of the senses, like awakening from a long hibernation. Even the scent of pollution, car exhaust, dust was exhilarating.

I had tried from Jordan to reach Ahlam and tell her I was coming but received no reply. No matter. I told myself she was simply too busy, caught up in her numerous projects. It made more sense simply to go there. After all, where else could she be? It wasn't as if she could pick up and leave. That was me—I was the person who could do that.

The manager at the Kuwaiti Hotel greeted me warmly and without surprise, as if he had been expecting me. My former room was occupied—I could have it back in a couple of days. In the meantime, for the same twenty dollars a night, I was given a room that was ridiculously large: eleven single beds arranged around the perimeter. The walls were pink, the ceiling mauve; it might have been meant for a family of lunatics. Noise rattled the windowpane—children's cries, a police whistle, the drumbeat of passing music, the rumble of motorcycle carts with bad engines. I couldn't make up my mind which bed I would sleep in, and in the end scattered my belongings everywhere so as not to feel lonely.

The first thing I did was call Ahlam. The phone rang for a long time but there was no answer. I waited, then called again, envisioning the room in which it must be ringing, the bare white walls, scuffed linoleum, the worn velvet sofa. No answer. She was never separated from her phone. I searched through my notebooks for the number of anyone who might know where she was. Mona. She would know how to reach Ahlam.

Mona answered on the first ring. I told her I was trying to reach Ahlam. "Have you seen her?"

Mona sounded guarded. She hadn't spoken to Ahlam lately and had no idea where she was.

I hung up, more worried now. I tried Ahlam's number again. If she didn't answer I would simply walk the five or six blocks to her apartment and pound on the door. The phone rang for a long time. Just as I was about to hang up she answered. Her voice sounded reedy and small, like a child's. She said she had been sleeping, though it was early in the evening. A half-hour later she was at the door of my hotel room.

The same person, though slightly diminished. She had lost weight, or the winter had bleached her skin. Behind her, in the hallway, stood a tall young scarecrow with a blue bandana wrapped hip-hop style around his head. Thinking he had followed her, or was dangerous, I ushered Ahlam inside and closed the door in his face.

"He's with me," she said, laughing, her composure restored. His name was Ali and he was her assistant.

"In that case," I said, revising my opinion and letting him in, "perhaps he can assist me in opening the bottle of wine I bought at the Duty Free." I had imagined celebrating.

There was no corkscrew in the kitchen, nor, Ahlam said, likely to be one anywhere else in Little Baghdad, so Ali operated on the cork with a kitchen knife, playing music on his phone and singing along, embracing the illicit nature of his task. As he went about it, bits of cork flying, Ahlam sat on one of the beds and explained why my emails and phone calls had gone unanswered.

First, her husband was gone. He had returned to Baghdad.

In my mind, a picture of her husband. Slightly stooped in the way of tall thin men, white hair thick as thatch, a pleasingly gaunt face. A kind man, was my impression, not unintelligent but not cunning in ways now mandatory. She told me he had been taunted by other men—even by the Syrian intelligence when they came to check on what she was up to. "They told him, 'You let your wife support you.'"

She lit a cigarette—at the Duty Free, where I had bought them for her, a carton of Marlboros sold for six US dollars—and I went to find an ashtray in the kitchen, where Ali was making progress. When I returned she continued.

Her husband had become involved in a business scheme that promised attractive returns. He had borrowed the money and of course the investment foundered, a scam all along. He wasn't able to pay the money back. There had been threats. Texts appearing on his phone, which she had found. "They said they would harm our children if he did not pay." When she confronted him he did not want to talk about it, telling her, "I will take care of this." But there was no possibility of taking care of it, of her, of anything.

He wanted Ahlam to return with him to Iraq. It was obvious she could not—she was already a target, had been seriously threatened.

She told the kids that their father had gone to find work in Aleppo. She didn't want to worry them or, because they were too young to keep secrets, have them spread the news. If word got out, she would be compromised, unable to continue her projects without tongues wagging. If her husband's decision to leave was a relief in some ways, she was also left with one less layer of protection.

Immediately she had been summoned by Captain Abu Yusuf. She found him at his office in the local intelligence headquarters, as usual behind his desk—pale, small moustache, ever the harried bureaucrat. But a bureaucrat with a gun.

"We hear your husband has left," he said, looking up from his paperwork.

So he knew. She hadn't told anyone, but he knew.

And then, as if he were operating a benevolence society: "We can help you with things."

"What things?" she asked.

"With anything," he said. "Fake passports, human smuggling. All we want from you are names."

"Whose names?"

"Anyone."

"What for?"

"It's time for you to do for Syria what you did for the Americans in Iraq."

She never tried to hide the fact that she had worked for the Americans. Others did. I had met them, on the run from threats to themselves and their families, branded as traitors to their country. She did not accept this verdict on her conduct. She believed she was helping her own people the only way she could: by working with those who held power to help those who had none. There was no government anymore—there was still no real government—so it was the Americans or nothing. "I was dealing with *reality*." Reality demanded nuanced thinking, a kind of moral reasoning from a world ever more black and white. Now, seated in front of her behind his desk, another kind of reality, a man who only understood giving and taking orders, and saw his chance to make something of her, and of himself.

Fake passports, human smuggling—he was dangling such incentives because he presumed she was the same sort of person he was. It was as comical as the room in which we now sat, as incongruous. And dangerous. He told her he wanted her to be his eyes and ears, to have her spy on other refugees and foreign reporters and report back to him.

She told him the truth: that she was grateful to Syria for its generosity. That if anyone threatened to do the country harm she would tell him.

"And would you?" I asked.

"Of course. If someone wants to plant a bomb or attack Syria? Even if he did not order me, I would tell him. Remember, this is the only country that gave us shelter. No other country would help us."

But she would not be his informant. That implied submission, an abandonment of moral agency.

She left his office feeling constricted, a tightness in the chest. Months earlier, when she first realized that Abu Yusuf had been sending men to follow her, he had phoned her to say, "My man saw you with someone from the BBC."

"Yes," she replied, "and there was someone from the Ministry of Information with us," knowing he wouldn't check. "He came to translate. All I did was take the journalist to interview Iraqi families. No Syrians, only Iraqis.

There are two million of us in your country and we need to find a solution for them. Anyway, I am no longer fixing for journalists."

But she had not been reporting to the Ministry of Information; and she had been working for two researchers from Human Rights Watch, an organization banned from entering Syria.

"You can't be serious," I said. "Ahlam! If he finds out you were working for them, it will be huge trouble."

"The researchers only stayed forty-eight hours," she said, waving aside my concerns. "Someone came to ask about them at their hotel, so they were afraid of being arrested."

Now Abu Yusuf was calling her every two or three weeks, asking, "What do you have for me?"

So she stopped working for journalists. Stopped responding to emails. She became more careful on the phone, not taking calls from overseas numbers. "That's why I didn't answer you. I didn't want to make trouble." The pains in her heart returned. Today was the first time she had left her bed in three days.

"What about Mona? Is she helping you with the classes?" I asked. I recalled the last time I had seen Mona, in Tarek's cellar apartment in the wall of the Old City, passed out drunk, her long hair fanned around her face. It was Tarek who had introduced Mona to Ahlam.

Mona, she said, had begun telling people that she, Mona, was running the classes for refugee girls. "I didn't mind," Ahlam said. "And she helped me find volunteers to teach English and French." But then, without warning, Mona stopped calling, stopped coming around, cut her off. Ahlam was hurt. She could run the classes on her own, but she had considered Mona her friend, her backup. She went to see Tarek to ask him what was going on.

"She's just a fool," Tarek told her. "She's jealous of you."

"Why?" asked Ahlam, astounded. She often missed such cues. The woman waving her hands, over tea, to show off gold.

"Because you are who you are."

Mona had volunteered at the UNHCR in media relations in order to make connections with journalists. "She wanted to be in the picture," he said. "She wanted to be famous. But the only fixer the journalists wanted to work with is you."

Ali brought the bottle from the kitchen, looking pleased with himself. I poured wine into a tea glass, bits of cork floating on the surface.

"You want some?" I asked Ahlam. "You might need a glass." She shook her head, laughed, and I drank alone. Ali, who spoke no English, was sitting on one of the beds playing music on his phone: Céline Dion, who had many Iraqi fans.

I had come on impulse, without a clear purpose besides assuring myself that Ahlam had not disappeared. Now I thought I should see if I could turn the time to good use. I decided to start work on background for the PTSD story. This time I didn't need Ahlam's help so need not put her at any further risk. I had plenty of contacts already in hand. I would continue my research on my own and meanwhile keep an eye on her.

On the first afternoon Ahlam took me downstairs from her apartment to show me the classrooms she had rented: a trio of simple rooms on the main floor of her building. Some volunteers had painted the walls with murals of bright flowers to make them less gloomy. In one of the classrooms, a young woman was giving a lesson in mathematics, writing equations on a whiteboard.

On the surface life seemed as it had been. Ahlam's apartment was still a lively community centre and town hall. Yet the atmosphere was different. Less focused, more manic, looser, as if whatever structural elements that had been holding up the walls were buckling. Young people were always coming and going from the classrooms, racing in and then stomping down the stairs. And since her husband had left, half a dozen young men had taken to hanging out here, wandering in around noon from whichever family or friends let them sleep on their floors, staying till well after dark, discussing plans for things they would never do; smoking, talking about girls, about their families in Iraq: who had been killed; who was missing; whose houses had been taken over by militias. Mostly they talked about nothing. Their conversation consisted of banter, jokes, uncertain plans. Their legs jerked as they sat on the battered sofa, ashing their cigarettes on the floor. They got up, sat down, got up, sat down. They wanted action, action, to do something. They could hardly stand to sit around but there was nothing for them to do. The hours of their days were long, since they could neither work legally in Syria nor afford the tuition fees charged to non-Syrian university students. And if they had had that kind of money, they would have tried to be smuggled out.

"You should be president of Iraq," one of them said to me. A charmer, slight as a fifteen-year-old though he was twenty-two, always impeccably dressed in the same neatly pressed black shirt and pants. It was one of his running lines. "You will be much better than the one we have."

"Then I will have to start my own Abu Ghraib," I told him. "And torture you the way you torture me by playing Céline Dion."

His phone rang. I listened to the boy arguing. His parents wanted him to come back home and get married. No! If he could not support himself, he told them, how could he support a wife, and then no doubt a child? He wanted to work again, he had been trained as a mechanic, but in Iraq, he told me, after closing his phone, there are only three job opportunities: "To be killed, to be about to be killed, or to be kidnapped."

In fact there were only two. He could join the security forces or join the militias, which amounted to the same thing. These young men, all of the ones I met here, were the kind that wars burn like fuel.

Ahlam channelled their surplus energy. They were her "assistants," Sherlock Holmes with his Baker Street Irregulars. When she was fixing, she dispatched them to find sources for journalists or human rights groups. Now she sent them to visit people in hospital or families of children with special needs and bring back an assessment—her own private intelligence network. She sent them to find out how the next-door neighbour, shot in the hip in Iraq, was faring; he could not move from his mattress so another neighbour came to take him to the bathroom. In another apartment six men who had been released from Abu Ghraib were sharing a single room. She sent the young men to find out how the men were making do. Once, when a baby was born prematurely to a refugee couple, Ahlam brought two of her assistants with her to the hospital. She gave them the newborn to hold while she shouted at a doctor until he found an incubator.

The baby died anyway, two days later. The young men, Ahlam told me, wept with her when they heard.

In the past she had left her son and daughter in the care of her husband when she went out. Now she was relying on one of the young men to babysit. Hamza had golden blond hair and blue eyes—his mother was Iranian, as fair as he was. He had been staying with Ahlam's family for the past year, sleeping at night on a blanket in the living room, and I had occasionally encountered him there. The first time I met him I had taken him for European. His Western looks—the looks of an occupier—were the reason he had fled. Once, when he went back to visit his family, he was so swiftly reported that his mother had had to hide him on the roof for six weeks while militias searched for him. Now in Damascus, he had no family and no job, so he earned his keep. Hamza was often doing housework, passing a broom across the floor, emptying ashtrays, clearing away tea glasses.

They were all of an age when they should have been assuming the mantle of adulthood, learning a trade or cramming for university exams, looking around for a mate, but the war had frozen them in time. The society that raised them no longer existed; its values and expectations no longer made sense. "They have no aim, no purpose, they are only breathing, so I make them see the suffering of others and do something to help," Ahlam said. They all called her "mother," and I wondered if they filled some of the void left in her heart by her eldest son.

They completed the tasks she set them willingly because those tasks filled the vacuum of dead time and earned them her praise: they felt they had finally done something right.

When they reported back from their missions she let them play their music as loud as they wanted. In her apartment they danced with abandon, as if to shake the last of the energy from their limbs. Sometimes Ahlam just laughed at their antics and sometimes she joined them. She could still do that, still get up and dance, and I took that as a positive sign.

While I was researching PTSD among the refugees for my next article, I made time to work on my Arabic. Each morning, at precisely ten a.m., a woman named Umm Sally met me at Ahlam's apartment to give me lessons. Fifty years old, bone thin, prim and schoolmarmish in a black pantsuit and wire-rimmed glasses, Umm Sally was one of the volunteers at Ahlam's school. She was an excellent teacher, praising me lavishly whenever I got things right. I would be fluent in a month, she was sure of it.

As I wrote down words in the decorative script—so lush, so elegant, like composing a symphony—Umm Sally veered into the details of her life. I practised the verb "to forget," and she told me she forgot to bring the picture of her husband, a professor. "He was beautiful," she recalled. In the past she used to sleep like an infant, awaking to drink orange juice and milk and do her morning calisthenics. For six months after his murder she slept hardly at all.

She taught me: *It is necessary to forget.*

She showed me instead a picture of her only child, a girl of twenty-two. Her daughter looked pale and serious, like a ghostly Emily Dickinson. She loved music, wanted to go to music school, her mother said, but such longings were as useful as melted wax. Also, she hated to cover her hair but that was necessary now because life was unstable and a girl without a father could not afford to take risks. So she refused to leave their apartment in Sayeda Zainab.

Sitting next to Umm Sally on the sofa, shifting around the protruding springs, I made lists of verb structures. I tried to get her to review the construction of the past tense as distinct from the present, which in the Semitic languages involves breaking the words apart. Umm Sally, her eyes glazing over, seemed not to hear me. "Past?" she said. "Iraq is in the past, not now."

One morning Umm Sally turned to me, her glasses sliding down her nose onto her chin. We had been practising the verb "to love."

"All my love is destroyed," she murmured. "Where will I go?"

I took her hand and we sat in silence. Her hand so cool and dry, the day so warm. And then, as if shaking herself from a troubled dream, she asked me if I knew the word for picnic.

A woman had come to Ahlam to discuss her desire to be resettled, or smuggled, whichever worked, to a stable country where she could build a future. The woman had an additional complication: she had rescued a cat, and the cat now had kittens, and she wanted to bring the cat and her kittens with her.

Ahlam's phone rang, and she turned her back from this hopeless case to take the call. I could hear her speaking in English, making arrangements—times, places, yeses and okays and whens. I saw that she was on her second phone.

"Who was that?" I asked when she had finished.

It was a producer for Al Jazeera's English channel who had hired her to work as their fixer on a story about the recent

Swedish crackdown on Iraqi asylum seekers. Sweden was being overrun. She gave a small laugh: Sweden didn't want all of Iraq to move to Sweden, nor their cats and kittens.

"I thought you said you'd stopped working," I said, surprise shading into alarm. "How do you know they aren't monitoring both your phones?"

She had the look I saw so often now. As if she couldn't really hear what I was saying. As if there were louder internal voices crowding out the present. I felt a pang of fear.

"You need to take this seriously," I said, disliking my hectoring tone. "You can't be working for journalists anymore." It was one thing to be at her apartment, another for her to be seen with a camera crew. I didn't like lecturing, telling her what to do. I don't tell friends what to do. But she wasn't a normal friend and this was by no means a normal situation. In the past it had been her job to tell me when to take precautions; now it seemed the tables had turned. I feared she didn't scrutinize the world with enough cynicism. I had enough cynicism for both of us. I pulled out the trump card. "What about your children?"

I knew she might not consider her own safety—there was a recklessness to her nature, and a romantic conceit that "right makes might," when that notion had by now been demonstrably discredited. But her children were another matter. If anything happened to her they would be orphaned. And they were spirited, excitable, prone to laughter and tears. Often they clung to her, demanding attention, worried that she could be taken from them again. Now that their father was gone she was all they had. "If anything happens to you," I said, pressing home the point, "what happens to them?"

If anything happens.

Finally she fished around in her handbag. She pulled out some coins. This was the last of her money. Enough to buy bread. The money I had brought her in January had been spent on rent for herself and the classrooms downstairs. It was May now. And she said, if we wanted to talk about the children, this was about the children; there were bills to pay, children to feed, and with her husband gone, no one but herself to rely upon. So she had returned to work after all, which she had neglected to tell me, not wanting me to get upset, as I was doing now. A week before I arrived, she confessed, she'd called her friend Khaled from Reuters, asking him to spread the word that she was back in business. Maybe it was dangerous but it was life. You did what you had to do to survive.

Then, remarkably, the day took a turn for a better. Ahlam had to go to the offices of the International Organization for Migration, a partner of the UNHCR. Like everyone, she was applying to be resettled abroad, and of course it probably wouldn't happen—no one wanted Iraqis—but you had to try. There was also the problem that her family had paid a ransom to her kidnappers, which automatically eliminated prospective refugees from being accepted to the United States since they had, by paying ransom, given "material aid" to terrorists. But she had several effusive letters of recommendation from high-up American officers for whom she had worked, and this bolstered her case.

We shared a taxi downtown, seated in the back with the windows rolled down so Ahlam could smoke. It was a perfect blue-sky day, like every day in Damascus in May: full of life and promise, not too hot. Dirt roads turned to gravel then paved highway, like an educational film on the development of modern infrastructure. A photo of a pair of smiling children swung from the driver's rear-view mirror; in the back window, an enlarged silhouette of President Assad—popular among taxi drivers. In the busy downtown streets, we passed beige and white low-rises interspersed with shops. Outside a florist, red bouquets poked from buckets of water. Through the window of a shoe store a woman was trying on a pair of silver sandals. A man walked by on the sidewalk, carrying a cage with a pair of songbirds, his other hand holding the hand of a little girl in a fuchsia sundress.

Now that her husband was gone, Ahlam needed to separate her application for resettlement abroad from his in order for the process to continue. When she and the children were resettled, she told me, she would get a divorce. I left her at the office, watching as she spoke to the security guard and was signed in, then I walked over to an Internet café.

Both of us were having difficulties with the men in our lives. I had received more emails. "You're gone so much, and even when you are here . . ." Every time I went away, the loneliness hit him harder, whereas I was usually too busy to feel lonely. He wrote that he wondered how other people in these situations, military spouses, for instance, resolved it: "I suppose some of them have affairs, but that just seems too messy." He reminded me of how helpless he had felt when I had been in trouble in Iran. In those days, he wrote, he discovered his first grey hairs. Now he was wrestling with "the dilemma," as he called it: if I stayed home he would be less lonely but I would suffer, and if I suffered then he would suffer, so all benefit would be lost.

In the crowded net café, reading through his latest email, I felt myself alone, and felt his aloneness too. He described our situation with a clarity that in the dim light of the computer screens was blinding. Compartmentalization came easily to me. There was work, there was home: different categories. And there was always something keeping us apart—half of our emails were about trouble connecting, being online at different times, phone calls that wouldn't go through, Skype calls disconnecting. I felt an urgent need to Skype with him now—to talk this all through, to soothe his loneliness, to reassure him that this relationship, the foundation on which we had known such happiness in the past, still mattered and could be saved. To say that he mattered. But it was four in the morning his time, and he had mentioned he had to get up early for work. There was a technology conference, or contract, that he had to fly to in North Carolina. As our careers had diverged over the past few years, I sometimes felt I understood his work no better than he did mine. On a gritty keyboard I typed that I missed him. I spoke of utter sadness. I tried to summon the courage his words exhibited in their raw honesty. "Is the real problem my leaving, or is it us, even when together?" It was the question he hadn't asked, but implied.

I pressed send, passed coins to the cashier, and walked back outside, stunned by sunlight. A gulp of warm air; the rush of street and sun; laughter from a couple passing by. Another compartment, a slipstream from one world to another. When Ahlam emerged from the migration office, she looked calmer, relieved, as if she had completed an important ritual. Neither of us spoke about ourselves.

Since we were already downtown we went to a restaurant, something we rarely did because there weren't any restaurants to speak of in Little Baghdad and I was on a budget, if one incomparable to hers. It was a small indulgence, worth even more for coming on a bad day. We ate Syrian food, which the world knows as Lebanese: little platters of mezze drenched in olive oil set on a white tablecloth. Sunlight was pouring in the window from the street.

Chapter 13

THE DISAPPEARANCE

THE DAY BEGAN LIKE any other. Awakened at dawn by the call to prayer, I fell back asleep for another hour. When I woke again I felt along the wall for the light switch, scanning for cockroaches before stepping barefoot to the kerosene stove, where I struck a match to heat water for coffee. I was glad to be back in my old Kuwaiti Hotel room, sized to fit my needs. I took a quick shower, since the water in this part of Damascus was not only undrinkable but in short supply, then pulled on a pair of jeans and a long-sleeved shirt that covered my arms to the wrist—there was no need to stand out any more than necessary. Descending the empty stairwell I entered the marvellous cacophony of a perfect late-spring day.

The morning light ignited the gold dome of the shrine. The rattle of taxis, motorcycle carts, vendors rolling up the metal shutters on their shops. Already the Internet cafés were filling up with Iraqi boys who spent all day playing first-person shooter games, pretending to be American soldiers on urban combat missions in neighbourhoods that must have reminded them of home. Outside a storefront, a swarm of happy little schoolgirls in uniform were lined up to buy sweets, giggling and jostling. A boy swerved past on an adult-sized bicycle, weaving precariously on through the gathering crowd.

As I turned past the shrine and crossed the busy main street, dodging taxis that slowed or honked at the sight of me, I realized that I would be leaving here soon. Worried as I was for Ahlam, I couldn't be here forever, and I had to earn my keep. With a few more interviews I could write another story. I stopped to buy a packet of cigarettes for her from a sidewalk stand, handing the boy exact change without being asked. I needed to go home, to my real home, and deal with my own reality.

As I wended my way through the alleyways towards Ahlam's apartment, I thought I felt something. A pair of eyes, a man standing next to a motorcycle, staring intently. The sense of being followed occurred to me but I abandoned it like a whim. After years spent working undercover in places where journalists were unwelcome, my radar could be oversensitive; as the only Westerner in the neighbourhood, I shrugged off curious stares.

By nine a.m. we were drinking tea alone at Ahlam's apartment—the teaspoons of sugar dissolving into a glass, my notebook as usual on my lap, reviewing Arabic verb conjugations from yesterday's lesson with Umm Sally—when a man knocked at the door. Ahlam went to answer it and stepped out into the stairwell. I could hear them speaking but not their words. Nevertheless I felt an immediate shift in the atmospheric pressure of the room. Without getting up I looked around, wondering where I might hide my notebook, estimating how long it would take to find something that had been concealed in here. Not long. The living room was a box except for a doorless closet crammed with her children's belongings. I placed the notebook back into my bag and sat there, waiting for her to return. The minutes stretched out, timed to the beating of my heart.

When she returned, the man walked into the room ahead of her. He was short, unsmiling, a vain little moustache like a hyphen above his mouth. The kind of man who, whatever he is wearing, always appears to be in uniform. I knew, without a word from either of them, that he was one of those responsible for keeping order among the newcomers, to ensure that the war did not come with them to Syria. A man of limited powers and yet—for those under his authority—unlimited.

She was to accompany him to their headquarters to answer some questions. Men were waiting downstairs to escort her in a car. They told her she would be gone for a few hours. This had happened before, such official summonings, at least half a dozen times. When she was sick in bed for a week after her husband left, they had panicked and sent a man to check on her: why was she staying at home, changing her patterns? But never before had a group of men come for her.

By now I was on my feet. It was a long and awkward moment as the three of us stood stock-still in the room, none of us moving or meeting the others' eyes. Finally he broke the silence. "Get rid of her," he said to Ahlam in Arabic.

She had been standing beside him and now she walked over to me. "Go," she said, her face close to mine. "Go to your hotel. Go now." In her voice was an urgency I had never heard before, though her face betrayed nothing. Her expression was flat as a becalmed lake. This vacancy, this flatness in someone always so animated, someone whose face I knew as a stage on which every sort of emotion played, was far more menacing than the presence of the stranger.

I took my bag with my notebook and left, retracing my steps of earlier that morning. I barely recall the walk back. Only the acid flush that carried up my face like a rash, the pulse in my ears, the sensation of being watched. And yet, when I looked around, no one was paying me the least attention. The locals were used to me now, a neighbourhood fixture. "Doktorah!" A shopkeeper I knew shouted greetings from the shadowy interior of his shop. His voice was friendly, unaffected. That feeling I had of being watched earlier this morning—was it as fabricated as the one I felt now?

At the door of the hotel, I studied the face of the young security guard who slept at night on a mattress inside the front door. He smiled, greeted me as usual, asked after my health. Up the flight of stairs, taken two at a time. In the glass-panelled office across from my room, the hotel manager was playing solitaire on his computer with his little son, a pale redhead, on his lap. He waved to me, indicating that I should join them for tea.

No one had been here to ask about me.

My room was like a cave, self-contained and insular. Inside, everything was as I had left it: my audio recorder still lying in a tangle of cords, books pell-mell, a half-made single bed, a towel drying on the door of the wardrobe that I never used. Through the window high up on the wall I could hear the sounds of the day unfolding as it should, horns honking, children laughing, the clatter of working life.

How strange that I had come to love it here.

The air-conditioning unit had a leak. The pot I had placed below it was about to overflow, so I emptied it into the sink and then lay down on the bed with the lights off.

Before, the leak had not bothered me but now each drop was a question that rippled outward. *Drip*—She is gone. *Drip*—Where has she been taken? *Drip*—Just a few hours, he had said.

This had happened before. It was nothing unusual. Was it my presence that had drawn them this time? Did they take me for a spy? Perhaps I had set off a tripwire. For all my bullshit lectures to her about not working with journalists and putting herself in needless danger, I had overlooked something. I was a journalist.

I had known the signs were bad. After all, that's why I had come back to find her. Because I had trusted in my own cover story, trusted it was a sound cloak of invisibility, I had not quite taken in Ahlam's vulnerabilities. Or I had taken them in, but then I must have grown complacent. Maybe because everyone here was vulnerable. Every day something bad happened to someone, and it was normal to be wary, to be worried, but also normal to think of it like a car bomb— always happening to somebody else. Or maybe I was the bomb. Or the two of us together were.

Drip. Drip. Drip.

An hour passed, and my phone rang. I answered, hoping to hear Ahlam's voice telling me that everything was fine, the coast was clear.

It was Umm Sally, my Arabic teacher.

"Where are you?" she asked. Her voice was kind, concerned, betraying no annoyance. She had come to Ahlam's apartment to meet me for my lesson and found no one there.

The children would be at school but where was everyone else? The apartment was empty. She had brought the picture of her husband to show me.

"I'm so sorry," I said. "Something came up."

How rude I must seem, the obnoxious entitled Westerner who did not consider the effects of her actions on others. I could not tell her what happened over the phone, could not say anything that might jeopardize her or anyone else. I would explain everything later, learn the words of apology, admire the photograph of her husband, so beautiful and gone. It did not occur to me that I would never see her again.

I thought it wise not to sleep in my room that night. Instead I stayed at an American friend's apartment on a busy downtown street, a two-bedroom above a convenience store. Awakening in the middle of the night in the dark, I couldn't remember where I was. The air was hot and sticky, claustrophobic, a ceiling fan barely nudging the air. The next morning she asked me to leave. She was a freelance journalist and didn't want trouble. For the first time I understood something that had managed to evade me all of my life: trouble is a contagious disease.

I took a collective taxi back to Sayeda Zainab, bumping along the pitted road in the van with the other passengers, comforted by their benign presence. When it stopped near the shrine I got out and walked the last block to the hotel. Another beautiful spring day. Dust and heat and people going about their ordinary lives. It was the first of June.

Nothing in my room appeared to have been touched, though I wondered if I ought to have rigged something—arranged a strand of hair as one reads about in novels—to know for sure. It was possible that Ahlam had already returned to her apartment but I didn't dare to phone her or any of the Iraqis who might know. Anything to do with Ahlam was now radioactive.

I went downstairs to the net café around the corner. There might be an email from her or someone who knew something. In the smoke-filled café, there was only one terminal available, the rest occupied by noisy gamers who shouted in pain or triumph as if they were experiencing the life on their screens. I was glad of that—they didn't look up when I sat down.

I scrolled through my emails. Nothing about Ahlam. There was only one of a personal nature—Gabriela, the Czech-American photographer I had met at Ahlam's last winter when she came over with Ahlam's friend Hamid, the hard-boiled fellow Iraqi fixer. Gabriela wondered if I had made it back to Damascus. *How exciting it must be to see old friends there.* She was finishing some work in Washington and planning her own trip back, wanting advice, wondering if conditions had worsened.

I typed a cryptic response: A. *may be in some new trouble with intel. She had to go to them yesterday and I haven't heard from her since . . . I'm worried about her, though she has a thousand lives . . .*

I logged off and walked back to my room. I had bought two cans of Tuborg beer at a liquor store downtown and opened one of them, lukewarm, as I sorted through my belongings. I considered my audio recordings, but my recorded interviews didn't mention names; I kept those separately in my notebooks. Looking through my notes I tore up the pages with names into tiny pieces and flushed them down the toilet. My laptop? That was probably okay—my sources here didn't email me; they texted. I deleted every phone number, every text message from my phone, copying the most important numbers onto an inside page of my notebook in code.

I was startled by the sound of my phone ringing. It was a voice I recognized. The American editor at *Syria Today*, an English-language newsmagazine. "Come to the office." Something to speak to me about. He insisted. "Come *now*." And then I remembered. He had introduced me to the Syrian journalist who brought me to meet Ahlam almost a year ago.

An hour later I was at the magazine office sitting across from him and the Syrian journalist.

"Ahlam has been arrested," the journalist informed me.

"How do you know?" I assumed he had channels—after all he was a journalist—but then he explained that he had heard about it from the Iraqi woman who cleaned his office.

"Really? How would she know?"

"They are saying you are Mossad or CIA," he continued, without clarifying. "That's why she was taken."

"If I'm a spy, it's only for myself," I said. "And I should pay myself better." My voice sounded tinny and defensive. And wait: "Who are 'they'?"

"They" were the community, the street, where information was rumour and innuendo. "They" said she was in prison, but then again, they knew nothing. All we knew for a fact was that she was gone.

He told me I had to move out of Little Baghdad. Now. Today. Immediately. A Westerner like me attracted too much attention there and they might be lying in wait. But I should stay in Syria. If I left I could be captured at the border and it would look like I was fleeing.

And so it begins. The paranoia. The fear. It spreads out in waves and infects everyone around you. It infects your mind, your thoughts. You begin to monitor your actions, your words, to see how the watcher might view them, and it is always the same way: with suspicion. You begin to regard others in the same paranoid fashion: Is that person asking me questions, so nonchalantly, seeking information on behalf of someone else? Am I replying appropriately, reacting in a way that could be construed as having nothing to hide?

I began to wonder about Ahlam, whom I'd thought I knew. About the Syrian journalist, and how he knew what he said he knew. About my own role in Ahlam's disappearance. And all those who surrounded her, needed her, availed themselves of any help she might offer, and occasionally envied her too, this woman whose power derived from no one but herself.

Chapter 14

THE CAGE

I FOUND A ROOM at the Sultan, a backpacker's hotel near the railway station outside the Old City walls. It was a musty place filled with decorative cushions and a film of dust as old as the hippie trail. A French couple chain-smoked in the breakfast room, arguing over a guidebook.

It was a short walk from the Sultan through stark morning sunlight that left me feeling exposed to Souk al-Hamidiyeh, the covered bazaar in the Old City. It seemed like a good idea to play the tourist. Besides, I needed the souk: a dim and cavernous tunnel where I could dissolve into the cosmopolitan stew of nationalities and religions. Greek Orthodox priests in flowing robes striding past women in jeans and men in business suits; white headscarves, no headscarves, nuns in habits, kids in school uniforms, tourists in shorts. This mix of peoples was the best thing about Damascus, the thing I always loved. I could not have imagined that I was witnessing a final act—that this age-old tradition of pluralism would shortly disappear, adding millions of Syrians to the millions of Iraqis seeking refuge in the outside world.

Like Ahlam. Two more days had passed without a word. In the taxi from the journalist's office I had called a woman I knew at the UNHCR and asked her to meet me for a drink. Sitting in an upscale bar filled with the after-work set, she wanted to know why I hadn't told her about this over the phone.

"Over the phone?" I had said. "You want me to tell you this *over the phone*?"

After that meeting I spoke daily to the staff at the refugee agency. They were investigating her disappearance, they told me, meeting with the Ministry of Foreign Affairs. They did not yet know where her children were. I pointed out that it was a good thing Ahlam had worked for them, because it meant they had a level of responsibility for her well-being. I offered to write an article, but they urged me in the strongest terms not to publicize her arrest. If I did she might be deported to Iraq, and we all knew what that meant. And if I had it in my head to involve the human rights groups she had worked for—Amnesty, Human Rights Watch, Refugees International—it would only make it harder for the authorities to back down. "The international groups can scream and shout," said the protection officer in charge of her case. "It will do nothing." The same, he implied, went for me.

Now I pushed through the crowds, ignoring the overtures of vendors touting garish belly-dance costumes, lizard skins marketed as miracle cures, knock-off versions of brand-name perfumes, samovars as tall as a man. A man in a wheelchair had parked himself directly in the path of passersby, selling flesh-toned balloons printed with Chinese characters. There was, as always, a lineup outside Bakdash, the nineteenth-century brass-and-wood pistachio ice cream shop that was a Damascus landmark.

I had no idea what I was looking for. Escape. Oblivion. The comfort of timelessness. That's always why I came to the Old City, to lose myself within ancient walls that spoke of endurance, solidity, immunity to cataclysm. I passed beneath the Roman columns of the Temple of Jupiter into the wide sun-drenched square and turned down a narrow stone passageway. There, across from a rainbow of carpet shops, an artist's studio caught my eye. In the dirt-smeared windows were small naive portraits of veiled women. Some revealed a single eye and others were merely black shrouds. Yet they were oddly cheerful, like a set of Russian dolls. They reminded me of Ahlam, who had managed to maintain her humanity within constraints that would have crippled anyone else.

Pushing open the door, I found an old man brewing tea over a stove on the floor, a cigarette in his mouth. The air hung with a curtain of pungent brown smoke as thick as my depression. Brushing aside piles of papers and books, he invited me to take a seat. He was an artist, he said in fluent English. He had adopted the profession at the age of fifty-one after he was unable to find a publisher for his last book, *Temptations of the Devil*.

So, a heretic then?

"No—a Sufi." The mystics of Islam.

He made me tea—"You like mint?"—and insisted I join him with a Gauloise. Then, while we sat on low stools across from one another, he read me his philosophical meanderings, rendered in Arabic calligraphy and framed around the shop.

My God, when I met you after all this suffering from searching for you, I found myself in front of myself!

My God, I think that all the language in the world cannot explain my feelings when you said to me you have no hell.

"No hell—and no paradise," he said, putting aside his musings. "We are working with God to perfect this life."

Sitting there, amid the narcotic comforts of art and tea and nicotine, the outside world faded. Breathe. I could almost breathe.

The old man told me he had once been married to a Palestinian woman, and once to a beautiful German anthropologist who had left him to marry an African prince. "He was so tall! So black!" And she as pale as milk.

He had come to Sufism on his own. "God does not want us to pray to him, to build a temple. No, no, no! No. To develop this life *with* him."

It was a perfect description of Ahlam's cosmology. "Wherever you are, begin," she often said, quoting her father. "Begin and the rest will follow."

But begin how? And what would follow?

The eyes of the women in the paintings watched me from shelves around the small studio. Though they were clad in black, the artist had surrounded them in bright pointillist colours as though they were emitting light. As though, through art, he had freed them.

I remembered what Ahlam had told me about her girlhood on the Tigris, sitting with her bare feet dangling out of her bedroom window overlooking the river as she read books about other lives and worlds. I remembered what her father had said when she was still that girl. "You are a free bird. Don't let anyone put you in a cage."

Somewhere, in this city, she was in a cage, and I could think of no way to pry open the bars.

—

Back at the Sultan, the man at the front desk was chatty, pointing out a bookcase bulging with airport novels that guests had left behind, and suggesting a travel book that might be of interest. I pretended to care. That was why I was here, to see the sights. He handed me my room key, along with my passport which he had taken to complete my registration.

I unlocked the door of my room and locked it again behind me. Looking around at the faded furnishings, still holding my passport, I realized I could not stay here. In another day or two, a photocopy of my passport would make it onto somebody's desk. Perhaps it was sitting there already, waiting for a bored state employee to return from lunch. After that it might only be a matter of time before someone came here to ask the man at the front desk about me.

I couldn't stay here, but I couldn't leave Damascus either. If I left, I would leave Syria altogether, and were I to be detained at the border—"come this way, sit here," scenes I knew from past experience—I could imagine waiting in a drab office while a junior clerk or career-minded lieutenant typed a simple web search and pulled up, instantaneously, my article on the refugees from Iraq. If he had any English at all he would skim to the part where I wrote about the woman in Sayeda Zainab. Name changed or not, it would be easy to identify her. They would already know she was the key fixer on anything to do with refugees. If they were looking for reasons to hold her, working for an undercover journalist would fit the slot.

I perched on the worn coverlet at the foot of the bed and looked through my wallet, mentally calculating what remained in my bank account. There was a bank I had discovered here, registered in Lebanon, that allowed me to take out money, though the statements made it appear that I had withdrawn it from Beirut. Funds would still be tight. There was teaching awaiting me in Vancouver in September, three months away, by which time my Syria visa would have expired. Meanwhile I couldn't file stories from Damascus without drawing attention to my byline, or take assignments elsewhere.

There was only one assignment anyway. Since I was here and she was there—wherever "there" was—that was my assignment: to look for her. That was where I had to begin.

For that I needed freedom. Freedom to move around, ask questions, talk to people without being watched. If I had to stay in Damascus, I would have to go underground.

First I tried to get my old apartment back, the one I'd rented the year before. It seemed to me that if I could stay there, everything would go back to being the way it had been. Ahlam would go on being—what? It made no logical sense but in the irresistible magical thinking that overtook me, if I could return to that tidy studio apartment with its flamingo-pink terrace overlooking the city, I would be safe and she would be conjured back into existence.

I found the telephone number of the landlord in the back of one of my old notebooks. At least I hadn't torn that number up. It seemed like a good sign—I still had his number—and he was obliging on the phone, but explained that his son was back from medical school in the United States and was using the apartment to study. He offered to speak to his son on my behalf, and for a brief time I was under the illusion my plan would actually work. I would move back to the top of those stairs and Ahlam would return unharmed, like a film running backward. But when I called him again it turned out his son would not agree to help me turn back time: he had his future to think of, his exams.

I considered two other apartments. The first was too expensive and on the ground floor. Anyone could break in at any time. The second, on the top floor of a walk-up next to a department store, was almost perfect. It had a stale, locker-room smell, but I could live with that. I was ready to tell the landlord, a short stocky man in a suit, that I would take it, when a couple scuttled out of the bedroom I hadn't even bothered to check. The man, so tall his head almost touched the low ceiling, was buttoning his shirt, while the heavily made-up girl ran a hand through tangled hair. "That's my brother and his wife," said the landlord stiffly. Not unless they had different fathers. Otherwise the place was renting by the hour.

Instead I found an ersatz version of my first apartment, a handful of blocks away, in a walk-up ensconced between a wine bar and a European clothing store that sold clubwear: ripped jeans, glitter T-shirts, see-through tops. A Westerner would be expected to live somewhere like this. I would not stand out.

I paid cash to the owners, who wished to avoid paying taxes and so did not register with the authorities. They had asked for two months up front, so in the back office of a garment factory, amid the clamour of sewing machines, I counted out a thousand dollars' worth of Syrian pounds.

The apartment was dusty, almost squalid, uncared for, but it was on the top storey, its front door accessible only off an enclosed central terrace. From the artifacts abandoned by former tenants—rolling papers, a Paulo Coelho novel, a love letter in broken English to someone named Giorgio from a girl who sought a future in their Damascus fling, beginner Arabic translations ("in the morning I drink coffee")—I assumed it had previously been rented by European students living the hash-smoking Orientalist fantasy. Someone had tried, and failed, to paint Che Guevara's face on a canvas rolled up in a corner of the terrace.

Inside, I turned on the air conditioning and opened my notebook to the last interview I had done, the day before Ahlam went missing. It was with a psychiatrist who had practised in Baghdad, a solemn, intelligent man, now a refugee himself. I had written down his thoughts about a teenaged patient of his who had witnessed her father being kidnapped. She suffered sleep disturbances, paranoia, certain that at any moment she and her mother would be next. "There was a question of how to treat her," he said. "Was this an irrational fear?"

After that the notebook was blank. White pages, like an expunged memory. Only a line I had written since. *I have a nightmare where I hear the sound of electric drills and wake in a state of raw fear.*

Even jotting down that dream—borrowed threads of the sort of torture described to me in interviews with Iraqis—took enormous effort. To write about the nightmare of Ahlam's disappearance was another matter. I lacked the clarity of thought, the stillness that writing demands. Even if I wanted to defy the UN staffers and publish something about what had happened, I'm not sure I could have strung the sentences together. I could feel my mind going in uncertain directions, shadows contorting into phantasms. I was afraid: afraid of being watched, being taken, being tortured. I was equally afraid of myself: that my presence put others at risk. I wanted to contact the young men who had made Ahlam's apartment their clubhouse—her assistants—to find out what they knew and where her children were; or her brother Salaam, who might be here from Baghdad already, looking for her. But Ahlam had been my link to them, and she was missing—the missing link. And I had begun to fear my own words, my data trail, as if I held the power of life and death in my hands. If I had put her in danger, anyone who talked to me could be in danger too. *Was this an irrational fear?*

I went to the kitchen to boil water for coffee. With the shutters on the window closed against the blinding afternoon, it was dark and stuffy. When had this kitchen last been cleaned?

I was still able to step back and regard my situation with some equanimity. I had been in dangerous situations before: hiding in a house in Bethlehem surrounded by gunfire when a child was shot in the head; on the Iranian border with Iraq, where I was held and interrogated overnight in a police station. Did I know, they asked, government buildings had been bombed, the blame placed on the British troops directly across the border in Basra? Perhaps I was their spy? (It took several hours, and several phone calls to Tehran in the middle of the night that went unanswered, for the jackbooted official with the three-days-growth beard to decide that a woman, by definition, could not be a spy.) Never forgotten was the time I was told by a colonel in the formidably named Disciplinary Force of the Islamic Republic of Iran in Tehran that if I tried to renew my visa one more time he would personally see to it that I was arrested (that was the time, when I phoned home to alert my boyfriend, that my phone card ran out, leaving him for days not knowing if I was alive or dead. It would be a turning point in our relationship). Yet in none of these situations, arguably more dangerous, was I as anxious as I was now.

Perhaps I had been too absorbed by what was happening in the moment to think about the future. Perhaps because it was only my own safety that was at stake, I figured I could take whatever came, that if they hurt me they could only hurt *me*. And I had my passport, and all the protections it afforded. This was different. This implicated me, it may have been because of me, but I wasn't the one imprisoned.

Was she taken because of me? The question plagued me. She had taken many risks, and I was one of them; I had taken risks—she was one of them. She knew everyone; any of those everyones could have been the reason: Al Jazeera, which had employed her for their story three days before her arrest; the BBC, which had aired a documentary in which she featured some weeks earlier, broadcasting it throughout the Arab world. Amnesty had her face on the cover of their latest report. Indeed, the mere fact that Ahlam knew everyone could be the reason in itself: it was presumably the reason Abu Yusuf had pressed her to spy on other refugees and foreign reporters.

As the water boiled, I rummaged in a cupboard. A previous tenant had left behind half a bag of sugar, and I still had the coffee I'd packed in my hasty move from the Kuwaiti Hotel in Little Baghdad, paying my tab to the manager at the Kuwaiti while smiling as naturally as I could, promising to come back soon. I knew that I wouldn't. The year before, when the alleys and apartments there were still a mystery to me, I had been edgy, cautious, afraid of being watched, then had had those fears stilled by Ahlam's fearlessness, which, just like fear, was contagious. I had been right to be worried: she had been wrong.

And even if this was not my fault, even if her arrest had nothing to do with me—and I thought that was possible, from certain vantage points even likely—I was still responsible for her. We had been a team. If our positions had been reversed, if during our fieldwork I had been the one hauled away, I was certain she wouldn't have simply gone on without looking for me. Our friendship had been forged through the work, and it was the work she did—on behalf of me, and all of us—that had put her in danger.

So what, I asked myself, could I actually do? I wished Ahlam was there to give me advice. Locating disappeared prisoners had been her specialty in Baghdad. I remembered what she had told me about her methods, how she had persuaded an American general to give her the names of the prisoners under his command; and when the commander of another prison ignored her requests, found a translator to secretly pass her information. When she told me what she had done, she said, "Your situation forces you to do something official and something unofficial."

Official channels were the least likely to cause problems, but whenever I phoned the UN High Commissioner for Refugees, the status of her case was like a weather report that never changed. She had been gone for a week now, and I called every day. They continued to tell me they were working on it. They said that if they pushed too hard, they could jeopardize all the other people in prison.

So how hard would they push? How many resources could they devote to a single life when they were considering the whole venture, all the millions of refugees with all their millions of problems? They all but said as much to me.

I understood one critical thing: they didn't know as much as I did about where she had come from, whom she knew, who she was, or how crucial she had been to getting these stories out into the world; nor would they be devoted to this single task, the only assignment I had.

The coffee was bitter. I had to buy milk. Food—that would also be a good idea. Dumping the coffee down the drain and rinsing the glass under the tap, I considered whom to talk to next. I recalled stories about the Red Cross visiting prisoners in wartime. A neutral body. On the side of the ordinary person caught in the war machine. Was that still the case? I had met a Frenchman at Ahlam's apartment who used to work for the Red Cross in Iraq.

I locked the door behind me—a satisfyingly solid door, with a deadbolt—and headed downstairs to the Internet café to look up the Red Cross.

Chapter 15

OFFICIALDOM

THE DAMASCUS HEADQUARTERS OF the International Committee of the Red Cross turned out to be within walking distance. It felt good to be on my way somewhere, showered and smartly dressed, leather satchel worn crosswise, like someone headed to a promising job interview. Passing a sun-bleached park where children were playing, I stopped at a stand to buy a card with phone time. I would have liked to have a phone not registered to my name, but all SIM cards had to be registered with official ID so there was nothing to be done about that. Whenever I talked on the phone or wrote an email I asked myself: How would someone else interpret this? When I needed to call someone about Ahlam, I tried to use the landline in my flat.

The neighbourhood I was walking through looked vaguely familiar. I recalled the apartment I had visited around here with Ahlam in the winter—a pair of Serbs, friends of Mona—she had been getting ready for a party. That seemed like another world, another life. It had crossed my mind to call Mona again, but I abandoned the idea since it seemed to me she had abandoned Ahlam. Whatever Mona's problems were, instinctively I didn't want her to know I was still around and looking for Ahlam.

The Red Cross headquarters was a typical spartan NGO set-up. The chief of mission welcomed me into his office. He was slim, late middle-aged, with a genial, cultured manner. A classic Swiss, ready to hear me out. Taking the proffered seat, I explained everything: my work with Ahlam over the past year, the arrest, its possible context. When I told him of the many people who had been coming and going from her place, including Westerners, an amused smile played on his lips. "The authorities love that, don't they?" he said, by which he meant the opposite. When I told him how she had been working as a fixer for international media in both Iraq and Syria, he added, "I'm surprised she wasn't stopped long ago."

He sat with his ankles crossed, fingers pressed together, thinking. "The government here suffers from a form of paranoia." So do I, I thought, but managed not to say so. It was a relief to talk to someone who took me seriously. I didn't want to give him any reason to discount my concerns.

For that brief hour I felt blanketed in diplomatic immunity. Not crazy, not a threat, not a carrier of the plague. In the end he agreed to press his contacts on her behalf. He would talk to the UNHCR, add his voice. He stood to see me out. "Don't be optimistic," he said. And then, as if to blunt the force of that pronouncement, "It is good that you came here."

Walking back from his office, buoyed yet wondering whether anything would come of it, I considered my other options. Official channels. The summer before, I had interviewed two Syrian government officials to ask about the effects of the refugees on the economy. Ordinary Syrians were hurting because of inflation, and the refugees were bringing social problems such as prostitution and black market labour, and exacerbating fears of the war spreading over the borders. The government was anxious about US intentions; quite rightly too. Washington's war planners had made threats to take down Syria after Iraq, and the government was dangerously isolated in this time of heightened sectarian tensions. Syria, with a minority of Shia-derived Alawites ruling a majority Sunni population, was a photographic negative of pre-war Iraq.

The first official I had met was a suspicious, Cold War type who only warmed up when we discussed Graham Greene, the topic of his PhD dissertation. But he had confirmed something I had been investigating: the Americans wanted to cherry-pick the refugees, taking those who had worked for them—like Ahlam, it occurred to me now—and leaving behind the widows, the orphans, the disabled, the war-wounded. As usual the UNHCR was caught in the middle. The other official was young, easygoing, disarmingly confident, one of the new breed of technocrats bent on turning Syria from a socialist economy to a free-market one. An engaging, chubby guy in a well-cut suit who joked about his weight, he was a Catholic, educated at the London School of Economics.

But which official to trust?

I had liked the LSE guy. He was funny, not your average drab economist. More the kind of person who believed that with the right manoeuvring of numbers and policy tweaks you could remake society into some sort of automatic capitalist utopia, like a self-winding watch. But maybe I just liked him because his sort was familiar to me, a product of my own culture's aspirations.

But if I talked to either of them I would be forcing them to consider what to do about me. I would lose the one advantage I had, the ability to move around unnoticed. And if they were upset about Ahlam's work as a fixer, and thought she had broken the rules by working unofficially, any noise from me would simply confirm their suspicions. I would have to explain how I knew her and might be interrogated myself. It seemed better not to put myself in a situation I couldn't control.

The only person I could think of who knew Ahlam, and might have reason to be concerned about her as much as I was, was her friend, the other Iraqi fixer, Hamid. I had been impressed with him when he came over to Ahlam's apartment with Gabriela. He was well-connected, reliable, and Ahlam's equal—with an equivalent competence and toughness. Hamid would be a good person to talk to, but I had already written to Gabriela and hadn't heard whether she'd talked to him. In the meantime I didn't want to contact him directly. I had put one fixer at risk; I didn't want to endanger another. Tracking down people for information I needed was my profession, yet this time I had no idea where to start. Every possibility seemed to have a corresponding and equally powerful argument against it. The voices in my head were at odds with one another, in a tug-of-war that neither side could win.

On to the next possibility: to contact other journalists who knew Ahlam and see whether, like the Red Cross, they could work their back channels and do something.

—

A few blocks from my new apartment was an air-conditioned café with free Wi-Fi where I often went to check email. The café had been my haunt the year before when I still had my flamingo-pink terrace and the confidence that I could observe events without becoming ensnared. It was a popular place jammed with young couples drinking milkshakes and surfing on their laptops or watching soccer games on big-screen TVs. Staff in black-and-white uniforms walked around, refreshing the dying coals on water pipes or delivering ketchup and fries. The windows of the café were made of one-way mirrors so you could look outside but no one could see in. It was one of the reasons young people came here—to avoid their elders' prying eyes. Every afternoon I took a discreet table in a backroom where I could see out into the main room but wasn't immediately visible.

I wrote to my boyfriend to tell him about Ahlam, careful not to raise too much alarm. I didn't want my words to convey my fears, in case someone else was reading them, and I didn't want to worry him, knowing there was nothing he could do. *Do you think this puts you in any danger?* he emailed back, seeing through my words. And then: *I have learned to trust your instincts.* He wrote that he was struggling now with *creating enough emotional distance from you so that I am not going insane from missing you, but not so much that I disconnect.*

I knew, unhappily, that it was impossible for me to focus on two dilemmas at once. I was not capable of giving my full attention to one without neglecting the other, nor of being present in two places at once. As perhaps had been the case for a long time now.

Journalists: I had to turn my mind to the journalists Ahlam knew. I spent several days writing and responding to contacts. I wrote to Deborah Amos, a correspondent I had met at the National Press Club in Washington. She often reported from Syria and had filed a piece on Ahlam for NPR, as had journalists for *Salon.com*, the *Nation*, the *Washington Post*. She wrote me back, alarmed, offering to talk to people she knew at the UN. She had heard that Ahlam was on a watch list, but to arrest her? Why? she wondered, as I did.

Al Jazeera was next. I wondered if they even knew what had happened after her last assignment. The satellite news channel was launched in the mid-1990s in the tiny Gulf emirate of Qatar by a group of BBC-trained Arab journalists who had tried to start a BBC affiliate in Saudi Arabia but had quickly been censored. Qatar, under a new and younger emir (he had overthrown his father while the old man was holidaying in Switzerland), agreed to put its money—and there was a lot of it, from their natural gas fields—into the Arabic broadcast initiative. Now they had also started an English channel that was putting other broadcasters around the world to shame. This was partly because they put real money into reporting, and partly because they often hired good fixers who had been doing stories behind the scenes for other English-language media and made them on-air correspondents. They had expert reporters deeply immersed in their regions reporting from all over the world at a time when every other broadcaster was cutting back.

I remembered the name of the producer Ahlam had worked with and found him on their website. I sent him an email.

He called me the next day from London, sounding worried—
he hadn't known—and promised to do whatever he could.
He got in touch with Al Jazeera's Damascus bureau chief,
but, he emailed back to say, the bureau chief was unable to
find out anything. Ahlam was a fixer. Not an employee. She
worked contract to contract—like most magazine journalists,
a situation I knew well—and so had no immunity, no aura of
power to shield her. Though he didn't say as much, I understood that she was on her own.

One afternoon, looking up from my laptop at my backroom table, I saw another foreigner amid the throng of
Syrians in the main room. Blue eyes, a big bald head bent
over his computer. I went over and introduced myself. He
was British, working as a photographer for international
magazines and making his home in Damascus. We had—
an unsurprising sign of the small world we worked in—
colleagues in common. He complained about the business,
I complained about the business—a primal bonding exer-
cise among journalists.

They say that in times of fear people form kinship alli-
ances, and they are right. In a split second my now-chronic
reticence, which squelched speech and even thought, was
overcome by a visceral desire to trust. Invited to join him at
his table, I told him I had run into some trouble. A friend
of mine, a fixer, had been arrested, I wasn't sure why. The
story soon poured out. How comforting in times of trouble
to speak frankly with the assurance of being understood,
not having to define one's terms or explain how such things
come about. After I had finished talking he related his
own story.

He was married to a Syrian woman. One day she was summoned to a meeting with one of the intelligence agencies. They presented her with a fat file containing transcripts of all his emails painstakingly translated from English into Arabic, and ordered her to spy on him. From that point on he began emailing himself long extracts from medical websites. "Elephantiasis of the testicles and the like," he said. "Let them translate that."

I sent a superfluous message home recounting the beauty of Damascus, the glorious weather. Let them translate that. But a couple of days later, returning to the same café, I was unable to connect to the Internet. The manager came over to apologize. A new regulation. I must change the settings on my laptop and insert a code. Not their choice, he explained, pointing at the ceiling: an order from above.

After that I went to different Internet cafés, using different computers, never staying longer than twenty minutes, though I wasn't sure it made the slightest difference.

I felt helpless in the face of a great impenetrable system, a fortress that had neither windows nor doors. I was accustomed to obstacles in my work, but something always gave way eventually. Even when the path ahead involved diversions or dead ends, there was always a way in, or out. I remembered the prison I had visited in Beirut, when I'd gone there to report my passport missing—how I had walked up the staircase and out of there freely, with a sense of my own capability, my own capacity for action, intact. I could hardly remember the person who had done that. She had believed there were solutions to every problem. She had believed she could watch and ask questions and analyze without being

caught up in any of it. It was part of the reason I had not connected my presence at Ahlam's apartment with the dangers
it posed for her.

Ahlam saw what needed doing and did it. Perhaps that
was why I had found her so appealing. Now that my belief
in freedom of action, in *agency*, was gone, it seemed to me
that it must have been an illusion all along. Just a luxury
wrought by a worldview in which individuals believe they
shape their own destinies—and a curse as well. In the West
we are taught this from birth: that the course of our life is
determined by how well we play our cards. The weak are
weak because they did something wrong; the powerful have
power because they earned it. Only now was I coming to
understand the sense of fatalism so common in the East,
where most of what happens is determined by forces beyond
one's control.

I remembered what Ahlam had told me about being abandoned in the river as a girl, and fighting the current. "The
difficulty isn't to learn to swim in the water," she had said.
"The difficulty is to learn to swim in life." She had faced the
currents, the obstacles, and survived. Now she was caught in
a current I could neither see nor understand. I felt it overwhelming me too, pulling me down.

In the past, before it became clear what can happen to those
who operate outside the system and act as if they are free to
do whatever they like, I would have thought nothing of the
day when the power was cut to my apartment.

It happened in the mid-morning, an hour when I usually walked down the four flights to go check email. Each
day I stepped over a killing field of dead cockroaches in

the stairwell. The woman who lived on the second floor was militant about them, spraying daily. And for that I was glad: if the cockroaches couldn't make it any farther up the stairs, perhaps no one could.

I waited an hour in the sweltering heat, expecting the power to come back on as usual. Power outages had increased with the influx of refugees weighing down an outdated power grid—Iraqis liked to joke that it was a way of making them feel at home. When it didn't come back on I stepped into the stairwell and listened. I could hear the sounds of electric life whirring in other apartments. It was only out in mine.

My landlady, a pious Sunni with a PhD in physics, came over the next day with her entire family to fix the electrical system. It was nothing, then, just a failure in a badly maintained flat. I began to relax. All was well, I was well, the A/C was working again.

The following day, towards noon, I heard a pounding on the front door. I had just returned from checking email and was standing in the kitchen, contemplating the lack of food in the fridge. At the sound of knocking I froze. I wasn't expecting anyone. Hardly anyone knew I was here, and they would have phoned. I stayed silent, not making a sound. The pounding continued for a long time and finally ceased.

A quarter of an hour later there was a clattering on the roof. I went out onto the terrace and looked up. A man was on the roof, attempting to lower a ladder down onto my terrace.

I shouted. The word "police" translates into many languages. I saw a stick lying among the debris on the terrace and grabbed it, waving it at him like a sword. I would kill him with it if I had to, beat him to death. He pulled the ladder back up over the roof and fled.

I wanted to call the police, and in a normal situation I might have. Now I feared them more than I feared the intruder. What if he *was* the police? In the past I would have interpreted this as nothing more than another strange coincidence, rather than a plot directed at me. And—it was coincidence. Within a couple of days, after urgent discussions with my landlady, I learned that the stranger on the roof was the neighbour across the hall, a shadowy figure I now recalled peering at me on several occasions through a crack in his door as I went downstairs. He was single at forty, living with his parents in the apartment next door, and had seen me coming and going. His parents were away and he wanted to "introduce himself," as my landlady put it. She told me he was convinced that his dramatic overture would be welcome and was apparently shocked that I did not see it that way.

And yet . . . I was deeply shaken. I felt as if the conventions of civilization were disintegrating. Maybe those too had been a fiction all along. Maybe my landlady was telling the truth when she assured me he would not bother me again—but she also wanted to calm me down; it was illegal to rent me this apartment in the first place, off the books.

I could no longer, no matter what anyone said, separate coincidence from intentional threat. I remembered years ago reading J.M. Coetzee's book of essays on censorship, *Giving Offense*. "When certain kinds of writing and speech, even certain thoughts," he wrote, "become surreptitious activities, then the paranoia of the state is on its way to being reproduced in the psyche of the subject, and the state can look forward to a future in which the bureaucracies of supervision can be allowed to wither away, their function having been, in effect, privatized." And, "All writers under censorship are at least potentially touched by paranoia, not just those who have their work suppressed."[33]

And so it happens. Where I had once been ready to dismiss anomalies, I now interpreted every event as a message. These two events—a power cut *to my apartment*, a foiled break-in *to my apartment*—were anomalous and singular, and in this way resembled gifts that are chosen with a specific recipient in mind. It is the same way the censor becomes internalized. He works his way into our private thoughts so deeply that he is always with us, always watching, even when he's not there.

Ahlam had been gone without a trace for eleven days.

Chapter 16

THE FIXER'S FIXER

PLZ CONTACT ME.

I stared at the screen on the computer. The net café was quiet. The bored girl at the front desk had handed me the access code without a second look.

Two phone numbers followed the message. One for a mobile phone, the other a landline. I wrote them down, transposing two of the numbers. It wouldn't take a high-level code-breaker to figure it out, but it would be a hassle.

I called the landline from my own landline in the apartment—an old rotary phone that was not registered to me.

"How did you find me?" I asked.

Hamid's voice was like a gravel-crusher. "Gabriela told me," he said. "She was worried after getting your email." We agreed to meet the following afternoon at the Royal Café, across the street from the Cham Palace Hotel.

The Royal was one of those old-style Arab coffeehouses: smoke-filled, large as a warehouse, packed exclusively with men except for one young couple gazing longingly at each other across a table. I arrived exactly at five, taking a table at the back. Hamid arrived a few minutes later, having scoped the place first. He sat down heavily across from me and looked around. He had the kind of face that revealed nothing unless he wanted it to. "Let's go somewhere else," he said.

We decided, after some debate, to go to my apartment where we could talk unseen. It was risky, but we could not think of a safer place.

I walked on ahead, through the crowds heading home from work. Men in suits, women in dresses. People were stepping out of a patisserie, carrying little white boxes wrapped with string. There was a line outside the window wicket where a fat man in a white chef's uniform sold hummus and baba ghanoush by the kilo, ladled into plastic bags.

Hamid trailed me at a distance. After I had gone upstairs he waited a few more minutes and then buzzed up. By the time he reached my floor he was huffing and clutching his chest.

He blamed his heart trouble on a recent visit to Baghdad to check on his home. His house was near the airport, a place of intense fighting. After his family fled he had rented it to a woman he knew, but the violence was such that he could no longer charge her anything: it was a comfort just to have someone watching the place. When he finally managed to get there she told him that she, too, had moved to Syria for a while—she herself had only just returned to check on her furniture. When she reached the house she had found it occupied by a group of young militiamen who thanked her politely for the use of a very good house and left. A few days later they came back. They had forgotten something. They went into the backyard and lifted a sewer grate, pulling out two large rockets that they carted away.

Later, when she cleaned her furniture, she turned over the chairs and found papers stashed beneath them with lists of names. "She burned them," Hamid said, "into ash."

As I put on water for coffee, he sighed and said that if the war ever ended he would change his name to Salaam—peace. I told him about the theory that it takes ten years after a war for a society to return to the status quo ante.

"Even after ten years we won't be back to zero," he said, "because of the mentality of this new generation. This generation and the next two generations. They aren't being educated anymore, they see nothing but violence. They've become easy to brainwash and they are caught between Saudi Arabia and Iran." His goal, which he was devoting himself to these days, was getting his own children out. One son was already studying in the United States; another had a lead on a university scholarship there. After that, only one more to go.

He looked around my apartment, taking it in. "This place is weird."

"I know." I handed him a mug.

I told him about the break-in. The neighbour on the roof with the ladder.

"You should move," Hamid said, stirring in sugar. "It's not safe. Anyone can come in here over the roof. What if he comes back?"

What if, undaunted by my reaction, he chose to try again? That was my fear as well. "I already paid two months' rent in advance. I'm broke. And where am I going to go? I can't leave right now." Not without finding out what had happened to

Ahlam. We took our coffees and two kitchen chairs onto the terrace, sitting side by side, looking out as twilight fell and the city darkened into points of light. A wind came up, scattering dust. My eyes blurred, but no tears fell. I hadn't wept. A flock of birds flew overhead, black as bats. Where did they go at night? I wondered.

We ran through the possible reasons for Ahlam's arrest: her unofficial work with journalists, the unofficial school, someone with a grudge making a false report. Jealousies, petty slights—you never knew whom you could trust. And she had become the unofficial representative of Iraqis in Syria. Not everyone was pleased to have an activist in their midst.

"You know what the people call her?" Hamid said. "They call her 'Mother of the Iraqis.'"

But that would have upset some, this status of Ahlam's. He had once mentioned her name to a high-ranking female member of Iraq's Baath Party who was living in Damascus. She had stiffened, calling Ahlam "a one-woman NGO." It was not a compliment. The implication was that Ahlam did whatever she wanted, working outside the system. Officialdom doesn't trust such a person. From where do they get their power? What gives them the idea they can do whatever they want?

"Maybe it has nothing to do with the Syrians. Maybe it has to do with Ahlam's work in Iraq," I said. "Before she came here . . ."

Hamid knew she had angered some Iraqi factions because she did not distinguish between sects and refused to ally with any of them. Civil war breaks society into shards. Those who fall outside the new divisions—the minorities, the intellectuals, all who refuse to take sides—are left with no one to protect them. There was also the problem that she had helped the Americans in Iraq. Everyone who had done so was a target.

Just before Ahlam was arrested I had met a middle-aged woman who had been a high-school teacher in Baghdad until a few months before, when US troops came to see her school. Given her fluency in English, she acted as the interpreter for their visit. The troop commander commended her English skills and, in front of the entire staff and students, suggested she might see them about a job. She declined, shocked that he would mention such an offer in public. The next day he sent someone to the school to inquire again as to whether she would like to work as an interpreter. She declined again, but word soon spread among her colleagues that she was in league with the US military. One afternoon a man approached her in the street. He was a large man, "very ugly," she told me. "You are too old to rape and too poor to kidnap, so this is for you," he said, holding out a bullet, her gift for "working with the Americans." She fled to Syria.

I had thought I had a convincing cover story—a visiting professor—but whoever was watching her might have seen right through it. It wouldn't be that hard to put together the pieces, or at least become suspicious. I asked Hamid if he thought it was my fault. It was a hard question to ask, because I was afraid of his answer, but he didn't seem to hear me. He was worrying aloud about what her arrest meant for other Iraqis in Syria. "Arrest someone like her, someone everybody knows, and it sends a message. So we all shut up." Adding, "Especially because she's a fixer." A link from the refugees to the outside world. As he was.

Both of us, staring into the blackness of that Damascus

night, were interpreting her arrest through our own lenses like a piece of conceptual art.

What we did not discuss was the most terrifying prospect of all: that she might have been arrested for nothing. This had been the case for many of the prisoners Ahlam had known in Iraq, picked up on baseless suspicions, over grudges, held forever and a day for nothing at all. With no good reason to arrest her, there would be no good reason to set her free. If Abu Yusuf's motivation was anger at her refusal to cooperate, her arrest could fall into that category. If no logical principles were at work, we were dealing with a form of madness.

It's sometimes said that the simplest answer is usually the right one, but the people who say that haven't spent much time reporting in the Middle East. Here, if the cause of something seems obvious, it is probably because it was designed to look that way, to steer one away from what is really going on.

I lit a cigarette.

"Can I have one of those? Don't tell my wife," he said, as I handed him the packet and the lighter. "I'm supposed to quit because of my—" He pounded his chest.

We smoked in silence, side by side in the dark, like a pair of detectives on a late-night stakeout, or a pair of fugitives with nowhere to go.

"So what do we do? I've exhausted the official channels," I said.

"UNHCR?" he asked.

"I'm talking to them. Every day. They're not telling me much. I think they are tired of me, actually. You could try."

He nodded. He would do that. He knew people there.

"And the guys who used to be at her apartment, who hung out there all the time. One of them was living there." Hamza, with the blond hair and blue eyes. "I could try to reach him. He might know what's happened to her kids." Her kids. Who was taking care of them? "And how to reach her brother, Salaam."

He agreed. Good idea. "I know someone else who might help us," he offered. A friendly Syrian with connections to the country's military-security establishment. "We could pay him a visit."

We decided to do the only thing we could, the one thing we were both good at: fact-finding. As the streets below us filled with the sound of evening crowds—people heading to restaurants, meeting friends—we focused on our action plan: to find out where she was being held, the accusations against her, and the status of her case.

Chapter 17

ALONE TOGETHER

I DIDN'T WANT TO STAY in my apartment alone, so I called one of the two other people in Damascus who were still talking to me—amazing how quickly friends and colleagues had disappeared—and the only one who had nothing else to do. During the day Rana came over, but her parents expected her home at night: she had her teaching job, studies, and her married sister had recently had a baby, a sweet little boy she adored. So Kuki agreed to come and stay at night. When I asked if he had time in his schedule, he made the obvious point that "refugees don't have schedules." Plus he was currently living with two aunts and a bunch of small cousins, so was glad of an excuse to get out. Just for a few nights, I said, until I was sure the stranger next door wasn't coming back for me.

"That won't happen," said Kuki confidently, sipping the tumbler of wine I had poured him. His presence was a comfort and a distraction. He was self-absorbed, suffering from a keen awareness of his wasted youth. He had lost the past five years ("the five *best* years") and plenty of people who mattered in his life—relatives and friends kidnapped or murdered. I had been with him the day his aunt phoned to tell him a car bomb had gone off outside his parents' house in an upscale neighbourhood of Baghdad, blowing out the front door and killing the neighbour; he'd collapsed into a ball, expressing guilt at not being there to share their fate. No problem of mine could he take particularly seriously.

A heat wave was sweeping Damascus; a hot wind, stifling and oppressive. I pulled two mattresses from the bedroom into the living room, positioning them beneath the air-conditioning unit. The living room was musty, a tapestry of a hunting scene against one wall, an oil painting of a landscape, two ancient sofas that gave up clouds of dust when sat upon. Someone had once taken the trouble to make the place a home but that was long ago.

Kuki had majored in French in university but watched a lot of American movies. It was from movies, and from rap, that he had learned English. He could riff on 50 Cent, see deeper meaning in the lyrics. Sometimes he asked me to parse confounding lines. Now he told me he had renewed his residency permit in Syria with the assistance of an older Syrian actor who had influence. "He wants to help me," Kuki said.

"Yeah, he wants to *help* you. Is he good-looking?"

He smirked. "I have a boyfriend." He was still with the American from the Midwest whom he'd met through a website. "How are things with *your* man?" He often asked about my relationship, as if I had some secret formula for relationship longevity.

"We broke up, I think."

He looked shocked. A lot had been riding, apparently, on me serving as a successful example of couples who manage to make a long-distance relationship work.

"When?"

"Officially?" It had happened in the days before. Or years before. "We talked on the phone. I couldn't say much." You can't ask someone to be there for you when you've not been there for them. And you can't ask them to wait just because the timing is bad. "We couldn't talk very long—the phone line."

I breathed hard, stifling emotion. There wasn't time for weakness now, I told myself. There was so much to be upset about that it would be easy to let the current pull me under. But it felt like the last rope snapping, the final anchor to my old life, to the person I used to be.

I did not of course consider whether my emotional response to my personal trouble offered insight into Ahlam's response to her world falling apart: events so devastating as to make my struggles paltry. Yet there was a passing resemblance, I think now, in our instincts to deny in order to keep moving, to move in order to keep denying. Was her response to unbearable loss—burying herself in the problems of others—the only way she knew to survive? I ask this question only now because in the moment we are creatures of instinct—fight or flight—while true revelation takes time, if it ever comes. And though she had always been like this, a problem-solver, a fixer, her work had become an obsession for her the way my work did for me in hard times.

I poured myself another glass of wine. It wasn't helping, but was worth a try.

"You could go back, work things out from there," Kuki suggested, his mind still on my relationship.

I had been thinking of doing so before Ahlam disappeared—two and a half weeks ago. I realized I was measuring time in terms of before and after. "But I don't think it would make a difference," I replied. "We're moving in different directions. It's not just this—not just being apart."

I made Kuki tour the apartment, scout the perimeter, before we settled for the night, even though I knew he wasn't exactly the bodyguard type. No one was lying in wait; there was no one crouched behind a door or waiting to spring from an anteroom, but I felt as if there was. My judgement was off, my instincts, usually failsafe, were proving unreliable.

"What are you going to do when you get to New York?" I said when he returned, to change the subject. He had been called for interviews with the US Homeland Security, the next stage in his case for refugee resettlement. I considered it likely that he would be accepted: how many jihadists are both gay and out of the closet? Some could probably quote 50 Cent, but they couldn't dance to him.

I pulled sheets over the mattresses. No need for blankets. Even with the A/C running all night, it was hot.

"Maybe modeling, I don't know." But the reality was he was twenty-five. Aging out. "If not, I can cut hair. I always cut the hair for all my aunts and my cousins." His own shaggy mop gleamed with a new copper rinse.

He looked at my hair. My bangs were long and unkempt. Reaching out a hand, he tousled them and said, "I have scissors. Let me take care of that."

"Thank you," I said, moved in a way I could not explain.

He slept on the mattress next to mine, with his back to me. Listening to his reassuring, even breathing, I stayed up long into the night.

—

By the next afternoon Kuki was restless. He paced around. Checked his phone. Said he had heard about a party. We should go. I was waiting for Hamid to call, landline to landline, and in the meantime struggling with aimlessness, unsure what to do next.

"Come on, blondie. What else do you have to do? You can't stay here all the time. There might be important people there." Adding, portentously, "People who could help you find Ahlam."

On the face of it, it was a lie. But I didn't want to be alone. And maybe, by staying in, I would miss my chance to do something. I had often found answers to my questions by simply going everywhere, talking to everyone. As a journalist, you never knew where you'd catch a break.

That evening Kuki sat me on a chair, placed a glass of wine in my hand, and trimmed the strands that hung in front of my eyes, with utmost care.

I stood up and brushed myself off. He held up a mirror. "Looks good," I said. And it did.

I was wearing the same jeans I usually wore. "Not that," he said. "It's a party." He dug around in my suitcase for my one and only decent black dress, which could be hung in the steam from a shower and still do the job, and held it up. "This."

The party was on the rooftop of a fancy hotel, women dancing provocatively in the open air, men in tight black shirts who smelled like an explosion at a cologne factory. A society columnist for a local Damascus rag wanted to take our photograph but I bowed out—unimaginable, in these circumstances, to be seen out on the town, to have my face and name in print. Kuki, naturally, absorbed the limelight with élan.

While he hit the dance floor, wearing a T-shirt with his nickname on it, I talked to a Frenchman with leonine hair and a billowy white shirt, open at the neck, a caricature of the European intellectual. He looked like Bernard-Henri Lévy. He was in the business of prosthetic limbs—the market in the Middle East, he told me, was booming. He offered to buy me a cocktail but I declined. Then he made his hand into a pincer claw and directed it towards me: "Le Shark," he called it. "Le Shark."

I fled the Shark. The music was deafening, the crowd pressing in around me. I felt guilty for being here. In anguish I found a spot away from everyone else on the edge of the roof, where I could look out over the city. She was out there somewhere, I could feel it. *Where are you? Tell me where you are.*

The Royal Café, eight p.m.

I arrived there first. Punctuality—that I could do. This time Hamid didn't even bother to sit down. "Let's go," he said. I plunked down change for the coffee that had yet to come.

Through an Iraqi friend I had tracked down one of Ahlam's "assistants," who said he could put me in touch with Hamza. "Hamza's the one who always took care of the kids when Ahlam was out," I had told Hamid. "Maybe he knows something." We were meeting the two boys under the bridge near the university.

I followed him out to the street where he waved down a taxi.

"Can the boy be trusted?" Hamid asked.

"That I don't know."

The streets by the university were dark. The occasional cluster of students, passing on the sidewalk, gusts of sudden laughter and impassioned discussion. We walked towards the bridge.

I recognized Hamza immediately: his white face visible in the darkness, the boiled-blue eyes. He and the other boy were anxious, whispering, their faces close to ours, explaining how everyone around Ahlam had scattered after her arrest. Her disappearance had exploded the fragile world she had created, sending the survivors running for cover. They had thrown away their SIM cards, changed phone numbers, found new places to stay. Her apartment had been searched the day of her arrest. Agents had searched the classrooms too. All the books had been taken. I imagined the secret police puzzling over children's textbooks, trying to decode sinister messages. "The monkey lives in the jungle." The line Ahlam's daughter had taught me from her lesson book. "The monkey lives in the jungle," they would mutter to themselves, asking what it meant.

Hamza said the children were staying with him, that they were fine. But where? I asked. He would say no more, but showed me pictures of them on his phone. I was uneasy. I couldn't tell if they were recent since the children were both wearing the same track suits they had received in the winter, as presents for Eid. The pictures could have been taken long ago.

"What about Salaam?" I asked. Ahlam's brother.

"He is talking to the mukhabarat. Trying to get her released. Offering money."

"What do you think?" I asked Hamid after they had left. He had kept his own counsel while speaking to them, his face a mask. Now he let it slide.

"I don't trust them."

Two nights later we went to meet Hamid's Syrian contact. He reminded me of a movie-star cop: early thirties, handsome and square-jawed, picket-fence teeth, full of wisecracks. He was in his office answering phone calls when we arrived.

He shook my hand vigorously. "I'm Osama," he said, grinning broadly. "Osama bin Laden."

In his professional life "Osama" was a real-estate agent. His office resembled a doctor's waiting room, chairs stationed against the walls. He pointed to a woman who had just walked in the door. She wore pancake makeup, skintight jeans and a camouflage-patterned shirt, her eyebrows tweezed into a quizzical arc. "She's an Iraqi terrorist," he said, winking. "Just out of Guantánamo."

Hamid and I took seats while he answered another phone call. Osama's two young assistants greeted us. One of them immediately brought glasses of tea; the other brought over a month-old white kitten that he placed in my lap. At first it mewed as I petted its fur, and then curled up and fell asleep. Under my hand I could feel its rapid heartbeat. It was strangely comforting to comfort another being.

After Osama hung up, he and Hamid chatted briefly. Hamid filled him in on the man who had tried to break into my apartment. Osama's eyebrows shot up.

"You want me to take care of him?" he asked. This time he was serious.

No, no. That did not seem like a good idea. I could see that going very wrong. Nor was it a good idea to talk about Ahlam in a packed office with strangers coming and going and curious assistants listening in. After Osama had cleared away some paperwork and answered another phone call ("The President of Iran," he informed me, covering the phone with his hand), we walked outside to talk in his car. He agreed to look into the case of "the missing woman."

It was a week before Osama called back. We went to see him at his home, a simple but spacious apartment, lovingly decorated. He had a pretty blonde wife and two small children, a boy and a girl, who were taking lessons in English. They each sat on opposite arms of my chair, eager to practise. The boy, who was seven or eight, pointed at his older sister. "She's a donkey," he said, in a fit of giggles.

"That's a very bad word," I said. "You can't say that word."

"She's a donkey!" he said, almost falling off the chair he was laughing so hard.

Hamid was talking to Osama on the sofa. When we left he filled me in. According to Osama's contact inside the military-security establishment, who said he had read Ahlam's file, she stood accused of giving information to reporters. This part was obviously true. The rest of it was harder to believe. She was charged with running guns to Iraqi militias and operating a human smuggling ring. The contact said the atmosphere around the case was serious. "Don't go near it," he said.

We also learned where Ahlam was being held: at Douma Prison, on the outskirts of Damascus, just walking distance from the UNHCR office.

PART **THREE**

Chapter 18

AHLAM'S STORY
PART ONE

AHLAM WONDERED WHAT TIME it was, if it was day or night. She had spent two days in her cramped isolation cell, dreading what they were planning for her. Her cell was not wide enough to stretch out her arms fully, nor long enough for her to lie down, but the guards weren't letting her sleep anyway, and the fluorescent lights never switched off.

When they first brought her to the intelligence headquarters in Sayeda Zainab, a motorcycle escorting the station wagon with another car following behind, she was taken directly to Abu Yusuf's office. He was at his desk. She went to sit down.

"No, stand," he said. She stood back up. "Who was that blonde woman in your apartment?" he asked.

"She's a professor at a university in Vancouver."

"You think I don't know that! I know everything about her."

He took out his pistol, setting it in front of him on his desk. "We allowed you to open your school, to meet foreigners. Now it's time to pay up."

"What do you mean?" she asked.

He mentioned the name of an American correspondent who reported on the refugees in Syria. "We want you to go to work for her. See who she's talking to, what questions she's asking. And we want you to give us reports on the foreigners working for the UNHCR. Weekly reports."

"No." The word that would become her mantra.

"Take her to the next room," he said to one of his men.

She was led out of his office and allowed to sit down. The agent who had taken her from her apartment stood there, looking unhappy. He looked like he was feeling guilty, she thought. Some minutes later—perhaps Abu Yusuf had made a phone call—she was brought back into his office.

He repeated his demands: the journalist, the UNHCR. Weekly reports.

"Listen," Ahlam said, attempting reason. "I can't just ask a journalist if I can work for her." She tried to explain that this was not the way such things were done. "The journalist asks for you, you don't ask to work for her. She will become suspicious. I will be taken for a fool." And, she added, the foreigners at the UNHCR were just humanitarian workers, so she wouldn't spy on them.

"You're a traitor," he snarled. "You betrayed Iraq by cooperating with American forces. Now you are trying to do the same in Syria." He waved to his men.

They blindfolded her, took her outside and put her in a car. She couldn't tell in which direction they were driving. Finally, they stopped.

"You're at Douma Prison," someone said, "where you belong."

But they didn't let her out.

"Why is it taking so long?" she heard the driver ask.

"We're waiting for permission."

It struck Ahlam that the prison wasn't expecting her, that this was Abu Yusuf's idea.

Finally permission came through. She was taken from the car and led down a set of stairs into a basement. In an office a guard took her purse and her phones, and removed her blindfold. He wanted to take the cord from her neck with the picture of her son. "No," she said, clutching it. "You're not taking that."

The guard was an older man with grey-black hair. Tall and big-boned, an imposing figure, yet with something humorous or human about him, a broad open face. His name was Sadiq, he told her. "Look," he said, "anyone who sees that will take it from you because they will think you might hang yourself with it. So if you want it, hide it." She tucked it under her shirt.

On her third day in the isolation cell, the door opened. She was blindfolded and handcuffed and marched down a hallway, turning right down a longer corridor. Though she could see nothing, she would later come to understand that hers was one of a row of eight or nine isolation cells, and that the longer corridor held the larger multi-person cells: on her left she was passing a cell for female prisoners next to a similar cell for male prisoners; and next to that another cell whose purpose, for some time, remained mysterious. When the guards reached the end of the corridor they ushered her into the final room. As she entered she heard the voice she already knew meant trouble.

"We hear you want to spy on our country," Abu Yusuf began. "We hear you want to destroy us." He walked over to the chair where the guards had set her down and began kicking her feet, hitting her arms. "You're a criminal. You don't deserve to live. We give you shelter and peace. We give you food that deserves to go to my people. We let you make your living. And this is how you repay us." He slapped her so hard that she was knocked from her chair. She pulled herself up and felt for the chair, then sat back down as if nothing had happened.

"She's not affected by my slaps," he said, whether to himself or an onlooker, she could not tell, "so maybe she will be affected by this." Moments later a stick sliced across her shoulders. Even then she would not give him the satisfaction of any reaction.

He recounted his favours to her: permission to work, permission to open a school. When she had gone to him the previous summer to ask permission to run the school, he had said, "You seem like a poor woman, so why do you give these lessons for free?"

"To serve the community and take the children from the street and educate them. That's all."

"Good point," he had said. "And we will support you in that. But we will need your help in the future."

"I'm at your service." She had not known that this was what he had in mind all along.

Now, bringing up the school again, he said, "If all you are doing is teaching girls then why are all these security agencies interested in you?"

Why indeed? Before he had thought of her as a simple woman, a refugee, no one of consequence; now he seemed to have the idea she was all-powerful.

The journalist, he repeated. That's all he wanted—for her to spy on the journalist the way she had spied for the Americans. Then she would be released, free to go.

"I'm sorry," said Ahlam. "I can't do what you ask." She had the feeling that he had promised to deliver a prize, to turn her into an informant, and her refusal was somehow personal: a humiliation, a failure in front of his superiors. If that was so, it made him a dangerous man.

The next day she was again taken from her cell in solitary, marched down the hallway, turning right down the longer corridor to the interrogation room at the end. This time Abu Yusuf had the letters of commendation she had received from US officials in Iraq, which had now been translated into Arabic. Months ago, she had hidden these documents, but when the agents had searched her apartment while she waited for them to take her away, they'd wasted no time finding what they were looking for: a child's schoolbag at the bottom of the doorless closet piled high with a hundred other objects. As if they'd somehow known exactly where to look.

These testimonies were essential to her refugee claim, but she knew that in the wrong hands they could also be dangerous. The first letter, from April 2005, was from Major Daniel J. Barzyk, a civil military affairs officer who praised her "tireless efforts" to help the poor and disadvantaged through her work as deputy director of operations at the General Information Center. He recommended she be sent on an outreach mission to the United States as an "Ambassador for Hope" to coordinate aid efforts and "raise awareness of the dire conditions that many people in Baghdad are living in."

The second letter, from May 2005, was from Ahlam's supervisor, Captain Cinnie L. Mullins, head of the Iraqi Assistance Center–Baghdad. It called her a "creative and original thinker" with "a great deal of common sense that she applied to finding solutions to the problems of the Iraqi people." The letter ended with a request: "Please assist her endeavor to secure aid to improve schools, increase housing and care for the orphaned, handicapped and displaced people of this once great land."

The third and last letter was dated August 2005. Major Adam Shilling reported that she had been kidnapped the month before while on her way to work, released one week later after "suffering physical abuse resulting in several long-term injuries." He noted that ongoing threats to her, her family and co-workers meant she could no longer work for them and was planning to leave Iraq. "Please render whatever assistance you can to her and her family."

Here was proof, Abu Yusuf said, of her collaboration with the enemy. "You helped them invade Iraq and now you are helping them invade Syria. You are their spy in Damascus."

The same words that been used when she was kidnapped: you're a traitor, you're a spy. Hearing the accusations, blindfolded as he beat her viciously about the head, or on the shoulder that had been injured during her kidnapping, as if he instinctively sensed her weakness, she flashed back to those days when she had wondered if she would live or die. She answered his demands the same way she had answered her kidnappers: no, no, no.

The interrogations continued daily and the demand was always the same: "We want you to gather information on the journalist." She was to go and offer her services as a fixer, and report back.

He knew all about her work for Al Jazeera English—they had been listening to both of her phones. Fortunately she still had the list of questions the Al Jazeera journalist had given her to ask inside her purse: nothing more than a boring inquiry into Swedish asylum laws. But he had not yet discovered her work for Human Rights Watch. It was just the sort of thing he wanted, concrete proof of treachery.

He said she was a spy for the Mossad, for the CIA. "Just confess and you will be released." But she remained silent, accepting his blows without a murmur, ignoring the instinct to flinch or show pain, knowing that to give in on any one point would be to start a process that would never end.

In one session she tried to explain that working for journalists was just a sideline, something she did because she spoke English and knew a lot of people. That her real work was helping Iraqis.

"Yes, we hear you are some kind of Mother Teresa." His voice had a mocking tone.

Ahlam had heard of the work of Mother Teresa and respected her; it was an insult to compare them. "Don't call me that! I am nothing next to that great woman, God bless her soul."

"You're so tough even your husband is afraid of you. That's why he ran away!"

"I'm tough? If you're so tough, why did you have to send three men to follow me around?"

She heard a deep belly laugh coming from somewhere behind her. Normally Abu Yusuf was alone, but on occasion another man joined them in the interrogation room. She was unable to see his face, but unlike Abu Yusuf, who called her bitch, slut, whore, he addressed her respectfully.

"Is there anything you need?" he asked her once.

"I need to know about my children," she told him.

"Don't worry about your children," he said. "Your children are fine." But she didn't know whether to believe him.

Maybe it was a case of good cop/bad cop. Or maybe the man who laughed out loud was Abu Yusuf's superior. If so, it was looking bad for him.

"Why did I send my men to follow you?" Abu Yusuf retorted. "Because you're a traitor! You were working for the Americans."

And on and on. From her cell in solitary, she prayed, meditating on her children and on staying strong. With the exception of three days when she was denied food and water for being "uncooperative," she was fed three times a day from the prison kitchen. In the morning, white cheese and bread. Lunch, bad watery soup, which she refused to eat, and bread. Dinner, a boiled egg or halaweh, a sugar and sesame sweet. If they were feeling generous, a tomato or boiled potato.

The guards were aggressive, shouting, "What do you want?" if they spoke to her at all. Only Sadiq, who had warned her to hide her pendant of her son, treated her with respect, asking, "What can I do for you, sister? I know you don't deserve this."

Twice a day he took her down the hall to the toilets. Finally she told Sadiq she had only one kidney, from birth, and had to go more than two times a day. He went to the warden to get permission; and after that he took her three times: morning, noon, afternoon.

It may have been this report that Sadiq made about her kidney that convinced the warden to move her out of solitary confinement. Or it may have been that Abu Yusuf was tiring of the daily beatings and interrogations that went nowhere. Because after thirty-three days of interrogation she was moved.

Chapter 19

WE ACCEPT EVERYTHING

"DOUMA," I SAID, LEANING over the seat to make sure the driver could hear me. He was very old—he looked about ninety—and tore through narrow side streets at a terrifying speed. It was ironic that I was going to the neighbourhood where we believed Ahlam was being held. Douma Prison, named for the suburb of Damascus where it was located, was less than two hundred metres from the UNHCR office. I had made an appointment by phone to tell the refugee agency what I had gleaned about Ahlam's case from my meetings with Osama, since news of this import had to be delivered in person.

"Douma," I said to the driver, shouting this time, showing him the address written in Arabic.

"*Insha'Allah!*" he shouted back. Lord willing. It was a term I really didn't like applied to something as simple as driving across town, but he seemed almost deaf and, in enormously thick spectacles, possibly blind. He shot through another cross street without bothering to look.

The Lord willed. He dropped me off at the UNHCR office building, where I signed in with a security guard before being escorted upstairs to the office of an information officer who had been my press liaison when I'd visited the refugee registration centre last summer. An Englishwoman with the wilted complexion of someone who didn't take well to the heat, she had seemed capable but overworked. Today, as I sat down excitedly across from her in her small drab office, she looked merely impatient. I had been calling them every day for almost a month now; she probably thought today would be more of the same. But I was elated—I had news for her. News for which I was certain she would be grateful.

I gave her a quick précis, telling her that Ahlam was likely nearby in Douma Prison, describing the charges that had been outlined to me.

"Who told you this?" She sounded annoyed.

I explained in vague terms that I had been talking to people.

"What people?" she said.

I said I'd rather not say. I could not bring Hamid into this. Or his Syrian sometime-real-estate-contact Osama.

"Why are they talking to you?" Her voice was cold. "If they have information they should come to us."

This was not how I had expected the meeting to go. She seemed less interested in what I had to say than in the fact that I had news to share. "But they don't do that, do they?" I said. "They don't come to you." I maintained a level tone, not wanting to be rude by spelling it out for her. The UNHCR was engaged in a balancing act that left them trusted by no side. The refugees, who had to reveal why they had fled in order to receive a registration certificate, and feared answering that infernal question about their sect, often told me they suspected the UNHCR of spying for the Syrians; the Syrian authorities, meanwhile, thought the UNHCR were agents of American foreign policy. It was a thankless task for the refugee agency. But my implication had not been lost on the official because she stood up from her desk, no longer merely impatient but furious.

"You should get out of here," she said heatedly, indicating the door. "Out of Damascus. Out of Syria. You are making things worse. Leave Ahlam to us."

"That's done a lot of good so far," I said, my tone rising to meet hers.

We ended the meeting in a shouting match.

My good mood of the morning was over. Whatever sense of purpose or empowerment the information had given me was gone.

In the taxi back to my apartment my thoughts veered between anger and self-approbation. *Of course* I was making things worse for the UNHCR—that was the whole point. I wanted them to feel pressure to do something. And no doubt, because of me, they had heard from the Red Cross and the journalists I had informed. No doubt they were tired of my constant badgering. Well, too bad. But—here my anger crumbled into depression—what if the official was right? What if, as she implied, I was only making things worse *for Ahlam*? Then what the hell was I doing here?

I had arranged to meet Rana that day, and she came to my apartment. I was relieved to see her, someone who actually wanted to talk to me. It was just past noon but I kept the shutters closed all the time now so the dusty rooms were in permanent twilight. She sat across from me at the kitchen table, hands folded. She was elegantly dressed as always, and composed. She had opted for lemon yellow today, from skirt to blouse to headscarf.

I buried my face in my hands. Nothing I did worked. Everything I touched turned bad. I could no longer be sure anything I did was in Ahlam's interest. I wondered if I was starting to lose my grip. For the first time since Ahlam disappeared I wept.

When I had recovered, I said, "I used to feel like a normal person in Syria. Like I could go about my life. Now I feel trapped in a police state." I met Rana's gaze. "How can you live like this?"

My tone must have sounded accusatory—as if this were in some way her fault. I felt ashamed. Here I was, behaving as badly as the Englishwoman, who herself must be on the verge of burnout, overwhelmed by the impossible tasks she confronted.

But Rana was silent, not reacting but thinking. After a long moment she spoke.

"This is the price people pay when they don't want civil war," she said. "Look what happened in Lebanon." Fifteen years of bitter sectarian war. "Look at Iraq." Iraq was the object lesson, the fate everyone feared. "How is that better?" Her voice was low and measured. "Because we hate war," she said softly, "we accept everything."

Her words punctured my self-righteousness. Sometimes you have to live with the unacceptable because the alternative is so much worse. I had daily seen the strengths of Syria— its tolerance of difference, its warmth, the sympathy for the survivors of war. On every street, down every alleyway, I met kind and intelligent and generous people—Rana was one of them. And so long as they did not involve themselves in politics, they were free to go about their lives as they chose. On a political level, compared to other countries in the region, Syria's government was no different and in many ways better: women like Rana were free to work and drive and go to university, have boyfriends or reject them, and wear a lemon yellow headscarf or a miniskirt if they preferred. A tradition of tolerance was a point of pride among Syrians. There were, of course, tensions between city-dwellers and the farm folk who were moving to the cities because of the drought—it had been another record bad year for rain—but these were class-based, not sectarian, pressures. They could be Kurdish, Alawite, Sunni, Shia, Druze, Armenian, Ismaili, Turkmen, Palestinian, Christian; no one asked and no one cared.

And I had seen for myself what had become of Iraqis. Not only was their nation destroyed, but so were the bonds of trust between people. They longed for the days of Saddam—"Not for him," they told me, "for the security"—so they could go back to the lives they had loved, walk down the streets of their neighbourhoods, send their children to school with the assurance they would see them at day's end.

At that moment, though, I also understood that I did not have to accept everything. I could leave. And it was true that the words of the Englishwoman had stung. What if she was right, and by staying here I was actually endangering Ahlam? I should go. I had to go. I began packing my bags, throwing things into them untidily.

"Please," I said, handing Rana the keys to the apartment. She often talked about her wish to live alone, which she couldn't afford on her schoolteacher's salary, the equivalent of two hundred US dollars a month. "I'm going to go away for a few days. Not long. I'm just not sure I am doing any good here . . . Maybe I can do more from outside. If you want to stay at the apartment, you can. The rent is paid."

An hour later I left by taxi for Beirut.

Chapter 20

AHLAM'S STORY
PART TWO

THE GUARDS AT DOUMA Prison were not allowed to search the women. Since the rape of two teenaged runaways, for which the guard responsible spent six months in solitary, the only person with keys to the women's cell was the chief warden, who looked on as the girl who would be Ahlam's cellmate was ordered to pat her down.

The black steel door slammed shut behind them. The key turned in the lock. How strange, in a cell measuring not more than four by four metres, for Ahlam to find herself with a green-eyed brown-haired beauty with a pierced lip and a stud in her tongue.

The girl, whose name was Leila, watched with interest as Ahlam took in the tiny bathroom to the left of the door, the metal shelf along the back wall piled with thin blankets, the noisy fan near the ceiling behind which the faintest strains of daylight could be seen. Under the stark glare of fluorescents, Ahlam surveyed the army of cockroaches scuttling fearlessly across the walls. "Don't bother yourself about them," Leila said nonchalantly. "We have a peace agreement."

Ahlam immediately signed on to the agreement. At mealtimes the two of them laid down a line of crumbs on the far side of the cell so they would not be disturbed. The treaty was honoured unless the cockroaches broke it by climbing over their faces while they slept.

"What's your story?" Leila asked, sitting next to Ahlam on the whitewashed floor. She was dressed in the silky black pajamas she had been wearing continuously since the night of her arrest four months ago. The pajamas, now somewhat the worse for wear, had at least been new when she was arrested.

Ahlam told her that she had been taken from her children for working for journalists and humanitarian groups, and had been interrogated over the course of a month. "What do you think will happen to me?" she asked. Though only twenty, Leila was the old hand.

"You need to talk to a lawyer," Leila said.

"Where am I going to find a lawyer?"

"In the next cell."

Along the back wall of the cell stretched a heating pipe. Leila got up and went to the far corner, crouching down beside it. "I'll speak to him," she said. With her mouth close to the pipe, she spoke into it. "Where is the lawyer?" she said. "I want to talk to him."

There was a scramble of male voices, then a man asking what she needed.

"There's an Iraqi lady here," Leila said into the pipe. "She spent a whole month in solitary, in an isolation cell. She has two children, a girl and a boy, and no one's taking care of them. We're wondering how to get her released."

"Tell him my interrogation is finished," Ahlam said.

After the last interrogation session, before she was moved, she had been given a questionnaire to fill out.

Where are the American forces in Iraq? it asked.

Did they think she was a leader of the American forces?

She took the pen and wrote her answer: *I don't know.*

Where are the militias in Iraq?

Her answer: *I don't know.*

She figured this meant they had finished with her and she would shortly be released.

Ahlam could hear the man's voice through the pipe and she felt her heart compress as she took in his words. "Even if the interrogation is finished," he said, "I suspect she's going to be here for at least four months."

On the white washed walls of the cell, where past prisoners had marked their names or longings, Ahlam scratched out two hearts and inside them wrote "Abdullah" and "Roqayah." But she found she couldn't stand to look at their names—her heart began to race with worry—so she rubbed them out with her hands.

Her eldest son did not need a heart; he was in her heart. In her cell she did something she had rarely allowed herself to do. She wept for him.

The days quickly developed a pattern. Waking at dawn, signalled by the distant strains of a mosque through the one small opening at the top of the cell where the fan rattled loudly. Hurriedly washing and filling plastic bottles under the meagre pipe in the stall-sized washroom which at least, unlike her cell in solitary, had its own squat toilet. The water pipe shut off at noon, and being summer, it was hot, so she and Leila took turns rinsing off in the morning and, when the water came back on at night, once again before bed. There was no soap or shampoo, no way to eradicate the sweat and grime and itch of the lice that plagued them, and no change of clothing, so after they had showered they put their stinking garments back on.

It was the conviction of the guards that women could not be criminals—women could be stupid but not wicked—and it was their fear that the women prisoners would pray to God to curse them. So they tried to curry favour with the women and thus with God. After midnight, when the warden had gone home, they slid open the metal slat on the cell door. Through the slat they shared whatever they had: food their wives had packed, newspapers, cigarettes, information, even (though it was forbidden) a copy of the Koran. Most of the guards were Druze or Alawite—Abu Yusuf was Christian—but in the main they were ordinary folk. What they feared most was punishment, which is why they had treated Ahlam so rudely in isolation, having been ordered to have no contact with her.

At first they spoke only to Leila, the longest serving prisoner, and the most beautiful. When they ascertained that Ahlam had serious charges against her and could not have been planted there to spy on them for Syrian intelligence, they began to talk to her. And, not surprisingly, in Ahlam they found a confidante. It had always been this way, people talked to her. They confessed their sorrows and secrets: the negligent wife who would no longer sleep with them, the lazy good-for-nothing son, various adventures with girlfriends.

Sadiq, who had guarded her in the isolation cell, was one of the guards for the women here, too, but he distinguished himself. He always had a book with him, so at night Ahlam and Leila stood by the eye-level slat and listened as he read to them. While reading from Babylonian history he served them Arabic coffee—strong and black, an unfathomable luxury, more delicious than any coffee they had ever tasted. Fearful of leaving any sign that he had allowed the women to smoke (for which he would receive an automatic six-month sentence, the same as for rape), he held a cigarette to their lips through the slat.

He told them he had worked in the prison for twenty years. He told them stories: one about a prison in the desert of Palmyra with a dozen floors below ground that no one knew about until the prisoners—those still alive—were released in 2000 after Bashar al-Assad came to power. "Thank God you don't live in Bashar's father's time," he said to Ahlam, speaking of the Syrian president's fearsome predecessor. "He would just have put a bullet in your head."

Ahlam and Leila passed the hours talking. Leila told her of the nightclubs where she used to go. "We'd go to Beirut. We went to drink, smoke hash, and returned to Damascus the next day. We just wanted to be wild." She knew all the top DJs, all the best clubs, had partied across Lebanon and Jordan. Playing with the stud in her tongue, or pacing the cell—a panther in its cage—she spoke about her past. How she had been raped as a little girl by a shopkeeper, how her father refused to press charges. How her parents, both doctors, fought all the time. Leila was fluent in English, having been taught by them. After their bitter divorce her father married a woman who had only one arm; the other she had lost in a car accident. By this time her father was injecting himself with morphine he stole from the hospital where he worked, and her stepmother treated her as the family slave, awakening her at five in the morning to clean, run errands and serve them until midnight. At thirteen, she ran away to her mother's house but nobody watched over her and her only contact with her father was through the bank machine: whenever she needed money she could take whatever she wanted. By fourteen, she was drinking, hanging out with a group of wild teenagers in Damascus. Then she discovered cocaine and her fiancé, who was now in another sector of the prison.

One evening the warden unlocked the door to the cell. "Get ready," he barked, as Ahlam was handcuffed and blindfolded. "They're going to interrogate you."

She was brought to the familiar room three doors down, where Abu Yusuf was waiting for her. She had not been here in several days, but she remembered his voice very well. He beat her with the stick and reminded her that she was a traitor. Then abruptly he stopped. The door opened and someone was brought in.

"Don't say a word," Abu Yusuf ordered her. "If he hears you, we're going to beat him."

Behind her a confused voice was asking why he had been handcuffed and blindfolded, why had they arrested him, why had they brought him here—what had he done? She knew that voice, and knew her brother's cologne.

Chapter 21

BEIRUT

"SO WHAT BRINGS YOU back to Beirut?" the Emperor asked, rising from behind his desk to kiss me on alternate cheeks. It was close to midnight at MusicHall—the middle of the Emperor's workday, and the end of a very long day for me. I had showered and changed at the hotel room. The giant bouncer at the end of the red carpet leading up to the club had pointed me to the private office behind the coat check.

It was quiet in the office but for the pounding of music in the packed cabaret, where the winter before I had watched red velvet curtains part on a young man who brought the house down with Edith Piaf's anthem regretting nothing. I wished I shared that sentiment. But I needed to talk to the most connected man in Lebanon.

"I had some . . . trouble in Damascus," I explained, sliding into a chair in front of his desk. MusicHall was Beirut's version of Rick's Café in *Casablanca*, though Michel Elefteriades, the Greek-Lebanese impresario who styled himself as "Emperor Michel I of Nowheristan," looked less like Humphrey Bogart and more like the leader of a Gypsy caravan spliced with Che Guevara. I'd interviewed him in the winter, thinking that at some point I would write about this place. I hadn't done so, but the two of us had become friends.

Twirling his sceptre, his cape draped on the back of his chair, he looked pleased to see me, a change from my morning's debacle at the UNHCR office in Douma. Unlike the Englishwoman who had wanted me gone, the Emperor liked having journalists around, passing on rumours or coming to him to confirm them, mixing with the British or French or Spanish ambassadors who paid him homage in his back office, along with politicians, UN officials, spies, and aspiring singers hoping to be discovered. He'd become famous as a judge on the Arab version of the televised singing contest *The X Factor*, but at heart he was a political operator. To him, politics was just another form of theatre.

"Why did you call me from the border?" he asked. "What was the urgency?"

Crossing from Syria into Lebanon had been a problem, but not for the reason I had feared. When I arrived at the customs wicket and presented my passport, the Lebanese border guard had looked from me to his computer screen, from the screen to me. "You," he said, "made a mistake." When I'd misplaced my passport in the winter, I had reported it missing to Lebanese intelligence. Having recovered it immediately afterward, and having had a plane to catch, I had neglected to inform them that the case was closed. Their computer, however, had not forgotten. At least he used that lovely word—mistake—which implied not guilt but incompetence, and could see from my passport photo that I was me.

"Just go back to Damascus," he had said. "We can resolve this in a few days."

"I couldn't go back there," I told the Emperor. I couldn't face the prospect. In Damascus lay confusion, uncertainty, fear, loss, and the distinct possibility that my presence there was doing Ahlam more harm than good. I had to get to Beirut and find some perspective. Even the air along the border smelled fresher, carrying on it the promise of the Mediterranean. The sky seemed higher, less oppressive. Taking out my phone I had called the Emperor, who called someone he knew, and after two hours the border guard waved me through. The officer in charge of the crossing had somehow got the idea that I was booked to perform at MusicHall that night. I realized his misconception when he asked me what instrument I played. "Electric guitar," I said after a moment's pause, fervently hoping someone wouldn't drag a Stratocaster out of a backroom and demand a recital while I protested that the acoustics weren't quite right. Fortunately that did not happen. But they had confiscated my passport—they said I could pick it up at the General Security headquarters in Beirut.

"You were in Syria again," the Emperor said. "With your people, the refugees?" Through the walls I could hear a woman's voice belting out "Unchain My Heart." Customers would be dancing in the aisles by now, waiters uncorking champagne.

"Yes." I explained the broad outlines of Ahlam's arrest. "The charges against her—providing weapons to militias, running a human trafficking operation—it's all bullshit. It has to be. Maybe they're upset because she was talking to reporters, working for journalists, even when they'd told her

to stop." I was coming around to Hamid's interpretation—
that this was somehow about her work as a fixer, though
exactly how wasn't clear to me. Hamid thought the arrest
was meant to send a signal to other Iraqis who worked with
journalists and to the refugees for whom she was a prominent figure, to keep them in line.

The Emperor tugged on his goatee, thinking. A waiter
entered, bringing me a glass of Riesling on a tray. The
Emperor was drinking Red Bull. He liked to be sober when
nobody else was because his drug of choice was information.

"Have you spoken to—?" He reeled off a list of names,
most of whom I had already contacted.

"I'm planning to go to the UNHCR here," I said. "And
Human Rights Watch. She worked for them both."

Through the walls came thunderous applause. The singer
would be taking her bow. "She's one of my new discoveries,"
the Emperor said, smiling.

"How long do you think they will hold Ahlam?" I persisted.

"A few months. Three, four. If they are sending a message
they will want to make it stick. Then, when she comes out,
she will know to do as she's told. And because of the gravity
of the charges against her, she won't be able to talk about
what happened."

It made sense. The charges were serious, the sort that
you'd accuse people of if you want to ensure they will say
nothing later on—if they are ever released. In an atmosphere
of distrust, ludicrous allegations were all too easy to believe.
Had she simply been accused of working for media, or being
too bold in advocating for refugees, it would look like political repression. But not this way. This way, the victim became
the guilty party, responsible for her own fate.

The Emperor offered to talk to people he knew. He held out a hand laden with silver rings.

"Anything. Thank you," I said, taking his hand.

To be without a passport is to lose your freedom. Until I could get it back I was in bureaucratic limbo. And getting it back was not as easy as I had been led to expect. I had thought I would stay in Beirut for three or four days, maybe a week—just long enough to catch my breath—but I had not counted on having it confiscated, or the runaround that would ensue.

"Oh, they can hold your passport for months," an American journalist I met in Beirut told me. We were sitting in a rooftop restaurant above Hamra Street, watching the camera crew that had commandeered the street below. Beirut is never more Beirut than after a conflict: less than two months ago there had been fighting here between Sunni militiamen— said to be supported by the US and Saudi Arabia, which hoped to divide the region between Sunni and Shia spheres, isolating Iran and Syria—and Lebanese Shia Hezbollah.[34] Some of the Sunni fighters were said to be Salafi jihadists who had earned their stripes in Iraq, but they were handily beaten. The Lebanese army had remained on the sidelines to avoid a civil war, and with each street that was captured, the fighters from Hezbollah handed the army control. Five minutes after the ceasefire, café owners were busy moving chairs out onto terraces. The large plate-glass window in the women's shoe shop next to my hotel still had a bullet hole, but otherwise all evidence of the fighting had been cleaned up as if it never happened. Tonight the crew was filming a music video—under strong lights, a young man with a bouquet of roses ran after a girl in a red dress.

"Months?" I said, incredulous. "You think it could take *months*?"

Having felt trapped in Damascus, I had somehow, in my attempted escape, landed in another trap. Every time I went to the General Security headquarters in downtown Beirut, handing over my phone, passing through a metal detector, descending into the cement holding pen in the basement, I waited two or three hours until an officer told me to come back again in a few days when the matter would be sorted. I knew I should probably offer to pay a "fee," but no one had offered the opportunity.

It was disturbing to be back inside the prison of this vast intelligence complex, silently watching an officer clean his gun or question a poor Ethiopian runaway maid until her employer showed up in his business suit to claim her, all the while knowing that Ahlam was in a prison somewhere like this in Damascus—only worse, because she would be locked in one of the cells, and I feared what her interrogations were like. Was she being beaten? Was she being tortured?

To distract myself and pass the time I borrowed a copy of Hemingway's A *Moveable Feast* from the prison library, putting it back when I gave up for the day, knowing I could finish it the next time.

In between, thanks to the Emperor, I made headway over the next two weeks. I spoke with Nadim Khoury, the deputy director of Human Rights Watch's Middle East and North Africa division. We met at an elegant restaurant downtown, part of the old historic bazaar that had been destroyed in

Lebanon's civil war and had only now, more than fifteen years after the war ended, been rebuilt. This was a sanitized, corporatized version of the ancient souk, people complained, without the soul of the original, a cash grab for elites who had privatized it. But at least wars end, I thought. At least people rebuild.

We stalled on the first idea—his offer to write a letter to the Syrian president demanding her release. "What if that just confirms that she worked for you?" I asked. "What if we're only giving them the proof they are looking for?" If they were after her for her work as an unofficial fixer, there were few worse crimes than illegally fixing for a human rights organization that was not supposed to be in Syria at all.

The UNHCR staff in Beirut couldn't do much that the Damascus branch hadn't, but they were happier to talk to me. They appeared less paranoid than their colleagues in Damascus, perhaps because they had less reason to be, because they were less infected by whatever hung in the air there. I felt the same way—Beirut was good for my state of mind even if I felt miserable most of the time. I was able to write emails and make phone calls without censoring myself, and walk down the streets without looking over my shoulder. People sat on café terraces, staring at their phones and gossiping, the women so brazenly dressed that I looked like a prude by comparison. There were good days and bad, but I found that keeping myself busy was the best way to manage depression, so I didn't mind going to General Security for the fifth and sixth time, and finishing Hemingway's memoir of the lost generation in Paris after the First World War.

I was in touch with Marianne and Alessandro, who were also trying to help Ahlam. Her arrest happened to coincide with their multi-family wedding in Italy, so they had diverted through Damascus on their honeymoon. Over Skype to Damascus I told them what I had learned—that she was imprisoned in Douma, and the allegations. And Marianne, in her quiet, steely way, had been active. She told me she had contacted a lawyer she knew who had worked at UNHCR in Damascus—of course, as luck would have it, the lawyer had left the refugee agency the week before—but she was also in touch with someone who knew someone at the US State Department, who said that Ahlam had been cleared for resettlement to the US around the time of her arrest. Ahlam hadn't said anything to me, but that was easy to understand: being cleared for resettlement simply meant you should expect to wait around for a year or two while nothing happened, if it ever did.

Marianne had just met with the UNHCR protection officer handling Ahlam's case. "He says they don't know which prison she is in, or what the accusations are against her. He says it's a black hole."

"They know," I replied. It was near sunset and I was sitting on the balcony of my hotel room. One of the reasons it was cheap was that it overlooked a vacant lot where a huge machine spent most daylight hours boring an enormous and apparently pointless hole in the ground, scattering rocks and sand, never appearing to make any progress. It struck me as an apt metaphor for my life at the moment. "They know, but they don't want us to get in their way." We were supposed to stay outside the yellow tape while the experts got on with things.

The protection officer gave Marianne the same advice he had given to me: don't go public—no big human rights campaigns—since anything we did on her behalf could be used against her. After talking to him, Marianne had spoken to an official at the French embassy in Damascus, who told her they had a hard time even getting their own citizens out of prison. "Essentially, it would be the job of the Iraqi embassy to get Ahlam out," she said. That wasn't even worth discussing. It was discouraging news.

She and Alessandro were about to leave Damascus and wanted to see me in Lebanon. They asked me to meet them at a lodge in the mountains, and overrode my protests that I couldn't afford it and considered myself terrible company, a possible hex on romantic relationships. I took a collective taxi, a large white van that rattled up hills, moving from the smoggy July haze over Beirut to greener and cleaner climes, seated next to an excitable girl who wore a small crucifix on a slim silver chain. Passing Bsharri, the quaint village where the poet Khalil Gibran was born, and apricot trees spilling their ripe fruit onto the road, I reached the lodge next to the last stand of the famous cedars of Lebanon. A stone wall, a few acres: a tree museum.

That evening Alessandro ignored the signs forbidding him to do so and clambered onto the stone wall. He walked around it, arms outspread against a sunset that dyed the whole sky red. Marianne shouted warnings that he ignored, to our delight. Their happiness together was stronger than my unhappiness, an antidote. Late into the night, in the wood-panelled dining room and up in rooms decorated with bright handmade carpets, we discussed Ahlam and what to do over very good red wine that seemed to have restorative powers.

We talked about my return to Damascus as soon as I could get my passport back. "Ahlam's brother must know something,"

I said. They hadn't met Salaam, or any of the young men I'd come to know at Ahlam's apartment, but I thought I might be able to reach Salaam safely through Hamza, Ahlam's assistant. Hamza had told me that the children were fine, and that Salaam was talking to the mukhabarat. I had to get there soon, while I still had a few more weeks left on my Syrian visa; and money was short so I had best use my time wisely. By the time I left them, two days later, and descended to the seaside of Beirut, something of my former self had returned to me. I was feeling bloody-minded. I descended further, into the basement of the intelligence complex, and again found the officer who was supposed to be handling my case.

"My brother is getting married," I told him, meeting his gaze. "In three days. In Jordan. My family is expecting me. I need my passport immediately—they will be heartbroken by my absence."

"Come back tomorrow," he said.

"You always say that." Only he didn't. He usually said to come back in a few days. "I have been here seven times."

"Come back tomorrow," he repeated.

When I appeared the next day, he reached into a drawer in his desk and handed me my passport. It must have been there the whole time.

That night, I took a collective taxi back to Damascus to look for Salaam, but it was too late.

Chapter 22

THE CHILDREN

THE MORNING THEIR MOTHER disappeared, Abdullah and Roqayah had gone to school as usual. It was the last day of classes, the beginning of the summer break, so they picked up their diplomas, wishing their mother was there to see the ceremony. But their mother wasn't at home, either, when they returned. No one was there except Hamza, the young man who lived with them. Later that day, a middle-aged cousin came and took them to her home. It was then that they heard their mother was in jail. She wasn't coming back.

When Roqayah asked people why her mother had been arrested, she heard different answers:

"It's your dad's fault."

"It's because of the Iraqis getting her in trouble."

"It's the foreigners she worked with."

"Her friend Mona informed on her."

She didn't know what to think, and her older brother seemed even more confused that she was, as if it was normal that their mother was in prison and they were sleeping on the floor at a widowed cousin's along with her five kids. In fact, the cousin was hardly ever around. Since her husband had been murdered, she had become a wealthy man's second wife, so she often left the younger children in the care of her teenaged daughters when she went to join him.

After a couple of weeks, one of the refugees—an Iraqi man who had been tortured in Abu Ghraib under the Americans and never quite recovered, and had often been in their apartment asking their mother for this or that—told their cousin that he would take them to the police station in Little Baghdad. Maybe if the police saw the two orphans, he said, they would realize they needed their mother and free her.

"How are you related to them?" an officer asked the man.

"I'm their uncle." It was a lie.

"Why don't *you* take them then?"

Perhaps that's when the idea came to him, or perhaps he'd had it all along. He took them to his home instead of returning them to their cousin's apartment. His own flat was filthy: insects crawling on the floor, a flooded kitchen, a big pile of dirty laundry in the bathroom that reeked of mildew. His wife, an angry and depressed woman, ordered her husband around incessantly; he seemed afraid of her. That night the man called their father, who was still in Baghdad, and put the kids on the phone. When he took the phone back there was something said about money. Within a few days they had moved with the man and his wife to a big new apartment.

Every night the children spoke by phone to their father in their village outside Baghdad. He could not come to them because he had been threatened in Damascus over unpaid debts. They also sometimes spoke to their aunt Tutu, their mother's sister. Roqayah didn't like to complain—at nine years of age she had accepted the fact that complaints changed nothing—but one evening she confessed to her aunt that the man they were staying with frightened her; he often walked around the children in nothing but his underwear. Frantic with worry, Tutu made the dangerous journey from Baghdad to Damascus to claim them.

Salaam had been working all this time, or he would have claimed them sooner. Now, with his sister Tutu there to help him, he rented an apartment for the four of them in Sayeda Zainab. They made a point of spoiling the kids, taking them to a nearby amusement park, paying for them to go on rides. Safe in the arms of family, smothered with attention, the children seemed almost okay.

On the morning of July 1, Salaam stopped by a transportation company to pick up the money he was owed for his work as a driver. The man who worked at the office stalled him. "Just wait," he said. "Come back in a bit."

Salaam decided to use the time to pick up a load of clean clothes from the laundry, thinking to bring it back to his apartment and take a shower. He was a good-looking man, if carrying a bit of extra weight that was a professional hazard for drivers, and took pains with his appearance. He looked forward to spending time with his nephew and niece who were at the apartment with Tutu.

Salaam had been meeting people from the mukhabarat to try to find out more about his other sister, but he had soon realized there were many Syrian security and intelligence departments and they didn't all communicate. That day he was determined, after he had picked up his laundry and taken a shower, to try again to find someone who could help him. He had helped raise the money to pay for Ahlam's ransom in Baghdad; if he could find the right person to bribe, he would gladly pay for her to be released again.

But at the laundry, he saw the man from the transportation company. He was pointing him out to a group of men. The men arrested him right there.

At intelligence headquarters, four agents stood around a man seated at a desk who introduced himself as Captain Abu Yusuf.

"What's going on?" Salaam asked him. "Why did you bring me here?"

He was shown photos of Ahlam and her husband with the American military outside their house in Baghdad. The Americans had given Ahlam the photos as a souvenir; she had hidden them with her documents.

"That's my sister," Salaam told them. "And that's her husband."

"Where is he?"

"Not here. He's in Iraq."

With that Salaam was handcuffed, wrists behind his back, and driven to his apartment. Tutu opened the door. Abu Yusuf marched past her into the apartment. The terrified children ran to their aunt. "Where's your machine gun?" he demanded of Salaam, who denied having a weapon.

Calmly and methodically, they tore the place apart. With Abu Yusuf directing, the four agents turned over mattresses, pulled everything from the cupboards and closets. Looked under the fridge, inside the fridge. After they had searched the living room, they directed the family to sit there. Tutu chain-smoked. Salaam asked if he could smoke but was told, "Not now."

They found nothing. An hour later Salaam was blindfolded in addition to being handcuffed and taken back to the vehicle. They took him to Douma Prison, the same prison where Ahlam was being held, though he did not know this.

The guards took his wallet and his clothing, leaving him in his underwear. He would only be allowed to dress when he went into interrogation. In the meantime he was taken to a solitary cell in the basement of the north sector of the building. The guards didn't speak except to call him a son of a bitch, and to insult his mother and sister.

It was one month and a day from his sister's arrest.

Two and a half weeks after Salaam was arrested, I crossed from Lebanon through the Syrian border without incident. This could mean one of two things. Either I was not being watched, or I was and they did not want me to know it. But something had changed. I was no longer afraid. Go ahead. Follow me around. Arrest me. I realized that I could accept many things. I could accept not fulfilling whatever ambitions had landed me here in the first place. I could accept the knowledge that nothing I wrote or would ever write would change a thing and that the world would continue to create and destroy and create and destroy as it always did. I could accept living without a relationship. I would still be okay. What I could not accept was Ahlam being gone. It was unthinkable that she had been missing for almost seven weeks. Unthinkable that she could be lost and never heard from again. Unthinkable that I could do nothing. Even though I knew how many other people in other prisons had been missing for years until everyone who had known them forgot or moved on.

My first call was to Hamid. This time we arranged to meet at the downtown apartment where I had spent that first claustrophobic night after Ahlam disappeared, off a busy main street filled with women's shoe shops, overtop a convenience store. The freelance journalist who had rented it had flown home early so was no longer worried that my troubles might be contagious. She had generously offered that I could stay there. It was too dangerous to return to the apartment I'd been at before and I didn't want to: I had felt powerless there.

In the living room was a small TV and a couple of heavy books—one about genocide, another about the civil war in Lebanon, that she must have deemed too cumbersome to pack. Hamid and I sat on chairs with the lights off. In the window stood cactus plants, needles out like armed sentries. Hamid's face looked grey, the skin slack around his eyes. He was smoking again, not even bothering to claim otherwise.

"What happened to you?" I asked. I had received a distressed email from Gabriela, the Czech-American photojournalist, who had been planning to come back to Syria, saying he had told her he couldn't be her fixer anymore; he had stopped that line of work. Gabriela could tell he seemed demoralized. She wondered if it was because his youngest son, suffering the disruptions, had done poorly on his final high-school exams, making it difficult to apply to universities abroad. And that was the sole aim of Hamid's life: getting his children out.

But of course it wasn't that. Or not only that.

While I was in Lebanon, Hamid told me, he had been called in for questioning by one of the intelligence agencies. Forced to sit for days in a waiting room, ordered back in each morning, leaving at closing time, coming back the next day. No one told him why he had been summoned. "It's a technique," he said. "It breaks you down."

When at last he had an audience with an intelligence official, he could not figure out from their line of questioning why they had called him in. "They didn't say her name." Ahlam's, he meant. If her arrest had been intended to send a message, the message had been received. Hamid stopped fixing.

Meeting with me now placed him in danger. I knew he only did so because loyalty was built into his marrow, a quality even self-preservation could not trump. But as he explained bluntly though with diplomacy—it was nothing personal—he could not help me anymore.

I understood. And was grateful for the help and support he had given, a solid presence when I had felt myself sinking. And it was thanks to Hamid, indirectly, that I learned the fate of Ahlam's younger brother.

It was Hamza who told me. The blue-eyed one who had met us under the bridge by the university after dark the month before. When I phoned Hamid upon arriving in Damascus, I'd called one of the numbers listed as "H" in my notebook— not the most sophisticated coding system: Hamza answered. But he was glad I had called, and eager to see me again. I arranged to see him on my own, keeping in mind that Hamid had told me he didn't trust him.

We met at the Umayyad Cave, a dank cellar restaurant down a back street in the Old City. Descending the stone staircase, I found myself in what appeared to be a clandestine meeting place for couples. Lovers' murmured conversations filled the darkness. Taking an empty table in a corner, I ordered tea and nuts in Arabic from the old man who ran the place. Hamza and I had agreed to arrive and leave separately, removing the batteries from our phones.

Hamza brought an English-speaking friend in his early twenties, another of the young guys who used to hang out at

Ahlam's apartment. It occurred to me that without Ahlam to direct their energies and keep them out of trouble, these boys were amoral, good or bad depending on the winds, but mainly concerned with their own survival. All of them, Hamza said, had been practising the answer to whether or not they knew Ahlam. "Who's she?" he quipped, laughing nervously. When you're in enough trouble, nobody knows your name.

I pressed Hamza on what had happened to Ahlam's children. He told me the kids were fine, that he knew where they were staying. "But they took Salaam," he said.

"Took him where?"

Hamza didn't know anything more, except that in trying to have his sister released, Salaam had been arrested himself.

The restaurant manager, grey and thin, hovered over our table, pressing us to order more or get out. I could tell from his leering smile that he thought I was involved in some sort of ménage à trois. This place was run like a hot-sheet motel. I ordered a bottle of water to make him go away. "I want to see the kids," I said.

Not possible. Too dangerous. But if I gave Hamza money he would arrange for me to talk to them; he'd put them on the phone. I pulled out my wallet and counted out three thousand pounds—the equivalent of sixty dollars. It would be worth it if I got some answers. If not he could support himself for a few weeks.

The next day Hamza rang. He put a young boy on the line. I didn't recognize the voice. It could have been any child—any kid on the street.

Hamid was right. They were lying to me.

Chapter 23

UNEXPECTED REVELATIONS

"I HAVE A SURPRISE FOR YOU," said Rana. She was wearing all red today. Bright as a strawberry. We were at our designated meeting place in the square outside the Umayyad Mosque in the Old City. I took off my sunglasses to greet her. The square was flush with sunshine, with tourists, pigeons, and hundreds of Iranians on pilgrimage. One of the pilgrims had his video camera trained on the pretty Syrian girls walking past. Not very pious, I thought.

"What surprise?"

She looked excited, in her typical understated way. "We are going to the hammam."

I had long been talking about going to one of the public baths. There had never been time. I had always been working, or thinking about work. It was strange how little any of that mattered anymore.

Rana, however, was on a mission to turn me back into a human being. She had taken me shopping the day before.

"You can't only wear black," she said. She hated black. Never wore it. She was always a festival of colour.

"I actually *like* wearing black," I said. "Black goes with everything. It goes with black."

She took me to a French shop in Sha'alan and insisted I try on something *not* black. I left with a turquoise knit shirt that she approved of, and a pale blue dress the colour of the sky at dawn. In another week I had to leave. The flight had been booked out of Jordan months ago and my visa was set to expire. The only consolation was that I had exhausted everything I could do here for Ahlam so must see what could be done for her from the outside.

I followed Rana around behind the mosque, away from the crowds. She took me towards an obscure doorway that I never would have found on my own.

One day a week the hammam was reserved for women. In the reception area we paid the small fee and undressed, hanging our clothes on pegs on the wall. Beneath her red headscarf Rana had a chin-length curly bob. With her low, throaty voice, she looked and sounded like a jazz singer in 1930s Paris.

I hung up my jeans, then my shirt. "All my clothes?" I asked. "Everything?" I took my time, unsure of how to do this, feeling out of my element. The receptionist had handed each of us a shard of olive oil soap and a towel not much bigger than a napkin. I tried various methods of arranging the tiny towel around myself, each of which involved sacrificing something else. Passing through the wooden door into the baths, a thick cloud of steam enveloped us. Warmth and water, acres of white marble. Hot water running from taps onto the floor, bowls with which to douse yourself. Young and old women mixed, the body's timeline of blossom and decay. An old woman with long hair in a thin white braid overturned a bowl and begun drumming, singing a folk song as her grandbabies tottered around her. I was struck, not for the first time, by how much more comfortable Muslim women are with their bodies than we are in the West.

After an hour, my skin had softened and I began to feel lighter. As I sat there, blanketed in steam, pouring hot water over my back, a large woman with thick arms lumbered in. She wore a cotton housedress over strong bare legs. "Go with her," said Rana, as the woman seized me by the shoulders.

She pulled me into a side room, indicating a table where I should lie down. I lay down on my stomach while she gave me the sort of massage that felt like a beating. Pounding my arms, my shoulders, my back, my legs. So hard it must have left bruises. When she deigned to release me, I stumbled back into the main chamber, aware that I hadn't thought of a single one of my problems during the massage.

"How was it?" Rana asked, pouring a bowl of hot water over her back.

"I got out alive," I said. "Your turn now."

When the masseuse came back with Rana, it was my turn again. This time I was made to lie down on the marble floor in front of everyone and with an abrasive mitt the woman scraped the entire outer layer of skin off my body, treating me like a pot that had burned on the stove. Rana started laughing.

"Why are you laughing?"

"You're so dirty."

"It only looks that way because I'm so pale otherwise," I protested. "The dirt shows." The dark matter. The dark thoughts, the bad energy, sloughed off me. I should have come here long ago.

I still had no news of Ahlam's children, or the whereabouts of Salaam, but on my third to last evening in Damascus a tiny window opened in the fortress. A glimpse, however shadowy, of how things might have come to pass.

That night I was invited to the home of a man who was famous among the expat crowd. A tall handsome theatre director who taught Arabic to foreigners, he could also have taught the art of cool. Late forties, with a rope of coiled hair pulled back in a Rasta-like ponytail, he walked with a natural grace and seemed always to have an arm draped around one or more beautiful women. Mazen was also an excellent cook—someone who could disappear into his kitchen at the arrival of unexpected guests and emerge moments later with a feast.

It was a Thursday night—his weekly salon. I had been to one such gathering last year, after the opening ceremony for Ahlam's school when the tribe of Westerners in attendance, wishing to drink beer, had migrated here.

Like Ahlam, our host was the sort of person who knew everyone. They had known one another, of course, and it was for that reason that I sought him out that night. He had spent several years in a Syrian prison in the 1980s, the time of the Muslim Brotherhood uprisings and the vicious crackdown that followed, when he was falsely accused of being a communist.

"Prison cured me of politics," Mazen told me. Now he lived for the moment. He threw the best parties in all of Damascus. In the prison kitchen he had learned to cook for a crowd.

A book-filled bohemian house, world beats on the stereo, the place jammed with anthropologists and journalists and aid workers. Bottles arrived in brown paper bags, supplemented by our host's extensive liquor cabinet. He had an open-door policy—anyone was welcome at any time, the locals mixing with the foreigners. That way, according to the theory he outlined to me, he prevented suspicions from arising. If anyone wondered what he was up to, why people were coming and going at all hours, they were welcome to come over and join in.

Around midnight I was sitting alone at the table in his outdoor courtyard, vines trailing up the walls, drinking a third glass of wine and smoking apple tobacco from a water pipe. The evening air was cool, but I couldn't bear to be around so many people, making conversation.

A woman, young and pretty, came outside to introduce herself, having had me pointed out to her by our host. It turned out she was the Syrian wife of the British photographer I had met at the café, the one who had taken to sending himself extracts from medical websites about "elephantiasis of the testicles and the like" after she had been ordered to spy on him.

"You knew Ahlam, right?" She had to raise her voice to be heard over the music.

I nodded, exhaling a plume of smoke. She said she had heard about the arrest, and also the reasons why.

"Why?" I asked.

"For smuggling guns to Iraqi militias and human trafficking." She uttered the charges, which I had heard earlier, like a fact. Accusations that were laughable but extremely dangerous: rumours have an afterlife because rumour is soon treated as fact and becomes fact through repetition.

"Who," I asked, "told you that?"

"Mona," she said.

"Mona." It took a moment to register, pieces falling into place. Mona, in her belted raincoat, her gypsy hair and aura of permanent discontent. The unlikely bleeding heart. I had forgotten all about Mona. Had she been, all along, a spy?

Stunned, I envisioned various scenarios, all of which overlapped and intertwined like the vines snaking up the walls of the courtyard where I sat.

Scenario One: as a Syrian fixer, Mona would have to report to the Ministry of Information. Unlike Ahlam, who as an Iraqi worked unofficially, Mona would have to tell the Ministry every movement of her clients. Perhaps she had gained permission to work as a fixer in exchange for a little espionage on the side (Abu Yusuf's offer to Ahlam rang again in my mind), tracking Ahlam all along. Perhaps she had come up with the charges just to bolster her worth as an informant.

Scenario Two: more generously, perhaps, before or after Ahlam's arrest, she had been called in for questioning by intelligence and fed these lies, which she later repeated. Spreading the word, a smear campaign: equally effective in shutting Ahlam down.

Scenario Three: seeing Ahlam as a rival—"She wanted to be in the picture," Ahlam's friend Tarek had said, to be the fixer everyone wanted—she set out to destroy her main competition. Even if Ahlam did get out, with such charges following her, no journalist would go near her again.

I felt a rage so hot and fierce it had a cleansing force. "That's bullshit," I told the woman, "and you should know it. If Ahlam was involved in human smuggling, don't you think she would have smuggled herself and her children out first? And she hated the militias. They destroyed everything."

The woman turned and went back to the party. I picked up the water pipe, drawing on it until the coals glowed red. Was Mona involved? If so, how?

Chapter 24

AHLAM'S STORY
PART THREE

"WE'RE HAVING A MEETING," Leila told the other women in the cell. It was what she and Ahlam always said when the two of them squeezed into the bathroom stall after midnight to share a smoke, when the warden had left.

"You'll be caught," warned one of their new cellmates, "and we will all be punished because of you."

"They won't catch us," said Leila, smiling as she twirled the cigarette between her fingers. "They *gave* it to us."

Where the old guard, Sadiq, was careful only to hold the cigarettes to their lips, the younger guards were less wary, handing out cigarettes liberally, especially when Leila asked. The guards had also given them lighters, one of which had fuel but no flint, the other flint but no fuel, so they used the one to light the other, and otherwise hid them on the far side of the shelf so the warden would not find out and punish the guards.

In the bathroom they shared the cigarette back and forth, discussing their fates. Leila's fiancé was an underworld character who had come up with a fantastical scheme to sell uranium to the Israelis. One night when the two of them were partying at a hotel room in Jordan he'd dialled the Israeli embassy or consulate—Leila couldn't remember much, she was stoned out of her mind—and put her on the phone, telling her to make an appointment. The next day she returned to Damascus. Syrian agents, alerted by Jordanian intelligence, rousted her from her bed—she had been here ever since, awaiting trial for the past six months.

Like Leila, Ahlam had no idea when she would get out. After hearing Salaam's voice, smelling the cologne that lingered on his clothing, she pounded her own face in grief. The next day she was again brought to the interrogation room. This time Abu Yusuf had been replaced by a new interrogator who removed her blindfold and handcuffs. He was a dandy in a pink shirt with dyed black hair; a man of fifty who wanted to be twenty. He didn't lay a hand on her, only wanted her to answer a list of questions, most of which concerned Iraq. In particular he wanted to know whether she had heard any senior officers of the US military threatening to attack Syria. That, then, was the motivating fear: everything that had happened to her stemmed from it.

She answered his questions, and was about to do as instructed and put her thumbprint to the bottom of her testimony, then stopped and looked at him.

"What is it?" the dandy asked.

"I have only one question."

"What's that?"

"Why am I here?"

He was silent for a long time. Finally he said, "Because you're not cooperating with the officer." Captain Abu Yusuf. Whose career aspirations were going down the drain.

A guard came to take her back to the cell. "What are the charges against her?" the guard asked the interrogator. She was moved that he seemed to have spoken up for her.

"None of your business," he said, not looking up from his report.

She hadn't seen her brother again. She had asked the guards about Salaam, but they figured he was in another sector of the prison that they did not enter.

Dropping the cigarette into the squat toilet, Leila sprayed the air with a bottle of perfume a guard had given her. They squeezed back out of the bathroom and rejoined the women who now shared their cell.

Along with a surly Kurd, who was there for forty days, there were many other women coming and going from the same four-by-four metres that Leila patrolled with her endless pacing. All the prisoners had been arrested for stupid reasons. A Libyan woman of twenty-five who had run away to marry her Egyptian boyfriend, whose parents had sent word to the Libyan embassy in Damascus to round her up. Another Libyan had fled a husband who was demanding her back. A Palestinian whose son had been caught illegally selling gasoline ration vouchers; her husband had also been jailed for their son's crime.

Two Syrian women, Salafis who followed a strict, conservative version of Sunni Islam that sought an Islamic state, were the only ones who veiled their faces. The older woman had a husband imprisoned in Guantánamo, arrested by the Americans in Pakistan for involvement with al-Qaeda. Trying to reach her husband, whom she hadn't heard from in three years, she had enlisted the younger one to help her write to her lawyer in London, since she didn't know how to use email. The two of them had been accused of conspiring with their lawyer, who was Jewish. In fact, had their interrogators paid the least attention, they might have discovered that the women knew quite a bit about al-Qaeda's operations in Syria—operations that would soon transform all of Syria, and the region, as al-Qaeda alternatively broke from or joined the Islamic State.

Then there were the two wives of a man from Aleppo. The first wife, married off at the age of twelve, very pretty and very probably insane, had been arrested for singing a comic ditty mocking President Bashar. The second wife, very fat, was arrested for not turning in the first; she sat in a heap on the floor and cried that her brothers would kill her when she got out.

The two wives talked competitively about the costumes they wore for their husband, the dances they performed for him, since they split the nights. What infuriated the first wife most was not the fact of being in jail, nor even having her feet beaten during interrogations until they were so swollen that she could no longer wear shoes, but that the agents who searched her home had ransacked her teddy bear collection. She spent her time singing and dancing and trying to seduce the guards in exchange for cigarettes. One night she shouted and pounded the cell door so hard that the guards threw an entire pack through the slat and slammed it closed. Whenever any of the women prayed—and the Salafi women were usually praying—she mocked them. "You are just praying now because you're in trouble. If you weren't in trouble you would forget God!"

Four Ethiopian girls arrived, housemaids who had run away from their employers in Lebanon. They had been

caught with false passports in Syria. With them were captured several Iraqi men who had been trying to have themselves smuggled to Turkey in hope of making it to Greece
and jobs in Europe. The Ethiopian girls were eventually sent
to an immigration centre for deportation, while the Iraqis
were sent to the men's cell next door, from which Ahlam
heard the most terrible cries.

Twice a day the male prisoners from the cell next door
were shuffled in small groups into the hallway outside the
cells to use the bathroom, since unlike the women they did
not have a toilet. Every time, they were beaten with sticks
and strips of rubber tire along the way. With the women
the guards could be kind, playing the music of Fairuz for
them first thing in the morning, even letting them watch
an American movie on a TV they set up in front of the cell
door, sneaking them food or cigarettes. But to the men the
guards showed no mercy.

While being beaten the men were forced to repeat, again
and again, "Jail is a school to teach us how to behave." And
when the guards were bored, they went into the men's cell
and randomly whipped the prisoners.

One day a batch of male prisoners arrived from Aleppo.
They had been arrested for the crime of having tattoos. The
oldest was no more than twenty-five, the youngest barely in
his teens. They were beaten upon arrival, ten strokes each.
"We must teach you to be real Arab men and not to defile
your bodies," they were told.

One of the guards who often gave Ahlam cigarettes
handed his blood-spattered shirt to the women to rinse
under the thin shower in their bathroom, before the blood
could set. He showed Ahlam his hands, how the skin had

blistered from all the beatings he had delivered.

"How can you do this work?" Ahlam asked him. "These men are human beings."

"Listen to me," he told her. He was angry. "I know not everyone in this jail deserves to be here, but what can I do? I'm just a guard." He had taken the job because he had no education—even the most educated guard had not completed the sixth grade—and the salary of two hundred dollars a month fed and housed his family. If he wanted to quit, he would have to bribe someone and get a medical report to prove he could not finish his commitment. "You have to serve for twenty years."

Another of the guards, the youngest of all, refused to beat a thin old man who was obviously ill. Instead he slipped the old man food and allowed him to take showers in the heat of summer. When the warden found out, he beat the guard in front of the old man. From the slit beneath the door of her cell, Ahlam could hear blow follow blow.

After midnight, Leila talked to the men in the neighbouring cell through the heating pipe along the back wall, asking how their day was or what they'd had for lunch. There were thirty men in a cell the same size as theirs. They had to sleep in shifts, legs to head, the others standing until they changed places.

It was a mystery what was happening in the far cell on the other side of the men's. This was known as the "al-Qaeda cell," for the fifteen or so men who had been arrested as part of a crackdown designed to please the Americans. Ahlam already knew that Syria was cooperating with the US to prove they were coming down on al-Qaeda, though the cooperation went much further than she knew. Among the fifty-four countries involved with a top-secret CIA program that kidnapped and "extraordinarily rendered" terrorist suspects to be tortured abroad after 9/11, Syria, along with Jordan and Egypt, was one of the most common destinations.[35]

The prisoners in the al-Qaeda cell had been there for a long time—a year and a half according to the guards, who had strict orders not to go near them. But in all that time, the guards had heard no evidence against them.

The only time Ahlam saw anyone from the al-Qaeda cell was when those prisoners went on a hunger strike. One of them lost consciousness and a doctor was summoned. She heard him being carried into the corridor outside the cells. She pressed her eye to the small hole by the slat where the welding had chipped away. She could just make out a man who appeared to be in his fifties, and heard him talking weakly to the doctor in the hallway. "I have four children," the man was saying. "I fled Iraq to give them a secure life. I was targeted down there, I had to flee my house, and now they have arrested me because I have money. Is that a crime?" He began to cry. "Nobody knows where I am, not my children, not my wife, nobody."

It reminded Ahlam of what Abu Yusuf had said the last time he spoke to her. "You can stay here for years," were his final words, "and nobody will know where you are."

Before prison, Ahlam had dreamed of having forty-eight hours in a day: time to rest, to eat, to finish the tasks she had set herself. Now time stretched out as it had not done before. Never, with the exception of her kidnapping in Iraq, had she had nothing to do but wait. Her back ached from sleeping on the concrete floor. The thin blankets were infested with bed bugs. She pleaded with the guards for medication to help her sleep through the pain but it made her dizzy so she stopped taking it. She tried to remember how to do yoga. Stretching up and over, up and over, breathing from the stomach. The other women laughed, all except Leila, who joined her. Leila practised yoga. She was always active, pacing back and forth for hours, or nervously toying with the stud in her tongue.

One day a wealthy woman arrived wearing tight capri pants and a low-cut blouse. Brought to the cell, still asking after the gold jewellery that had been confiscated upon her arrest, she demanded to know where to find the air-conditioning unit. Ahlam pointed to the fan high up in the wall, where the faint hints of daylight came through. "That is our air conditioner," she said.

The rich, Ahlam deduced, usually landed in jail because they had offended someone in government or refused to pay off a high official. They were allowed special privileges: to walk around the hallways, to smoke as they pleased, to have their own food delivered to their cells. One of the male prisoners, the guards told her, had been caught with $70,000 in cash at Damascus airport. After he arrived, life became better for everyone.

At night the wealthy prisoner ordered takeout and ate at a table in the corridor with the guards: fried chicken with fries, pizza, good bread with meat or zaatar. He always gave his leftovers to the women. He also bought the women soap, shampoo, sanitary products to replace the strips of old cloth the guards had given them, which they had been forced to wash and reuse. He provided cigarettes for the guards to dispense. The male prisoners never got the leftovers but were given tomatoes and onions to supplement their prison meals and enough cigarettes that they were able to share one among four of them twice a day.

The old guard, Sadiq, had already given Ahlam a contraband toothbrush, though, ever cautious, he worried that any such item might be used for a suicide. One day, Ahlam saw blood on the clothes and hands of the guards. An elderly doctor who had been held in solitary confinement for three months had slashed his wrists with a shard of glass from his spectacles. As punishment for not preventing the man's death, the guards were forced to stay in the prison for ten days without leave.

The wealthy prisoner, when he heard that the women had no change of clothes, bought them three robes in different sizes that they could put on while they hung their laundry to dry from the shelf. Ahlam had not worn new garments since her son died, but she began wearing one of the robes at the urging of the Salafi woman whose husband was imprisoned in Guantánamo. "It's been two years," the woman told her kindly. "It is time to stop mourning."

Whenever chicken was served from the rich man's leftovers, a cat and her kitten came to the opening high in the cell, where the fan was, and Ahlam threw them scraps. The fan roared and clattered, keeping everyone awake at night. When the guards gave them a plastic broom to clean the cell, she or Leila began jamming the broomstick into the blades of the fan in order to sleep.

One night they broke the motor. The next day the fan was removed and taken away for repair. On that day, a small miracle happened.

Ahlam and Leila were sitting on the floor of the cell as usual when a silver-winged butterfly flew in through the opening where the fan had been. Seeing it, they began shouting, ecstatic to see something of the world outside. They were alive, they were not dead. They were living creatures. The youngest guard, the one who had taken a beating in place of the old man, ran over to see the commotion, sliding open the slat. He laughed to see the two of them up and jumping around, excited as children by the winged visitor.

"It's a sign!" he shouted. "It's a sign!"

As the summer gave way to fall, they waited for the sign to be fulfilled.

One night Ahlam dreamed of her son. A group of children wanted him to come outside and play with them. In the yard was a lovely garden with green trees, the children dressed all in white, but she refused to let her son join them. He would be with her always: she would not let him leave.

Sadiq slid open the slat on her cell and saw the tears on her face. "I have a child," he said. "I have a girl." Adding, "We are not the ones who put you in jail."

Taking pity on her, he promised to try to find out the charges against her.

He returned a few days later, holding her prison file. There were several charges against her, he said, and read them out: spying, involvement in human smuggling, and taking money for refugees and giving it to Iraqi militias to buy weapons.

"You are a good and respectable woman," Sadiq told her. "I can't believe this. But someone made this report against you. It is here in the file." He read out the name.

Chapter 25

FAILURE

I WAS LEAVING, AND all my efforts to help Ahlam had come to nothing.

I went over to the taxis bound for Jordan, clustered in a dirt lot next to the Damascus bus station. It was exactly a year since I had met Ahlam. Back then I had wondered how, in the randomness of fortune, I'd found the ideal person to take me to the other side.

I had come here to tell the story of those who lived out the war's inescapable logic; those who had to pay the price that had been set by those who planned their fates and would never be called to account—who might right now be writing policy prescriptions for a well-funded think tank or delivering a keynote address.[36] The article I had written had received some attention, created a ripple. But in the end it had accomplished nothing because it could not roll back time. Had I expected that? Had I harboured, even in my moments of doubt, a grandiose belief in the power of story to alter destiny? I had wanted to understand how the invasion had started a civil war that was dividing the region. There were many who refused those divisions, but the person I knew who most embodied that dignified refusal had vanished.

If I could roll back time, if I could rewind the film of Ahlam's life, editing out the war, she would still be living with her family in their large house on the bank of the Tigris, all of them alive, whole, together, happy or heartbroken in ordinary ways. And here I was, returning to my old life—perhaps in an altered form, perhaps diminished—but her old life had been swallowed long ago.

The sense of powerlessness was humbling. It is how most of the world lives.

I slid into a taxi, joined by three Jordanian businessmen in suits, and we pulled out of the parking lot, towards Amman.

The businessmen, all of whom were in that amorphous profession known as "import-export," spent part of the four-hour journey talking about Saddam Hussein.

A great man. Good for Iraq. Sorely missed.

You would think they were discussing the Dalai Lama.

"Don't you agree?" They tried to draw me into their discussion but I refused to share their high opinion of the man. By almost any measure Iraq was worse off now than it had been before, but his brutality was not in doubt.

On the long flight to New York, I thought about an earlier flight home, shortly after Saddam Hussein's execution at the end of 2006. An African-American in a bomber jacket emblazoned with the words "Operation Iraqi Freedom" had the seat next to mine. A US Navy man during the first Gulf War, he was heading home to Florida on a break from Baghdad, where he worked for a private contractor as a systems engineer. He was from the Deep South, he told me.

He was the only member of his family ever to own a house, and he hadn't seen his home in months.

Not only did he surprise me by being a harsh critic of the war, which he saw as a money-making venture for the likes of Bush, Cheney and Rumsfeld after a kind of mafia-style falling-out with their old friend Saddam, but he said something else that stayed with me.

I said something often said about the war: "This will end badly." He fixed me with an unblinking gaze, as if to compel me to remember, and answered: "This. Will. *Never*. End."

I stopped in New York for ten days on the way back to Vancouver. It was a kind of debriefing, and a chance to coordinate with Marianne and Alessandro, who lived a few blocks from a friend's apartment in Chelsea where I was staying. Walking down streets past art galleries, dog bakeries, and bistros serving twelve-dollar glasses of wine, I overheard anxious chatter about the economy, the stock market, complaints about bosses and bills; everywhere a cash register ringing.

So this is what normal people do . . . I had forgotten. I bought an old hardcover copy of *The Quiet American* from a grey-bearded sidewalk vendor and read it late at night, its pages yellow and musty, its words more real to me than anything I heard on the street. I met with Marianne and Alessandro and other people who knew Ahlam to talk about new avenues, new plans of action.

When I finally reached Vancouver, home, there was no one there to meet me. My luggage had been lost in transit. I was the last person standing at the baggage carousel, watching it go round and round.

PART **FOUR**

Chapter 26

AHLAM'S STORY
PART FOUR

IN THE LATTER HALF of October 2008, the key turned in the lock of the cell. The door swung open to reveal the warden. "Get ready," he said. "You're going home."

Ahlam had nothing to get ready. She said goodbye to the other prisoners in her cell, though the only one she would really miss was Leila, whose transfer the month before to stand trial had been devastating. Leila, though half her age, had become a friend.

She was led outside to a station wagon, where she saw her brother, already seated in the back. "Don't be afraid," Salaam whispered. "We are going home." His clothing hung loosely on his frame. Like her, his wrists were chained, but the chains were long enough for Salaam to reach his wallet, which had been returned with his money still in it. As the gate opened and the car pulled out to the street, he cupped an American hundred-dollar bill in his hand and slipped it in hers. "We might get separated and you will need this."

They were taken to an immigration prison, Salaam to a men's wing and Ahlam to a cell with two dozen women, most of them Africans. The four Ethiopian girls who had been with her in Douma recognized her immediately. "You are here," said the girls, so surprised, in their housemaids' English. "You are here." They told her they were supposed to be deported but the Ethiopian government refused to pay their airfare. "Maybe you will be luckier than us."

The authorities had returned her phones when she left Douma and the first thing Ahlam did was ask to be allowed to make a call. "I want to know about my kids. I'll pay you anything." For twenty dollars, a guard let her out of the cell to use the phone. She called through the numbers but nobody was picking up. Finally she reached Ali, her former assistant. He seemed frightened at the sound of her voice. About her children, he said only, "They've been smuggled to Iraq."

She didn't believe him. She no longer trusted anything anyone said. Her heart thundered in her chest as she wondered if her children were alive or dead.

In the immigration prison the prisoners had to pay for their own food, buying it from the guards, so whoever had money provided for the rest. Over the next three days, with Salaam's money, Ahlam bought chicken, rice, cigarettes, sharing these around. She was convinced she was being sent back to Iraq. Salaam had been immediately deported, to her dismay. She asked a guard why she hadn't been allowed to leave yet. "The buses were full," he said. "We're waiting on your turn."

The third day she was moved again, this time to a huge building where she was taken to a basement. Through the darkness she could make out men sitting on the floor, eating, and hear the sound of other men screaming. She was taken into a vast room the size of an aircraft hangar, and left with six other women who huddled together in complete darkness, except for a tiny window at the top of the wall where the yellow light was fading towards night. The woman next to her, from Aleppo, said she was here because her husband was accused of being al-Qaeda. "They have taken me to pressure my husband to surrender." A girl of about twenty with short black hair ran wildly back and forth, hiding behind her mother at any loud noise. Her mother told Ahlam they had been caught sneaking from Lebanon into Syria. They had no passports, they could probably not even conceive of such documents or how one might obtain them. Poor, uneducated, the daughter mentally ill, they had only wanted to visit the shrine of Sayeda Zainab.

They told her where she was: Military Intelligence Branch 235, the notorious torture prison otherwise known as Palestine Branch.

A door opened, and the girl cowered behind her mother. But this time food appeared—one boiled potato and two tomatoes per inmate. The girl gobbled hers down and began shouting, "I want food! I want food!" Ahlam, who could not eat, gave her meal to the girl.

That night she did not sleep. She sat stock-still in terror, convinced that she would never leave this place. Hours later the door opened. Her name was called.

"Yes," she said.

"Interrogation." That terrifying word.

She stood with great reluctance and followed the guard who would lead her to her fate.

"Please sit down," said the interrogator. A handsome man in his mid-twenties: pale skin, brown hair. "I'm sorry to give you this trouble," he said. "You are my mother's age." He spoke to her calmly in the diction of an educated man. His questions were mainly regarding her husband's business dealings, which had accumulated unpaid debts. He asked her nothing about the Americans, nothing about Iraq, nothing about the allegations in her file. He finally sent her back to her cell in the basement, where she sat next to the mother of the simpleton. Through the window at the top of the wall she watched the break of dawn.

The next day she was transferred back to Douma.

"What are you doing here?" one of the guards asked in surprise.

"This is my home," she told him. "You want to kick me out of my home?" She was overjoyed to be out of the dreaded Palestine Branch.

She was led back to her old cell. From the outside she pulled open the slat in the door and peeked inside. "What are you doing here?" the women asked, as surprised as the guards.

"I missed you so much I came back!"

For the next five days she returned to prison life. On the fifth day the warden came to tell her she was going home. Which could mean anything.

"Expect me to come back to you," she said to her cell-mates as she took her leave, "so don't be bad girls."

Since leaving Damascus, through September and into October, I had been in touch with many different agencies and NGOs, particularly Reporters Without Borders. I wrote a case study, an overview of Ahlam's work for media and human rights groups and the circumstances of her arrest that I was sending to anyone who might be able to help. Marianne had contacted the French foreign ministry, thinking the French government might be able to use their influence with the Syrians. Nothing seemed to be working. We began to talk about a public campaign, though we were still uncertain as to whether it would do more harm than good, as the UNHCR had warned.

In late October, my phone rang in the middle of the night. I groped for it in the dark. When I heard the voice talking on the other end, I came wide awake. "You're a friend of Ahlam?" the man asked. It was a researcher from Amnesty International, apologizing that he was unfamiliar with my time zone. Ahlam, he said, had been Amnesty's fixer-translator on four reports in 2007 and 2008. As I sat in the pre-dawn darkness of my new apartment in Vancouver, boxes of unpacked books stacked against the walls, we discussed details around her arrest. He asked me to email him the case study I had written. We talked about the possibility of launching an international media campaign if all else failed.

"We are going to give it one more week first," he said. Amnesty was speaking with the UNHCR about her case, letting them know they would soon be taking action. "If nothing happens, we go public."

From Douma Prison, Ahlam was taken back to the immigration prison where she had last seen her brother. She had no idea what was going on until she entered a bare office where a UNHCR officer she had worked with in the past was waiting for her. You are getting out, the woman told her. Out? What did she mean? "To the United States. We did something unique," she added, "something we've never done before." The woman didn't explain, and Ahlam could only wonder what strings had been pulled to effect her release.

From there she was driven to the UNHCR office in Douma, the same neighbourhood where she had spent the past five months in prison. In an office upstairs, she saw her husband and children.

She looked at them in shock. The children were so much thinner than when she had last seen them and stared at her with something like terror in their eyes. Their passports had been in her purse when she was arrested, so after Salaam's arrest their father had arranged to have them smuggled out of Syria to be with him. Then, three days ago, an official from the UNHCR had phoned him in Iraq. "You're being resettled to the United States with your wife and children," he said. "Come to Damascus. Immediately." They had returned only that morning, the children smuggled back into Syria on a bus the same way they had been smuggled out four months ago.

Abdullah ran up to embrace his mother, but Roqayah hung back, saying only a shy hello. She never showed fear, but later that day, when Ahlam used the excuse of brushing her daughter's long black hair just to touch her, she was shocked to see strands of white.

In the UNHCR office the story changed again. Now they were being told they were leaving immediately, but their father would not be going with them. There had been a snag, since his resettlement file had been separated from Ahlam's after he fled to Baghdad on his own; he would have to wait until the system could arrange for him to join them. Roqayah didn't want to leave either. Torn between her mother and father, recently wrenched from her childhood home for the second time, she wanted them all to go home, to their big house along the Tigris where she had just celebrated her tenth birthday surrounded by family who loved her and life had seemed almost like it used to be before the war.

"I'll follow you later," her father assured them as he kissed them goodbye. Then he paused. Everyone was waiting. There was no time to waste. "You have to go," he ordered the children. "Now."

Ahlam was allowed to phone Salaam, who had reached their village in Baghdad, and her sister Tutu. She only had time to say goodbye, having no idea when or if she would ever see them again. Then she and the children were rushed to a white SUV flying a UN flag and driven straight to Damascus International Airport. Another SUV accompanied them. Still wearing the same clothes she had worn for the past five months, Ahlam asked the four officials guarding her to stop and let her find a change of clothing, but they refused. They had orders not to let her out of their sight. She asked if they could stop somewhere for cigarettes. They refused. She was given a badge and a bag with the UNHCR insignia and told not to lose them. "This is your identity now."

At the airport the small family waited for six hours with the UN officials, who paced and looked at their watches. It was four in the morning by the time they were placed on a direct flight to Budapest, along with ten other Iraqi families who had been accepted for resettlement in various countries. From the sky, Ahlam looked out the window to see sunshine—the first full sun she had seen in five months.

Years ago, as a young woman, Ahlam had dreamed of being a flight attendant, and this was the first time she had ever flown on a plane. In Budapest airport she used the last of the money Salaam had given her to buy a pack of cigarettes. She smoked in an outdoor courtyard, shivering in the cold, not losing sight of her children for a single moment. From there, they changed planes to New York, joining a group of refugees who were heading to the US. Roqayah kept insisting she wanted to go home, and Abdullah, her happy-go-lucky son, never once stopped smiling.

Landing at JFK airport on October 27, 2008, Ahlam approached a man who was directing all the refugees.

"Where am I going?" she asked him.

He looked at her badge. "You are going to Chicago."

"Chicago? Where is Chicago?" she asked.

"You don't know where Chicago is?" he asked, amused.

She had no idea.

Five days after Ahlam landed in Chicago, I flew into O'Hare. She and the children were staying in Edgewater, a lakeshore community of north Chicago known for one of the highest concentrations of immigrants and refugees in the United States. The building she had been placed in by Heartland Alliance, an anti-poverty group that partnered with the US State Department to find housing for refugees, had fifty apartments, ten on each floor, and fifteen nationalities: Bosnians, Serbians, Colombians, Rwandans, Ethiopians, Eritreans, Congolese, Iraqis—you name the war. Down the street, outside the gaping entrance to the L-train station, local toughs in hooded parkas shuffled around in packs. "I fuck him up, bitch!" one of them shouted.

When I reached the apartment, I knocked nervously at the door. What would I find on the other side? I had spent so much time wondering if she was alive or dead, if she had been tortured. I wondered what she would be like now, if I would find myself talking to a stranger I no longer recognized.

It was the children who answered, as wide-eyed as I had ever seen them. "Where's your mom?" I said, looking past them into the unfurnished living room. The light through the window was dim and the room was silent. "Ahlam?"

She had been as nervous as I was. She emerged from the hallway, shyly, and we embraced.

"It's really you," I said. "You're really here." And then, "Why are we crying? We should be happy."

"We are crying for the past, for the present, for everything that happened in all this time."

I pulled away so I could look at her. "I thought you would be in bed," I said. "I came to make you soup, to take care of you. But you haven't changed at all."

"No," she said, grinning. "I haven't changed."

Now she sat across from me at a card table set up on the beige shag carpet of her new flat, jubilant. A week ago she had been sleeping on the cement floor of a prison cell, certain she would be there for the rest of her life. Looking down she spotted a cockroach crawling on the linoleum floor of the kitchen. "Oh, my old friend," she said, looking down at it. "I miss you so much." She killed it with a shoe. "I never did that in prison. We had a peace agreement. But peacetime is over!"

Twelve-year-old Abdullah, amazed at all the useful objects people threw out in Chicago, had brought two television sets into the apartment. He alerted his mother that he had seen a third television in another alleyway but she told him that was enough. He and his sister were watching a Disney movie on one of them while Ahlam and I talked.

"Why did they arrest you?" I asked her. "Was it because of me?"

"They wanted me to spy on a journalist. Not you. Deborah Amos. From NPR."

Amos, a prominent Mideast correspondent, had been covering the refugee story in Syria at much the same time that I had, going in and out of the country often as she gathered material for a book. She had met Ahlam before I came to Damascus, when she did a radio segment on Ahlam's kidnapping in Iraq. I had known the two of them were acquainted, which is why Amos was one of the first journalists I'd emailed from Damascus after her arrest.

"They thought you were a professor." Ahlam smiled. She explained how Abu Yusuf had asked her who the woman in her apartment was, then assured her, when she explained that I was a professor from Vancouver, that he already "knew everything" about me. She hadn't contradicted him. "It was good that we spread that rumour." He knew only my cover story, spread from bread seller to cigarette vendor to hotel security guard, reinforced by every refugee who saw me at Ahlam's apartment.

It was a revelation. I had, after all, eluded the secret police by working undercover. But although my sleight of hand had not jeopardized Ahlam after all, neither had it diminished the fear and guilt that had consumed me. The paranoia of the state, as J.M. Coetzee observed, had been reproduced in my psyche, such that the state had no need to bother with me. As Hamid had often observed, if her arrest had been meant to "send a message," that message had been received.

Deborah Amos had told me she was not working undercover, though she was conscious of the perils of being observed: having heard Ahlam was on a watch list, she'd deliberately steered clear of her. Amos had obtained an official journalist's visa through the Syrian embassy in Washington, DC. She had worked through all the right channels, done all the right things, which would have made her an easy target as someone to watch.

Whether this was a case of one branch of the security and intelligence agencies trampling on the decisions of another, a turf war among the more than a dozen overlapping agencies operating in Syria, Ahlam had no idea. It may simply have been one man's attempt to further his career.

"What do you think of Syria now?" I asked Ahlam.

"Don't forget, they took in more of us than any country in the world. No other country would help us."

She could still regard her experience with nuance. And she seemed well, even euphoric. For both of us the sense of relief was like a drug. As for how her release had been achieved, she thought Amnesty International might have had something to do with it, and certainly the UNHCR had pulled out the stops. The UN agencies weren't as powerful as people sometimes imagined, especially when working in dictatorships where their positions were tenuous. As Marianne put it: "They have to pick their battles." Yet faced with countless other cases like Ahlam's, countless other battles, they had chosen to fight this one. "What made Ahlam's case different was that she had so many people pulling for her," Marianne said. "She had so many friends."

Over that kitchen table, Ahlam, bending her head to light a cigarette, told me how the agents who searched her apartment had made a beeline for her letters from American officials in Iraq. "They knew exactly where to look."

"How could they?" I asked. "Who else knew?"

She had hidden her documents, she told me, months before her arrest. It was on a day when Mona had come by for a visit, back when relations between them were warm; it hadn't occurred to her to hide things from a friend. When the old guard, Sadiq, had taken pity on her and read to her from her prison file, he told her someone had informed on her. The name on the report was Mona's.

I asked her what she thought of Mona now. She went over to the window, painted so many times it no longer opened without a struggle. "It especially hurts when a friend betrays you," she said quietly. She had been told by Tarek, before anything happened, that Mona was jealous of her renown as a fixer, but it was hard for Ahlam to fathom jealousy—it wasn't in her nature. And Mona's youth, beauty, potential were such that it was hard to understand why she would be jealous of a refugee who had only come to Damascus because she'd been kidnapped, and wore a picture of her dead son around her neck. She knew, of course, that Syrian fixers sometimes made deals with the Ministry of Information—some even had to give them kickbacks in order to be allowed to work. Everyone in the know was aware that this was the case. But the personal nature of the betrayal, by someone she considered a friend: this she could not grasp.

A cold wind gusted through the open window. In the alley below, a homeless man was bedding down for the night. Soon it would start to snow.

A few weeks later Ahlam slipped on an icy sidewalk and broke her arm. Her family in Iraq, with whom she was now able to keep in touch over the Internet, asked if she had broken it skiing, since that must be what she did all day now that she was living the American Dream.

Ahlam's arrival in Chicago coincided with the financial crisis. Streets of boarded up shops with "For Lease" signs that already looked weathered, legions of homeless, many of them army veterans, who rode the trains all day to stay warm. These conditions did not bode well for refugees who were expected to be fully employed by the time their government assistance was cut off in eight months.

Within days other Iraqi refugees in Chicago had found her. A depressed widower raising three little boys, who needed Ahlam to help him fill out medical forms. A female journalist who had been raped in Baghdad and was now a single mother. A man with a brain injury who came on to the female journalist in the elevator, and his beleaguered wife who wept when she learned she was pregnant with a third child.

I came back to Chicago for the month of December. Having finished my teaching term, I wanted to interview her while details were still fresh. A woman from Amnesty International came to document her testimony. Beth Ann was about fifty, a pale redhead with grown children. Straightforward, with an intelligent blue-eyed gaze and an American directness, she had long worked on Amnesty's Iraq file and was sent to help Ahlam settle in.

By the time I left, Beth Ann had become Ahlam's close friend. She arranged the things Ahlam could not, emailing her daily to-do lists, browbeating her into showing up to doctor's appointments, finding her a dentist willing to work pro bono (she had, beneath the nicotine stains, lovely white teeth), and putting a moratorium on her use of the term *insha'Allah*. "It's like saying, 'I'll get to it if I get to it,' and if not, blame God."

The two of them concocted a plan to open an Iraqi Mutual Aid Society, a first for Chicago. Ahlam had always been good at coming up with ideas, but she didn't know the American system as Beth Ann did. With Ahlam's testimony, Beth Ann's superlative organizational skills, and funding organized with help from Marianne, they pulled it off.

In 2009, the society opened, dedicated to helping refugees adapt to their new home. At first they ran it from Ahlam's apartment, and then an article about Ahlam appeared in the *Chicago Tribune*. A wealthy philanthropist named Ann read the article and phoned, showing up with a check for $20,000, afterward supporting the Mutual Aid Society with $40,000 a year. The society was able to rent an office and begin their work in earnest. The following year Ahlam received an award from a local women's group.

Within a year her children were speaking good English. Roqayah's grades jumped from Ds to As. Taking off the headscarf as she moved into middle school, she emerged as a beautiful young woman, thirteen going on twenty, fluent in American schoolgirl slang. She admired Doctors Without Borders and was already talking about pre-med; Abdullah—a math whiz—about computer science.

I should end the story here. Happy ever after in the land of opportunity.

Chapter 27

ADAPTATION

AHLAM AND I HAD LONG engaged in banter that allowed us to stave off darkness. I would joke when I hadn't been able to reach her for several weeks—her number mysteriously changed or her phone switched off—that I thought she'd disappeared again. And she would quip, "Yeah, next time they're sending me to Guantánamo."

"I hear the weather's good there."

"Better than Chicago."

There are three stages people go through after arriving in a new place that has been envisioned as a kind of salvation. The first is the halcyon time in which they imagine that everything in the new place is perfect; everything back home bad, even horrible. The second is the gradual disillusionment, as the new life reveals its own troubles. Longing for the lost homeland, old friends, ways of life that have acquired the glow of nostalgia. Then comes the settling in, the adaptation. Letting go of the past and realizing there is no going back. People who talk of these stages say the process takes about five years.

When I came to see her in the summer of 2009, she had a car and a driver's licence. Jason Pape, commander of the tank unit that used to hang out at Ahlam's house in Baghdad, had heard she was looking for work. He knew she would need a car for that to happen so he had given her his old Mercury station wagon with enough money to pay for the registration. Pape's father had driven the car all the way from Kansas to Chicago.

Over the first year, while the Iraqi Mutual Aid Society was getting underway, Ahlam held a series of part-time jobs, some of which, like driving local children to and from school, seemed to cost her more in gas than she was earning. Flummoxed by Chicago's tyrannical parking laws, which appeared to be the backbone of the city's funding strategy, she accumulated a breathtaking number of tickets. This was money she could not afford, and she missed a couple of months' rent. She found herself struggling to focus, haunted by the past.

Beth Ann found her a therapist at the Marjorie Kovler Center, an institute established in Chicago to help survivors of torture. After each therapy session she was exhausted; her entire body ached for days. She went for a while, then dropped out.

"Was she always so disorganized?" Beth Ann called me to ask. "Was she always this depressed?" I could tell she could not quite believe the stories I told of Ahlam's competence, of triumphs that sounded now like myth. I had thought, when she was first released, that she hadn't changed at all, but what Beth Ann said suggested I was wrong.

I said I remembered times when she was so exhausted she would sleep for two days straight. But then wake up and be exemplary. "I think she needs a year off," I told Beth Ann, "to recover." Which of course was impossible. The poor do not take a year off in Chicago and keep a roof overhead. When Ahlam came across a pamphlet advertising "free" money in exchange for signing onto a credit offer, it was Beth Ann who explained that nothing is ever free in America.

But there was someone who could keep a roof over her head, and that was Ann, the generous philanthropist who had discovered Ahlam through the article in the *Tribune*. After two years in Edgewater, Ahlam and the children moved to a leafy suburb where Ann had found them a better two-bedroom and paid the difference on the rent. Both of the kids had experienced bullying, and this way they could go to a school that did not need a police car permanently stationed outside.

When I visited again in the summer of 2011, the entire city sang with cicadas—a lovely sound. I was staying with Ahlam in her new apartment in Evanston, and had come expecting to stay up all night talking, catching up, but she was dropping into bed exactly at eleven p.m., awaking at seven on the dot. The person I knew, the quixotic, insomniac, bold and funny person, had been replaced by a robot.

When she talked she seemed faroff, as if she were speaking from behind bulletproof glass. She told me there had been flashbacks. We were driving, I remember, through her new neighbourhood, green with parks and tree-lined streets, past shops selling gluten-free cupcakes and organic produce, dog-grooming, edible fruit arrangements, custom picture frames. There was more than one bookstore and a library, but the little girl who had read every book she could get her hands on now lacked the capacity for sustained concentration. There was too much chaos in her head.

"What triggers the flashbacks?" I asked.

"Sirens," she said. "Or a baby crying." She drove as if in a trance. She kept cigarettes on the backseat and reached for them, shaking one out. "I can't stand that sound." She told me about the day in 2004 when there had been a bombing near her office in Baghdad. It was during the festival of Ashura, when observant Shia mourn the loss of the battle in Karbala fourteen centuries ago that started the Sunni–Shia rift. Thousands of families poured in through the massive wooden doors of the shrine in the suburb of Kadhimiya, touching the brass knocker as they entered to worship. At least seventy-five people died there that day—another sixty during a simultaneous attack on pilgrims in Karbala. It was the worst day of violence since the fall of Saddam Hussein and was blamed on al-Qaeda, which wanted civil war. Hearing the explosions from her office, she ran the several blocks to the shrine. All she could hear amid the shouts and sirens, all she could recall hearing, was an infant's cries. She followed the cries until she found the baby and pulled him from his dead mother's arms. The woman's body had shielded her son from the blast and saved his life.

I awoke one morning to drink tea with Ahlam before she left for work. She stood up to light a cigarette and looked out the kitchen window at the new day. Her face was blank. I got up from the table and put my arms around her. "Where are you?" I asked. "Tell me where you are."

Between us was an overwhelming sadness. The full force of what she felt and what she could not feel was with us in the room. For the first time I understood that she was still captive to the traumas she had lived through. Her symptoms, common to sufferers of Post-Traumatic Stress Disorder, had been blunted by the drugs her doctors prescribed. This one to make you sleep the first half of the night, that one for the second half, this one to stop the flashbacks, another for the depression, another to combat the side effects of the others.

She spoke of her son who had died, whose mother hadn't managed to save him. "He will never see Chicago. He will never swim in the lake or walk in the snow."

He was eleven and a half. He would always be eleven and a half.

"Why did I live?" she asked me. "I feel I'm not alive."

She had been, when I knew her in Damascus, more alive than anyone I've ever known.

Perhaps I had idealized her. Easy to do that with people who have risked their lives for you. I began tracking down journalists and American military officials who had known her. I wanted them to give me perspective, but listened as if anticipating a blow. I feared they would tell me she wasn't the person I remembered, that it was self-deception. But all they could do, in the words of the first journalist she ever worked for, Stephen Glain, was "add to the heap of superlatives that Ahlam routinely inspires."

They called her honest, competent, tough. They said—this was Khaled Oweis, the Reuters bureau chief in Damascus—"she had all the qualities you associate with the great Iraqis, except she wasn't wealthy." They said she was charming, bold, outrageous. Brave. Generous. Warm. "Badass." Empathetic. Smart about what needed doing and did it. Was reliable, likeable, funny. Sometimes sad. Non-sectarian at a time when the Shia ascendancy in Iraq made that a rare quality indeed.

In Skype calls and phone calls and emails, I was given a picture of someone even more influential than I had known at the time—"Did you know she fixed for Jeremy Bowen at the BBC? And Lina Sinjab at the Beeb, Lina loved her." Perhaps because she had been that missing link, our bridge across the divide towards a common humanity. That was her gift to us. She represented the spirit of the places we had come to know through her, whether Baghdad or Damascus, that were no longer what they had been, and in the deepest sense had disappeared.

Chapter 28

AFTERMATH

IMMEDIATELY AFTER HE WAS separated from Ahlam at the immigration prison, having slipped her some money just in case, Salaam was deported from Syria with a stamp on his passport forbidding him from returning for five years. This meant he could no longer work as a driver crossing back and forth through the border. He went back to their village on the banks of the Tigris, and found an office job. But it was not that easy to recover. At night he was plagued by dreams in which he relived the torture he had suffered in Douma. He became fearful of falling asleep and was soon smoking four packs a day. Meanwhile word had spread through the village that Ahlam's arrest, like her kidnapping before it, was due to her work with the Americans. These rumours clung to him.

One morning, at six a.m., when Salaam normally left for work, a man was shot in the head on the main road in front of his house. From behind, the man looked exactly like him. Salaam fled at once to Thailand, one of the few countries still giving visas to Iraqis.

Despite that frightening news, Ahlam was homesick for Iraq. The early euphoria, the joy of survival, had faded. After two years, her husband had been accepted for resettlement and come to Chicago, but they had agreed to live apart, sharing custody of the children. Ahlam longed to see her mother, whom she'd heard might not have much longer to live. And life in the United States was hard: all people seemed to do was work. In spite of the violence and a chorus of friends and family members telling her it was madness, she returned to Baghdad in the summer of 2012 for a one-month visit.

The day before her departure we spoke on the phone. We had long talked of making this journey together, seeing the village where she had grown up, but one hundred and fifty journalists had been killed in Iraq since 2003, and nearly a hundred kidnapped.[37] Not to mention the toll on "media workers," the fixers and drivers and interpreters who die anonymously.

It was too dangerous for either of us. She knew I didn't want her to go.

"How do you feel?" I asked her.

Her voice sounded strained. "Bad."

"How come?"

"Ghosts of the past. Ghosts of the future." I could hear her light a cigarette, the gentle *whish*.

"Remember this," I said. "I'll kill you if you get killed. I'll track you down and kill you again."

The year before, in 2011, protest movements had swept the Arab world. The so-called Arab Spring. These were driven as much by widespread youth unemployment and rising food prices as by a grassroots desire for democracy. And all, with the shaky exception of Tunisia where the protests started, failed.

In Syria, several issues converged to set off the protests. A drought, the worst in nine hundred years, had caused a million farmers and their families to abandon their land for work in the cities.[38] At the same time traditional subsidies and social services that had long bound the countryside to the authoritarian state were being "modernized" under President Bashar al-Assad. The London-trained eye doctor, married to an investment banker, was eager to join the World Trade Organization. Having applied in 2001, Syria gained observer status in mid-2010. In the intervening years, farmer and worker unions had been de-funded, rent controls abolished, public services eroded in favour of faith-based charities. Education and health spending and agricultural and fuel subsidies were cut. Trade tariffs were lowered, and state land sold off cheaply. As foreign capital rolled in, real-estate speculation took off. For drought-ravaged rural areas, most of which were Sunni, help had been slashed when it was needed most.

What must it have been like for those displaced farm folk— conservative, humble, God-fearing—to come to Damascus and witness the nightly Mardi Gras in the city's wealthier quarters? Men and women flirting, checking their laptops, going to nightclubs and restaurants, shopping for designer jeans. Amid this spectacle of urban decadence, there weren't even low-wage jobs or cheap housing. The deluge of middle-class Iraqi refugees had already taken that.

"The most dangerous juncture for an authoritarian regime," writes Raymond Hinnebusch, director of the Centre for Syrian Studies at the University of St. Andrews, "is when it seeks to 'reform,' particularly when the path of reform combines neo-liberalism and crony capitalism." As Hinnebusch observed, Syria's president forsook the poor for the rich. "The gap was partly filled by the security services which, however, were underpaid, corrupt and lax."[39] Men like Abu Yusuf.

When the first protest broke out in a city filled with desperate migrant farmers, it came as a shock to the authorities, who must have thought everyone was out enjoying the new prosperity. It began with the arrest of fifteen schoolchildren for spraying anti-government graffiti on the walls of their school, echoing sentiments they heard from Egypt and Tunisia on satellite news. When their parents tried to have them released, they were taunted and sent away. Those who protested were arrested or fired on, spurring more protests that spread across the country. With no patronage left to cement the society, nothing to offset the rising inequality, the government reached for the only tool it had not abandoned: the army. Once again, the regime employed the scorched earth policy that had defeated—temporarily as it turned out—the Sunni Muslim Brotherhood thirty years earlier.

But now was different. Now Syria had outside enemies who saw opportunity in the prospect of civil war. Now Libya was in chaos following regime change; arms and Islamic fighters were in abundant supply. Now Saudi Arabia and Qatar, threatened by the rise of Iran since the removal of its archenemy Saddam Hussein, were vying for supremacy in the Sunni world. Now Turkey had visions of recovering its lost hegemony. Now, after Libya, Russia was not going to support American adventurism. Now Iran was looking at any war on an ally as one directed at itself. Now al-Qaeda in Iraq was looking for a place to regroup and build an "Islamic state" that would spread across the region—and the world.

With Gulf States and Turkey backing foreign fighters who saw Syria as a proxy battlefield—and the West blindly supporting the enemies of Assad whoever they might be—the worst fears of those quietly intellectual Syrians I knew in Damascus were fulfilled: the war had come to them.

Skyping with me from the darkness of her mother's house, Ahlam said, "I feel I'm back in prison." She was only half joking; her mother refused to let her step outside. In the past they had kept the front door open all the time. Now all the houses along the river were fenced and barricaded, everyone indoors and accounted for after dark.

The day after she touched down at Baghdad airport, headlines announced that ten locations had been attacked in the city's worst day of violence since the withdrawal of American troops six months before. Over the course of her month-long visit, three car bombs went off in her district, followed by sweeping government arrests that seemed to target all Sunni men.

As the Iraqi government continued to make life hell for its Sunni population, the civil war in Syria was flowing back into Iraq. Opposition fighters from Syria were flocking into Baghdad, urging the Sunnis to join them in wiping out the Shia. "They even tried to recruit one of my nephews," Ahlam said. Had he not had a loving family and other options, who knows? Meanwhile the US found itself in a bizarre contortion: supporting the same fighters in Syria that it wanted to see defeated in Iraq.

The Islamic State was born from the invasion of 2003.[40] After the leader of al-Qaeda in Iraq was killed by an American airstrike in 2006, the group reconfigured as the Islamic State of Iraq, a name they later changed to the Islamic State of Iraq and Syria, or ISIS (Daesh to its enemies) and finally to Islamic State.

The leader of Islamic State, Abu Bakr al-Baghdadi, had spent four years in one of the American prisons in Iraq that Ahlam had talked to me about: Camp Bucca, where she said detainees could be held for a year on nothing but suspicion. When she was kidnapped for her work—which included locating missing prisoners—by members of al-Qaeda, al-Baghdadi was in that prison assembling the team that would turn al-Qaeda into IS: a combination of radical Islamic fighters and secular ex-Baathist military men from the days of Saddam Hussein. The Islamists had zeal but no plan; the ex-Baathists had plans but no zeal. Each galvanized the other.

"If there was no American prison in Iraq, there would be no IS now," one of al-Baghdadi's fighters told the *Guardian*. "Bucca was a factory. It made us all. It built our ideology."[41] It was there that military men with nothing more to lose decided to collude with radical Islamists who believed they had God on their side. Together they found wealthy sponsors in Saudi Arabia, Qatar, Kuwait and other Gulf States who welcomed the prospect of funding an army to fight the non-Sunni governments in Iraq and Syria. From victories in Syria they would go on to erase the border with Iraq that Britain—with the help of Gertrude Bell and T.E. Lawrence—had drawn after the First World War.

At home on the banks of the Tigris, life was worse now than Ahlam remembered, not better. With electricity sporadic, jobs scarce, and constant threats from Iraqi security forces, feuds had started among people she thought she knew. She was shocked by many things, especially to find that instead of going to school girls were now being married off at the age of nine or ten to thirty-year-old men. Their parents argued that marriage was a way to keep their daughters safe from rampant sex trafficking, including a new method: online entrapment through Twitter and Facebook.

"I feel like a stranger here," she confessed over Skype. "If I say things need to change, people tell me that nothing can change. They tell me to go back to Chicago."

Which she did. The past, her past, had become a foreign country. There was no going back.

Chapter 29

EXILE

ONE AFTERNOON IN CHICAGO, Ahlam and I walked over to Lake Michigan. It was high spring, the perfect mix of sun and shore.

Over the past seven years our lives had gone in different directions. She wasn't my fixer anymore and I was taking a break from magazine writing. It was a thin time for journalism anyhow. What with the slow death by Internet and ownership consolidation, there was less and less money for in-depth reporting from foreign places, investigative work, and the long-form narrative writing I did. Tens of thousands of reporters across North America had lost their jobs since the crash of 2008. Pages were shrinking as quickly as pay rates. The only writers I knew who were still living from their words were making half what they had before the collapse. I had stopped being surprised by editors asking journalists to write for free, or by the lack of good coverage of urgent global affairs.

I was focused now on writing this book, on teaching, and on a life that had opened in the wake of everything falling apart. I had moved to an island in the Pacific Northwest, having met someone new—this time a writer. As always I rarely discussed my personal life with Ahlam but now it was for different reasons: while my life had moved on, for her the past few years had not been easy. She had resigned from the Iraqi Mutual Aid Society, had had surgery on her back after a fall, and her children were growing up fast.

I'd spent time with them over the past week, delighted by how they had matured. Abdullah, tall and strapping, was studying math and computer science in college while working at the fashion retailer Forever 21—he kindly offered to let me use his employee discount. He was proud to be helping out his father, who was driving taxi, while Roqayah helped her mother (it was she who cooked for all of us).

About to turn seventeen, Roqayah was an honours student in Advanced Placement classes, studying madly for the SAT exams, helped by a coach Ann had hired. After school and on weekends she worked long hours at Jimmy John's, a sandwich chain.

She had gone from seeing herself as the "refugee girl," to volunteering as a mentor for other young refugees. She was still thinking pre-med but was also interested in history, French and current affairs, and unwound from her late-night shifts at Jimmy John's by watching *Orange Is the New Black* on Netflix, which she admired for its take on gender and diversity.

She was finally ready to tell me what had happened to her and her brother after their uncle Salaam's arrest. I knew that their father, from Baghdad, had made arrangements to have them smuggled home, after Syrian agents returned to the apartment with guns drawn, asking after other members of Ahlam's family. Shortly after that, Abdullah and Roqayah were told to pack their bags. An old friend of their father's drove them to an empty road on the outskirts of Damascus, where the three of them waited until a bus pulled up. The man left them in the care of the driver, who was going to help them get through the frontier.

When they neared the border, the driver stopped the bus and pulled back his chair, revealing a secret compartment. The two children crawled inside. From the small, dark space they could hear the bus come to a halt, the murmur of voices as Iraqi officers came aboard and checked passports. Crushed together, barely able to breathe, they didn't make a sound.

On the long journey to Baghdad, traffic stopped and started. Sometimes the two of them crawled out and stood on the road together, staring at the night. An old woman spoke to them kindly. Finally two passengers got off. "I suggest you take those seats now; before someone else does," the driver said. Abdullah slept by the window and his sister in the aisle seat. She didn't wake until Baghdad. "Your dad's here," the driver said. As the two of them stepped out, they saw their father, who threw his arms around them.

When the UNHCR called and told them to return to Damascus, the children still had no passports, and their father arranged to have them smuggled once again. Moving through Iraqi checkpoints they were hidden in the luggage compartment under the floor, and then, at the border, behind the driver's seat. "I remember crying because I couldn't breathe, and my brother was crying thinking they were going to find us." The only thing that made it bearable was knowing their father was there with them on the bus.

In the coming months she would write her college application essay on how growing up as a refugee of war had taught her the value of adaptation.

—

Ahlam had returned to therapy, but the back surgery had laid her up again, and with both of her children busy with school and work she was often alone with her two cats, Misha and Angel.

In 2015 matters came to a crisis. On the ninth anniversary of their son Anas's death, Ahlam's husband held a memorial to which Ahlam and her dearest Chicago friends, Beth Ann, Ann and Zainab—an Iraqi pediatrician—were invited. Ahlam had argued, irrationally, that her husband should not speak about their son, not say his name. When he did, she fled the gathering and disappeared. She remembered little of what happened next. Everything went dark.

When she didn't answer her phone the next day, Beth Ann and Zainab came to find her. They rang the buzzer again and again, but she didn't hear it. "It was Angel who woke me," she told me—her blue-and-brown-eyed white Persian. Hearing the buzzer, Angel jumped up on the bed and kneaded her with her paws until she got up. She had been asleep for nineteen hours. Her friends phoned her therapist at the Kovler Center, who came over right away. I flew down when she called me.

The wind was blowing strongly off the lake, spreading dandelion fluff and lifting sand from the hardpack. "Maybe this had to happen," Ahlam said. "I had been carrying the burden for too long." She was feeling buoyed by her brother Salaam's arrival in Chicago the week before, his application for resettlement finally accepted. Ann had agreed to cover the rent on a three-bedroom apartment for the whole family for the coming year.

She was back at work for a different aid organization. Most of the refugees she helped these days were Syrians, among the millions who had fled that ravaged country. When I asked her how Syrians spoke about the war, she said they didn't. "It's a wound." She was more excited about a second job she had taken, driving for Uber on the early morning shift. "No four walls," she said. "No one asking me for help with their problems." She had always loved driving. Her passengers were usually heading to the airport. They were quiet, checking their phones, utterly incurious about the woman at the wheel.

As Ahlam and I walked, we talked about Beth Ann and Ann, Zainab and Marianne. We had just been to Ann's venerable art deco home on the outskirts of Chicago.

"You remember what Khaled said about me?" Ahlam asked.

I had told her I had interviewed Khaled Oweis, her friend at Reuters, who had fled Syria and was now working for a think tank in Berlin. "Yes. He said you had all the qualities associated with the great Iraqis, except you weren't wealthy."

"Except I *am* wealthy," she said. "I have so many good friends."

She took off her sandals when we passed from grass to beach. She was recalling her childhood. She had been telling her therapist about the day her father had taken her out into the open fields on her grandfather's land. "Run," her father told her. "Run! No one can stop you."

Her children were becoming Americans, but she, I thought, would always be an exile. She stood facing the water and opened her arms wide. She closed her eyes, remembering, and I could picture her on that open field, her father watching over her, the land warm beneath her feet. Around us thousands of birds on their annual migration raced along the shore.

ACKNOWLEDGEMENTS

This is a non-fiction book. No person or event has been invented. Some events appear out of sequence where strict chronology would be confusing; some people whose presence has no bearing on the story have been omitted. I have changed the names of many people in the book out of concern for their safety or the safety of their families. Given the number of articles and a documentary about Ahlam, and with her permission, I have used her real first name, though I have omitted her family name for their sake.

To Ahlam I owe the largest debt of gratitude. She is one of those influential fixers and local experts, seldom visible despite their importance, who have done so much to show the world to itself. Thanks also to Abdullah, Roqayah and Salaam.

I am grateful to the hundreds of Iraqis and Syrians who spoke to me, most of whom do not appear here, but whose testimonies greatly informed my observations. Thanks in particular to Rana, who lives in a suburb of Damascus to which she fled after her home was destroyed. To Kuki, who made it to New York. And Hamid, who succeeded in getting three of his grown children to the United States and now lives with his wife in Beirut. For their help in the field and beyond, thanks to Marianne Gimon, Alessandro D'Ansembourg, Gabriela Bulisova, Farah Nosh, Yasha Opera, Kate Brooks, and Michel Elefteriades, whose Empire of Nowheristan the world awaits. For patiently confirming and expanding upon details where I could not be present, thanks to Jason Pape, Adam Shilling, Stephen Glain, David Luhnow, Khaled Yacoub Oweis and Deborah Amos.

Thanks to *Harper's* magazine for the assignment that led to this book; to my agents Martha Webb and Anne McDermid; to my extraordinary editor Louise Dennys at Knopf Canada, and to Kate Icely and Angelika Glover; to the BC Arts Council, Canada Council for the Arts, and Access Copyright Foundation; to Alisa Smith, Ann Jones, Christy Fletcher and especially, always, Ronald Wright.

NOTES

1. A Pew Research Center study conducted in late 2007 of 111 journalists from twenty-nine news organizations (all but one US-based) who had worked or were working in Iraq found that a majority said most of the country was too dangerous to visit. More than seven out of ten said that travelling with chase cars and armed security details had become normal. Fifty-seven percent had had at least one of their Iraqi staffers kidnapped or killed over the previous year. "Welcome to the new world of journalism, boys and girls," one bureau chief stated. "This is where we lost our innocence. Security teams, body armor and armored cars will forever now be pushed in between journalism and stories." (See "Journalists in Iraq—A Survey of Reporters on the Front Lines.")

2. Ken Adelman, "Cakewalk in Iraq," A27. Adelman was one of the neoconservative hawks behind the Iraq War. A member of the Pentagon's influential Defense Policy Board, chaired by Richard Perle, he was close to Dick Cheney, Donald Rumsfeld and Paul Wolfowitz. The latter four were key members of the Project for the New American Century (PNAC), a Washington-based think tank established in 1997. In *They Knew They Were Right* Jacob Heilbrunn writes: PNAC "was essentially a front organization to champion the democratic crusade, and specifically, the overthrow of Saddam Hussein" (217). Ten signatories to PNAC's statement of

principles went on to serve in the administration of George W. Bush; nine members of the Defense Policy Board had ties to defense contractors.

On September 20, 2001, nine days after the attacks on the World Trade Center and the Pentagon, a letter from PNAC signed by forty neo-conservatives advised Bush that he had no choice but to remove Saddam Hussein from power "even if evidence does not link Iraq directly to the attack." On September 19–20, the Defense Policy Board, which included Henry Kissinger, met in Rumsfeld's conference room at the Pentagon with Ahmed Chalabi, a wealthy Shia Muslim Iraqi exile and convicted embezzler who had met Richard Perle and Paul Wolfowitz in the 1980s while completing his PhD at the University of Chicago (ibid., 250). They had been introduced by leading neoconservative mentor Professor Albert Wohlstetter (ibid., 258), a Cold War theorist who was one of the models for the title character in Stanley Kubrick's *Dr. Strangelove*.

Chalabi, tapped by Cheney and Rumsfeld to lead Iraq after Saddam Hussein, became a key source of the false allegations about Iraq's weapons of mass destruction that manufactured public support for the invasion. He later served as deputy prime minister of Iraq and was appointed by the Shia-led government to chair the highly destructive de-Baathification commission. As Jonathan Steele notes in the obituary for Ahmed Chalabi in the *Guardian*, "He used the position to purge hundreds of Sunni politicians who wanted to run for parliament in March 2010, thereby paving the way for the sectarian polarisation that provoked the emergence of the extremist Sunni group Islamic State."

3. Reported in the *New York Times*, CNN, the *Guardian*, and elsewhere. See, for example, Pamela Hess, "Rumsfeld: Looting Is Transition to Freedom," April 11, 2003.

4. Interview with Dr. Matanius Habib, 2007. He refuted the theory that terrorism has no roots in injustice. "The urgent task in front of the international community is to help the Iraqi refugees survive and raise their living standards. That will keep them from crime, terrorism and hate. If not, we will see instability and international terrorism that will affect not only the region but the developed countries."

5. The Office of Special Plans (OSP) was a shadow intelligence unit conceived by Paul Wolfowitz and Donald Rumsfeld to make the case for invading Iraq. Headed by Douglas Feith and reporting to Dick Cheney, the OSP

manipulated raw intelligence in an attempt to show that Iraq had weapons of mass destruction and that Saddam Hussein had links to al-Qaeda, overriding more credible reports from the CIA and State Department. It relied on information provided by Ahmed Chalabi. (See Julian Borger, "The Spies Who Pushed for War," and Seymour Hersh, "Selective Intelligence.")

The OSP was also involved in post-invasion planning. Paul Bremer's orders to "de-Baathify" Iraqi society and disband the Iraqi army were made over objections from more experienced military and intelligence officials who warned of dangerous consequences. Bremer stated that on May 9, 2003, Douglas Feith showed him a draft order for the "De-Baathification of Iraqi Society." Later that day he received his "marching orders" in a memo from Rumsfeld. (Paul Bremer, *My Year in Iraq*, 39, quoted in James P. Pfiffner, "US Blunders in Iraq," 78.) That same day Rumsfeld approved a draft plan to disband Iraq's security forces and recreate the Iraqi army from scratch. The plan was drafted by Walt Slocombe, a tax attorney who had previously held Rumsfeld's job in the Clinton administration. Slocombe admits to drafting the policy but says, "it was made not only by Bremer but also by Wolfowitz and Feith and other people in the department, including, I assume, Rumsfeld." (See "Where Did ISIS Come From?")

6. Douglas Feith, Under Secretary of Defense for Policy and head of the Office of Special Plans, worked on the de-Baathification plan with Ahmed Chalabi and presented it to President Bush on March 10, 2003, ten days before the invasion of Iraq. While Paul Bremer said that the order would affect only about 20,000 people, the total was between 85,000 and 100,000. According to former CIA director George Tenet, who resigned in mid-2004 for "personal reasons," these included "forty thousand schoolteachers, who had joined the Baath Party simply to keep their jobs." For an overview of the de-Baathification debacle, see Pfiffner, "US Blunders in Iraq," 76–85.

7. CPA, Order No. 2, *Dissolution of Entities*. While 500,000 is the number commonly cited, the full effect of the order was closer to 700,000. According to Thomas Ricks, this order formally terminated 385,000 people in the armed forces, 285,000 in the Interior Ministry, which included police and domestic security, and 50,000 in presidential security units (*Fiasco*, 162).

8. See Ned Parker, "Saudis' Role in Iraq Insurgency Outlined." According to US military figures, the largest number of foreign fighters targeting US military and Iraqi civilians, some 45 percent, came from Saudi Arabia, as did the largest number of suicide bombers. Nearly half of the 135 foreigners in US detention facilities in Iraq were Saudi.

9. See Juan Cole, "Brief History of Islamic State of Iraq."

10. Teru Kuwayama notes that fixers would have more "glamorous" job titles if they were North American or European. ("How to Shoot (and Not Get Shot) in a War Zone.")

11. *A Collection of Essays*, 312–313. Orwell goes on to state that "all writers are vain, selfish and lazy, and at the very bottom of their motives there lies a mystery." (Ibid., 316)

12. David Kilcullen and Nate Rosenblatt offer a useful overview of the way mass rural migration to Syria's cities "driven by economic necessity and persistent drought" created a vast urban underclass that formed the basis of domestic Syrian resistance to the regime. Such urban villagers do not have the means to wait out the war abroad. They accommodate foreign-funded Islamic militant groups because the Islamists have the money and training to provide economic necessities, services and law enforcement. As the authors note, armed groups have otherwise devoted as much time to fighting one another as they do the Syrian government. "Neighborhood gangs run rampant. Lawlessness is rife. Warlordism is on the rise." These factors help explain why extremists, including al-Qaeda–linked groups and offshoots such as Islamic State, are thriving: they are well-funded, well-armed and the "least corrupt organizations among opposition groups." ("The Rise of Syria's Urban Poor," 33–41.)

13. Sunni Arabs account for 60 to 65 percent of the rank-and-file of the Syrian army, a near precise correlation to their 65 percent of the total Syrian population. This is a strong indicator of the class-based nature of the conflict. One reason for the high Sunni Arab representation in pro-government forces is the perception of opposition Sunnis as rural, religious and poor, thus having little in common with urban, educated Sunnis. Another reason is their fear of the radical Sunni Islamists who dominate the opposition. If the civil war in Syria was truly sectarian,

Syria's Sunnis would abandon the army and the government would fall. See Chris Zambelis, "Syria's Sunnis and the Regime's Resilience."

14. It is a common misconception that all Alawites, who make up about 12 percent of the Syrian population, benefited from the Assad rule. This was not the case. Most Alawites are poor and suffered the same state repression as other groups. They have supported the state rather than the opposition out of fear of Sunni jihadists, who consider Alawites to be heretics and massacre them. Nevertheless Alawites have expressed anger at the stunning death toll of Alawites serving in the Syrian army. Pro-government fighters have suffered the largest proportion of casualties in Syria, according to the opposition Syrian Network for Human Rights. By 2015, as many as a third of the 250,000 Alawite men of military age were dead. See Lauren Williams, "Syria's Alawites Not Deserting Assad Yet, Despite Crackdown," and Ruth Sherlock, "In Syria's War, Alawites Pay Heavy Price."

15. For an in-depth exploration of the outsiders who "hijacked" the Syrian revolution, see Hugh Roberts, "The Hijackers," 5–10.

16. Robert L. Bateman, "Iraq and the Problem of Border Security," 41–47.

17. See Shane Harris and Matthew M. Aid, "CIA Files Prove America Helped Saddam as He Gassed Iran."

18. See Roger Morris, "A Tyrant 40 Years in the Making." Morris documents the first American regime change in Iraq in 1963, when the CIA under President John F. Kennedy orchestrated the overthrow of Iraqi prime minister Abdel Karim Kassem in collaboration with Saddam Hussein. "Washington's role in the coup went unreported at the time and has been little noted since. America's anti-Kassem intrigue has been widely substantiated, however, in disclosures by the Senate Committee on Intelligence and in the work of journalists and historians like David Wise, an authority on the CIA." Kassem, who had overthrown the Western-allied Iraqi monarchy in 1958, was regarded by Washington as a "danger-ous leader who must be removed." In the early 1960s, the CIA organized regime opponents, backing a small anti-Communist group, the Baath Party. "According to the former Baathist leader Hani Fkaiki, among party members colluding with the CIA in 1962 and 1963 was Saddam Hussein,

then a 25-year-old who had fled to Cairo after taking part in a failed assassination of Kassem in 1958." The coup began on February 8, 1963, culminating in Kassem's execution. "Almost certainly a gain for our side," Robert Komer, a National Security Council aide, wrote to Kennedy. In the purge that followed, the Baathists systematically murdered Iraqi elites suspected of communist sympathies using lists the CIA provided. The follow-up 1968 coup that brought Saddam Hussein closer to ultimate power was also backed by the CIA.

19. Souad Al-Azzawi, "Decline of Iraqi Women Empowerment Through Education Under the American Occupation of Iraq 2003–2011." Iraqi associate professor Souad Al-Azzawi notes that prior to the First Gulf War in 1991 women made up more than 30 percent of faculty members in Iraqi universities and research centres in Iraq and two-thirds of all teaching staff in primary and secondary schools. Since 2003, with kidnappings and assassinations of academics, teachers, health care specialists and other professionals, "it has become really hard for women to keep up their jobs and education status."

20. Phil Williams, "Criminals, Militias, and Insurgents: Organized Crime in Iraq."

21. Stephen Glain, "The Arab Street," 172–173.

22. Scott Anderson, *Lawrence in Arabia*, 112.

23. T.E. Lawrence, *Seven Pillars of Wisdom*, 24.

24. Margaret MacMillan, *Paris 1919*, 81.

25. Lawrence, "A Report on Mesopotamia."

26. Roberts, "The Hijackers."

27. Although an election took place the year the French left with the support of the United States—already engaged in the battle to contain communism in the Middle East—it was handily won by entrenched elites who seemed impervious to American influence. American business interests were soon frustrated with the new Syrian parliament, which stalled on approving a right-of-way for a pipeline that was intended to serve US oil concerns in Saudi Arabia. In *The Game of Nations*, a *New York Times* bestseller published in 1970, CIA agent Miles Copeland, a member of the team behind the 1949 coup, describes how events unfolded. They first befriended the head of the Syrian army, Husni al-Za'im: "The political

action team suggested to Za'im the idea of a coup d'etat, advised him how to go about it, guided him through the intricate preparations in laying the groundwork for it . . . Za'im was 'the American boy.'" One member of the American team, Deane Hinton, was less than enthusiastic about the plan. According to Copeland, Hinton said, "I want to go on record as saying that this is the stupidest, most irresponsible action a diplomatic mission like ours could get itself involved in, and that we've started a series of these things that will never end." Had the coup not taken place, transferring authority from an elected government to the military, it is unlikely that Hafez al-Assad would ever have come to power. Documentary filmmaker Adam Curtis tells part of the story for the BBC in "The Baby and the Baath Water." See also Jörg Michael Dostal, "Post-independence Syria and the Great Powers (1946–1958)."

28. AFP, "War in Syria's Aleppo Takes Toll on Storied Baron Hotel."

29. Jason Pape, "Winning with the People in Iraq," 36.

30. William Langewiesche, "Welcome to the Green Zone."

31. Camp Bucca and other American prisons in Iraq, write Jeremi Suri and Andrew Thompson in the *New York Times*, "became virtual terrorist universities: The hardened radicals were the professors, the other detainees were the students, and the prison authorities played the role of absent custodian" ("How America Helped Isis").

32. Brigitte Weidlich, "Namibia: Govt Shuts Down U.S. Firm."

33. J.M. Coetzee, *Giving Offense*, 35 and 37.

34. As early as 2006, Saudi Arabia, the leading Sunni regime, sought to reshape the regional conflicts as Sunni versus Shia. As Michael Slackman and Hassan M. Fattah reported in the *New York Times*, "The shift is occurring with encouragement from the Bush administration. Its goal is to see an American-backed alliance of Sunni Arab states including Saudi Arabia, Jordan, Lebanon and Egypt, along with a Fatah-led Palestine and Israel, opposing Iran, Syria and the radical groups they support." They add that, "Sectarian overtones aside, the battle is also about political power, national interests and preserving the status quo" ("In Public View, Saudis Counter Iran in Region"). This shift was a response to the ousting of Saddam Hussein and the transfer of power to a Shia-led Iraqi government allied with a resurgent Iran that no longer had to contend with

Saddam. Saudi Arabia increased its support for Sunni allies in Lebanon to combat the Iranian-allied Shia Lebanese Hezbollah; the decision to lower the price of oil was partly aimed at harming Iran's oil-based economy. In the Syrian war, Saudi Arabia along with Turkey and Gulf States financed and armed Islamist opposition fighters, including those close to al-Qaeda.

35. Open Society Justice Initiative, "Globalizing Torture: CIA Secret Detention and Extraordinary Rendition."

36. Where are they now? In 2015, Douglas Feith, of the Pentagon's Office of Special Plans, was Director of the Center for National Security Strategies at the Hudson Institute, publishing op-eds in the *Wall Street Journal* and *Politico*. Paul Wolfowitz was a visiting scholar at the American Enterprise Institute, and serving as foreign policy advisor to failed presidential candidate Jeb Bush. Fellow neoconservative John Bolton was advising Republican candidate Ted Cruz, while Elliott Abrams and PNAC founder William Kristol were supporting Cruz's failed rival Marco Rubio, who was also being briefed by former Cheney advisor Eric Edelman. (See John Walcott, "What Donald Rumsfeld Knew We Didn't Know About Iraq.") Richard Perle, along with Condoleezza Rice and Henry Kissinger, was on the board of advisors of the Washington Institute for Near East Policy; Perle was discovered to have been an advisor to Libyan dictator Muammar Qadaffi in 2006. (See Laura Rozen, "Among Libya's lobbyists.") Ken Adelman went from the Defense Policy Board under Bush to the Board of the National Center for Counter-Terrorism during the Obama Administration, and has since repudiated both; according to his website he "teaches executive leadership through the wisdom of William Shakespeare." In June 2015, Rumsfeld gave an interview to the *Times of London* in which he said, "I'm not one who thinks that our particular template of democracy is appropriate for other countries at every moment of their histories" (Melanie Phillips, "Bush Was Wrong on Iraq, Says Rumsfeld"). In November Ahmed Chalabi died of heart failure. In December Dick Cheney was making the case for re-invading parts of the Middle East to trounce ISIS ("Vice President Dick Cheney on San Bernardino, Obama's Foreign Policy, and Setting History Straight"). Paul Bremer said the same thing in the same week, adding that on the whole, Iraqis are "better off" since the invasion ("Paul Bremer Wants

US Troops Back in Iraq to Fight ISIL"). Meanwhile George W. Bush was on the speaker circuit, charging $100,000 to appear at a gala for a Texas homeless shelter (Michael Kruse, "On Talk Circuit, George W. Bush Makes Millions but Few Waves").

37. For a comparative look at the numbers of journalists kidnapped or killed in Iraq and Syria, see Zeina Karam, "Journalists in Syria Face Growing Risk of Kidnap."

38. The drought that began in 1998 is the worst in 900 years, according to NASA scientists who based their findings on tree rings (Benjamin I. Cooke et al., "Spatiotemporal Drought Variability in the Mediterranean over the Last 900 Years"). By 2010, a million Syrian farmers had been forced to leave their land (Wadid Erian et al., "Drought Vulnerability in the Arab Region: Syria"). "We were forced to flee," a Syrian farmer told the *New York Times* the year before the Syria war began. "Now we are at less than zero—no money, no job, no hope" (Robert F. Worth, "Earth Is Parched Where Syrian Farms Thrived"). According to the *Proceedings of the National Academy of Sciences*, climate change contributed to the Syrian civil war. "It was the worst drought in the instrumental record, causing widespread crop failure and a mass migration of farming families to the urban centers. . . . We conclude that human influences on the climate system are implicated in the current Syrian conflict" (Colin P. Kelly et al., "Climate Change in the Fertile Crescent and Implications of the Recent Syrian Drought").

39. Raymond Hinnebusch, "Syria: From 'Authoritarian Upgrading' to Revolution?"

40. Barack Obama said as much in a 2015 interview with *VICE News*. ISIS, he said, is "a direct outgrowth of al-Qaeda in Iraq that grew out of our invasion." ("President Obama Speaks with *Vice News*.")

41. Quoted in Martin Chulov, "Isis: the Inside Story." See also Terrence McCoy, "How the Islamic State Evolved in an American Prison."

BIBLIOGRAPHY

Adelman, Ken. "Cakewalk in Iraq." *Washington Post*, February 13, 2002.

AFP. "War in Syria's Aleppo Takes Toll on Storied Baron Hotel." *Daily Mail*, November 18, 2014. http://www.dailymail.co.uk/wires/afp/article-2839735 /War-Syrias-Aleppo-takes-toll-storied-Baron-Hotel.html

Al-Azzawi, Souad. "Decline of Iraqi Women Empowerment Through Education Under the American Occupation of Iraq 2003–2011." Paper presented at International Seminar on the Situation of the Iraqi Academics, Ghent University, Belgium, March 9–11, 2011.

Al Jazeera staff. "Paul Bremer Wants US Troops Back in Iraq to Fight ISIL." *Al Jazeera*, December 3, 2015. http://www.aljazeera.com/news/2015/12/paul -bremer-troops-iraq-fight-isil-151203132946691.html

Anderson, Scott. *Lawrence in Arabia: War, Deceit, Imperial Folly and the Making of the Modern Middle East*. Toronto: Signal, 2013.

Bateman, Robert L. "Iraq and the Problem of Border Security." *SAIS Review*, Vol. 26, No. 1, (Winter–Spring 2006): 41–47.

Bremer, Paul. *My Year in Iraq*. New York: Simon & Schuster, 2007.

Borger, Julian. "The Spies Who Pushed for War." *The Guardian*, July 17, 2003. http://www.theguardian.com/world/2003/jul/17/iraq.usa

Chandrasekaran, Rajiv. *Imperial Life in the Emerald City: Inside Iraq's Green Zone*. New York: Vintage Books, 2006.

Cheney, Dick. "Vice President Dick Cheney on San Bernardino, Obama's Foreign Policy, and Setting History Straight." *The Hugh Hewitt Show* (radio). December 7, 2015. http://www.hughhewitt.com/vice-president-dick -cheney-san-bernardino-obamas-foreign-policy-setting-history-straight/

Chulov, Martin. "Isis: the Inside Story." *The Guardian*, December 11, 2014. http://www.theguardian.com/world/2014/dec/11/-sp-isis-the-inside-story

Cockburn, Patrick. *The Rise of the Islamic State: ISIS and the New Sunni Revolution*. London, New York: Verso, 2015.

Coetzee, J.M. *Giving Offense: Essays on Censorship*. Chicago: Chicago University Press, 1996.

Cole, Juan. "Brief History of Islamic State of Iraq." *Informed Comment*, May 17, 2007. http://www.juancole.com/2007/05/brief-history-of-islamic-state-of-iraq.html

Cook, B.I., K.J. Anchukaitis, R. Touchan, D.M. Meko, and E.R. Cook. "Spatio-temporal Drought Variability in the Mediterranean over the Last 900 Years." *Journal of Geophysical Research-Amospheres*, 121 (March 4, 2016). doi:10.1002/2015JD023929

Copeland, Miles, *The Game of Nations: The Amorality of Power Politics*. New York: Simon & Schuster, 1970.

CPA. Order No. 1. *De-Ba'athification of Iraqi Society*. May 16, 2003. http://www.iraqcoalition.org/regulations/20030516_CPAORD_1_De-Ba_athification_of_Iraqi_Society_.pdf

CPA. Order No. 2. *Dissolution of Entities*. May 23, 2003. http://www.iraqcoalition.org/regulations/20030823_CPAORD_2_Dissolution_of_Entities_with_Annex_A.pdf

Curtis, Adam. "The Baby and the Baath Water." BBC.co.uk, June 16, 2011. http://www.bbc.co.uk/blogs/adamcurtis/2011/06/the_baby_and_the_baath_water.html

Dodge, Toby. "The Failure of Sanctions and the Evolution of International Policy towards Iraq, 1990–2003." *Contemporary Arab Affairs*, Vol. 3, No.1, (January 2010): 83–91. doi:10.1080/17550910903525952

Dostal, Jörg Michael. "Post-independence Syria and the Great Powers (1946–1958): How Western Power Politics Pushed the Country Toward the Soviet Union." Paper prepared for the annual meeting of the Academic Council on the United Nations System, Kadir Has University, Istanbul, June 19–21, 2014. http://acuns.org/wp-content/uploads/2013/01/Syria-Paper-1946-1958-for-ACUNS-Conference-Website-12-June-2014.pdf

Drower, E.S. *The Mandaeans of Iraq and Iran*. Oxford: Clarendon Press, 1937.

Erian, Wadid; Bassem Katlan and Ouldbdey Babah. "Drought Vulnerability in the Arab Region: Special Case Study: Syria." Global Assessment Report on Disaster Risk Reduction, UNISDR, Geneva, 2010. http://www.preventionweb.net/english/hyogo/gar/2011/en/bgdocs/Erian_Katlan_&_Babah_2010.pdf.

Fromkin, David. *A Peace to End All Peace: The Fall of the Ottoman Empire and the Creation of the Modern Middle East*. New York: Henry Holt, 1989.

Glain, Stephen. "The Arab Street." In *Handbook of US–Middle East Relations: Formative Factors and Regional Perspectives*, edited by Robert E. Looney, 167–175. London and New York: Routledge, 2009.

Glass, Charles. *Syria Burning: ISIS and the Death of the Arab Spring*. New York and London: OR Books, 2015.

Harris, Shane and Matthew M. Aid. "CIA Files Prove America Helped Saddam as He Gassed Iran." *Foreign Policy*, August 26, 2013. http://foreignpolicy.com/2013/08/26/exclusive-cia-files-prove-america-helped-saddam-as-he-gassed-iran/

Hartley, L.P. *The Go-Between*. London: Hamish Hamilton, 1953.

Heilbrunn, Jacob. *They Knew They Were Right*. New York: Doubleday, 2008.

Hemingway, Ernest. *A Moveable Feast*. London: Jonathan Cape, 1964.

Hersh, Seymour. "Selective Intelligence." *The New Yorker*, May 12, 2003. http://www.newyorker.com/magazine/2003/05/12/selective-intelligence

Hess, Pamela. "Rumsfeld: Looting Is Transition to Freedom.'" *UPI*, April 11, 2003. http://www.upi.com/Business_News/Security-Industry/2003/04/11/Rumsfeld-Looting-is-transition-to-freedom/63821050097983/

Hinnebusch, Raymond. "Syria: From 'Authoritarian Upgrading' to Revolution?" *International Affairs*, Vol.88, No.1 (2012): 95–113. doi:10.1111/j.1468-2346.2012.01059.x

Karam, Zeina. "Journalists in Syria Face Growing Risk of Kidnap." *Associated Press*, November 9, 2013. http://bigstory.ap.org/article/journalists-syria-face-growing-risk-kidnap

Kazimi, Nibras. "Zarqawi's Anti-Shia Legacy: Original or Borrowed?" *Current Trends in Islamist Ideology*, Vol. 4 (Hudson Institute, 2006): 53–72.

Kelly, Colin P. Shahrzad Mohtadib, Mark A. Canec, Richard Seagerc, and Yochanan Kushnir. "Climate Change in the Fertile Crescent and Implications of the Recent Syrian Drought." *PNAS*, Vol. 112, No. 11 (March 2, 2015): 3241–3246. doi:www.pnas.org/cgi/doi/10.1073/pnas.1421533112

Kilcullen, David and Nate Rosenblatt. "The Rise of Syria's Urban Poor: Why the War for Syria's Future Will Be Fought Over the Country's New Urban Villages." *PRISM*, National Defense University, Center for Complex Operations, Vol. 4, Syria Supplemental, (2014): 33–41. http://caerusassociates.com/wp-content/uploads/2014/02/PRISM-Syrian-Supplemental-20140214.pdf

Kruse, Michael. "On Talk Circuit, George W. Bush Makes Millions but Few Waves." *Politico*, July 6, 2015. http://www.politico.com/story/2015/06/on-talk-circuit-george-bush-makes-millions-but-few-waves-118697

Kuwayama, Teru. "Ask a Pro: How to Shoot (and Not Get Shot) in a War Zone." *Gizmodo.com*, August 30, 2009. http://gizmodo.com/5330715/ask-a-pro-how-to-shoot-and-not-get-shot-in-a-war-zone

Langewiesche, William. "Welcome to the Green Zone." *The Atlantic*, November 2004. http://www.theatlantic.com/magazine/archive/2004/11/welcome-to-the-green-zone/303547/

Lawrence, T.E. "A Report on Mesopotamia." *The Sunday Times,* August 22, 1920.

Lawrence, T.E. *Seven Pillars of Wisdom: A Triumph.* London: Penguin, 1962.

MacMillan, Margaret. *Paris 1919: Six Months that Changed the World.* New York: Random House, 2001.

Marozzi, Justin. *Baghdad: City of Peace, City of Blood; A History in Thirteen Centuries.* UK: Penguin, 2015.

McCoy, Terrence. "How the Islamic State Evolved in an American Prison." *The Washington Post,* November 4, 2014. http://www. washingtonpost.com/news/morning-mix/wp/2014/11/04/how-an-american -prison-helped-ignite-the-islamic-state/

Obama, Barack. "President Obama Speaks with VICE News," VICE News, March 17, 2015. https://news.vice.com/video/president-barack-obama -speaks-with-vice-news

Open Society Justice Initiative. "Globalizing Torture: CIA Secret Detention and Extraordinary Rendition." February 2013. https://www. opensocietyfoundations.org/sites/default/files/globalizing-torture -20120205.pdf

Orwell, George. "Why I Write." *A Collection of Essays.* 309–316. New York: Harcourt, 1981. (originally published in 1946)

Pape, Jason. "Winning with the People in Iraq." *Armor* (March–April 2005): 35–38, 42.

Parker, Ned. "Saudis' Role in Iraq Insurgency Outlined," *Los Angeles Times,* July 15, 2007. https://web.archive.org/web/20090223180041/http: //fairuse.100webcustomers.com/fairenough/latimesA98.html

Pelham, Nicholas. *A New Muslim Order: The Shia and the Middle East Sectarian Crisis.* London and New York: I.B. Taurus, 2008.

Pfiffner, James P. "US Blunders in Iraq: De-Baathification and Disbanding the Army." *Intelligence and National Security.* Vol. 25, No. 1, February 2010, 76–85. doi: 10.1080/02684521003588120

Phillips, Melanie. "Bush Was Wrong on Iraq, Says Rumsfeld." *Times of London,* June 6, 2015. http://www.thetimes.co.uk/tto/news/world/americas /article4462278.ece

Pew Research Center. "Journalists in Iraq: A Survey of Reporters on the Front Lines." Project for Excellence in Journalism, November 28, 2007. http: //www.journalism.org/files/legacy/PEJ%20FINAL%20Survey%20of%20 Journalists%20in%20IraqWITH%20SURVEY.pdf

Ranjan, Rakesh Kumar and Prakash C. Jain. "The Decline of Educational System in Iraq." *Journal of Peace Studies,* Vol. 16, Issue 1–2, (January–June 2009). http://icpsnet.org/adm/pdf/1251368150.pdf

Ricks, Thomas. *Fiasco*. New York: Penguin Press 2006.

Roberts, Hugh. "The Hijackers." Review of *From Deep State to Islamic State: The Arab Counter-Revolution and Its Jihadi Legacy*, by Jean-Pierre Filiu; *Syrian Notebooks: Inside the Homs Uprising*, by Jonathan Littell; *The Rise of Islamic State: Isis and the New Sunni Revolution*, by Patrick Cockburn; and *Isis: Inside the Army of Terror*, by Michael Weiss and Hassan Hassan. *London Review of Books* 37 no.14 (2015): 5–10. http://www.lrb.co.uk/v37/n14/hugh-roberts/the-hijackers

Rozen, Laura. "Among Libya's Lobbyists." *Politico*, Feb 21, 2011. http://www.politico.com/blogs/laurarozen/0211/Among_Libyas_lobbyists.html?showall.

Sassoon, Joseph. *The Iraqi Refugees: The New Crisis in the Middle East*. London: I.B. Tauris, 2009.

Saroyan, William. "Antranik of Armenia." In *Essential Saroyan*, edited by William E. Justice. Berkeley, CA: Santa Clara Heyday Books, 2005.

Seale, Patrick. *Asad: The Struggle for the Middle East*. London: I.B. Tauris, 1988.

Sherlock, Ruth. "In Syria's War, Alawites Pay Heavy Price for Loyalty to Bashar al-Assad." *The Telegraph*, April 7, 2015. http://www.telegraph.co.uk/news/worldnews/middleeast/syria/11518232/In-Syrias-war-Alawites-pay-heavy-price-for-loyalty-to-Bashar-al-Assad.html

Slackman, Michael and Hassan M. Fatah. "In Public View, Saudis Counter Iran in Region." *The New York Times*, Feb 6, 2007. http://www.nytimes.com/2007/02/06/world/middleeast/06saudi.html?pagewanted=print&_r=0

Steele, Jonathan. "Ahmed Chalabi Obituary." *The Guardian*, November 4, 2015. http://www.theguardian.com/world/2015/nov/04/ahmed-chalabi

Swidey, Neil. "Where Did ISIS Come From?" *Boston Globe*, March 10, 2016. http://www.bostonglobe.com/magazine/2016/03/10/where-did-isis-come-from-the-story-starts-here/eOHwJQgnZPNj8SE9IVw5hK/story.html

Taneja, Preti. "Assimilation, Exodus, Eradication: Iraq's minority communities since 2003." Minority Rights Group International (2007). http://reliefweb.int/sites/reliefweb.int/files/resources/BB2504FB14F54574C125728E005299B1-Full_Report.pdf

Tenet, George. *At the Center of the Storm: My Years at the CIA*, New York: HarperCollins, 2007.

Thompson, Andrew and Jeremi Suri. "How America Helped ISIS." *The New York Times*, October 1, 2014. http://www.nytimes.com/2014/10/02/opinion/how-america-helped-isis.html?_r=0

UNHCR, *Background Information on the Situation of non-Muslim Religious Minorities in Iraq*, (October 2005).

Verlöy, André and Daniel Politi. "Advisors of influence: Nine members of the Defense Policy Board have ties to defense contractors." The Center for Public Integrity, March 28, 2003. http://www.publicintegrity.org/2003/03/28/3157/advisors-influence-nine-members-defense-policy-board-have-ties-defense-contractors

Walcott, John. "What Donald Rumsfeld Knew We Didn't Know About Iraq." *Politico*, January 24, 2016. http://www.politico.com/magazine/story/2016/01/iraq-war-wmds-donald-rumsfeld-new-report-213530

Wallach, Janet. *Desert Queen: The Extraordinary Life of Gertrude Bell.* New York: Doubleday, 1996.

Weidlich, Brigitte. "Namibia: Govt Shuts Down U.S. Firm." *The Namibian*, October 15, 2007. http://allafrica.com/stories/200710150424.html

Williams, Lauren. "Syria's Alawites Not Deserting Assad Yet, Despite Crackdown." *Middle East Eye*, September 11, 2014. http://www.middleeasteye.net/in-depth/features/syrias-alawites-not-deserting-assad-yet-despite-crackdown-526622504

Williams, Phil. "Criminals, Militias, and Insurgents: Organized Crime in Iraq." *Strategic Studies Institute*, June 2009. http://www.strategicstudiesinstitute.army.mil/pdffiles/pub930.pdf

Worth, Robert F. "Earth Is Parched Where Syrian Farms Thrived." *The New York Times*, October 13, 2010. http://www.nytimes.com/2010/10/14/world/middleeast/14syria.html?adxnnl=1&adxnnlx=1330449407-yAiPXrD1kQsKbG2Bb5A61A&pagewanted=1

Zambelis, Chris. "Syria's Sunnis and the Regime's Resilience." *CTC Sentinel.* Combating Terrorism Center, West Point, Vol 8, Issue 5, (May 2015): 5–9. https://www.ctc.usma.edu/posts/syrias-sunnis-and-the-regimes-resilience

ABOUT THE AUTHOR

DEBORAH CAMPBELL is an award-winning writer who has reported from many countries around the world, including Iran, Syria, Jordan, Egypt, Lebanon, Israel, Palestine, Mexico, Cuba, and Russia. Her work, much of which involves spending long periods of time in the societies she covers, has appeared in *Harper's*, *The Economist*, *The Guardian*, *New Scientist*, and *Foreign Policy*, and she is the recipient of three National Magazine Awards for her foreign correspondence. *A Disappearance in Damascus* won the 2016 Hilary Weston Writers' Trust Prize for Nonfiction. Campbell has guest-lectured at Harvard, Berkeley, Zayed University in Dubai, and the National Press Club in Washington. She teaches at the University of British Columbia.